New Horizons in Philosophy

This outstanding volume in The Mentor Philosophers series presents a new interpretation of the philosophical conflicts of the 19th century, the period which bridged the 18th century "age of enlightenment" and our own 20th century "age of analysis."

Edited by a noted authority who presents the basic writings of this period with introduction and interlinking commentary, *The Age of Ideology* shows the radical shift in 19th century thinking from traditional philosophical paths of reasoning and subject matter to an emphasis on subjectivity, a differentiation between ideology and the findings of empirical science, and thorough-going and critical examination of previous disciplines and tenets.

In this arresting report, leading philosophers like Hegel, Marx, Kierkegaard, Comte, Spencer, and Nietzsche bring into philosophy new concepts, such as the effect of history on philosophy, theories of dialectic mexistentialism, sociology. culture. *The Ag19th century's attool of man's adwhich are forerunmatism.

Henry D. Aiken, now rofessor of Philosophy at Harvard University, has also been on the teaching staffs of Columbia University and the University of Washington.

THE

MENTOR PHILOSOPHERS

☆

A DISTINGUISHED SERIES of six volumes presenting, in historical order, the basic writings of the outstanding philosophers of the Western world—from the Middle Ages to the present time. Each volume is self-contained and presents a single phase of the great development. Each is edited by a noted scholar who contributes an introduction and interpretive commentary explaining in what way the significant thought of each period has influenced Western philosophy. The Mentor Philosophers are 50¢ and 75¢ per volume. (*See back of book for complete listing of this series.*)

Note: If your dealer does not have the books you want, you may order them by mail, enclosing the list price plus 5¢ a copy to cover mailing costs. The New American Library of World Literature, Inc., P.O. Box 2310, Grand Central Station, New York 17, N. Y.

The Mentor Philosophers

THE AGE
OF IDEOLOGY

The 19th Century Philosophers

SELECTED, WITH INTRODUCTION AND INTERPRETIVE COMMENTARY

by

HENRY D. AIKEN

A MENTOR BOOK
Published by The New American Library

© 1956 BY HENRY D. AIKEN

FIRST PRINTING, DECEMBER, 1956
SECOND PRINTING, APRIL, 1957
THIRD PRINTING, FEBRUARY, 1959
FOURTH PRINTING, JANUARY, 1960
FIFTH PRINTING, JANUARY, 1961
SIXTH PRINTING, MAY, 1962

ACKNOWLEDGMENTS AND COPYRIGHT NOTICES

The author wishes to thank the following publishers and authorized representatives for their kind permission to reprint from the books indicated below:

THE AMERICAN-SCANDINAVIAN FOUNDATION:
Sören Kierkegaard, *Concluding Unscientific Postscript*, translated by David F. Swenson and Walter Lowrie, Copyright, 1941, by Princeton University Press.

VICTOR GOLLANCZ LTD.:
Karl Marx, "Theses on Feuerbach" and Friedrich Engels, "Anti-Dühring," in *A Handbook of Marxism*, edited by Emile Burns.

LAWRENCE & WISHART LTD.:
Karl Marx, "Theses on Feuerbach" and Friedrich Engels, "Anti-Dühring," in *A Handbook of Marxism*, edited by Emile Burns.

THE LIBERAL ARTS PRESS, INC.:
Immanuel Kant, *The Prolegomena to Any Future Metaphysics*, edited by Lewis W. Beck (Library of Liberal Arts Edition), Copyright, 1950, by the Liberal Arts Press.

ROUTLEDGE & KEGAN PAUL, LTD.:
Johann Gottlieb Fichte, *The Science of Knowledge*, translated by A. E. Kroeger; Arthur Schopenhauer, *The World as Will and Idea*, translated by R. B. Haldane and J. Kemp; Auguste Comte, *The Positive Philosophy of Auguste Comte*, translated by Harriet Martineau.

WILLEY BOOK CO., INC.:
G. W. F. Hegel, *The Philosophy of History*, translated by J. Sibree, Copyright, 1900, by the Colonial Press.

A cloth-bound edition of *The Age of Ideology*
is published by Houghton Mifflin Co.

*MENTOR BOOKS are published by
The New American Library of World Literature, Inc.
501 Madison Avenue, New York 22, New York*

Preface

THE PHILOSOPHICAL THOUGHT OF ANY AGE IS ALWAYS
more varied and more complex that it at first appears to
be. With all due respect to its distinguished predecessors,
however, the nineteenth century considerably outdistances
the seventeenth and eighteenth centuries, at least in the
sheer bulk, variety and complexity of its philosophical
ideas. For this reason, it is unusually difficult to find one
great theme or issue with which most of the major thinkers
of this period are all centrally concerned. Indeed, the very
juxtaposition of such fabulous names as Hegel and
Nietzsche, Marx and Mill, Comte and Kierkegaard, at once
calls to mind unprecedented differences not only in philosophical temper and style, but also in background and
method. In the nineteenth century whole philosophical
dynasties rise and fall within a few brief years, and the
technical jargon of one school shortly becomes the gib-
berish of the next. As the century wears on, party lines
become increasingly confused, so that useful, unmislead-
ing classifications of philosophers become virtually impossible. Yet I have found, despite all this, that underlying
most of the perplexities presented to the historian and
anthologist by nineteenth-century philosophy as a whole,
there is a central cluster of problems to which most of its
strangeness and difficulty are due. Beginning with Kant,
the very conception of the philosophical enterprise that
had prevailed since the time of Aristotle underwent a profound sea-change, with the consequence that the meanings
of even such basic terms of the traditional philosophical

vocabulary as "metaphysics" and "logic" were altered beyond recognition. Questions, the point or significance of which had not been challenged for two thousand years, were now found to be simply meaningless and were replaced by others that had hitherto not been contemplated. Much of the obscurity that pervades nineteenth-century philosophical writing is directly related to this fact. Undoubtedly this has increased the depth and originality of the nineteenth-century philosophers, but it has not made them more perspicuous or readable.

Choice of particular philosophers to be represented in this volume has been further complicated by limitations of space. I realized from the outset that not every philosopher of major importance within this period could be included if the book was not to degenerate into a meaningless catalogue of names, tendencies, and quotations. My ultimate choices were based upon the three considerations of originality, historical influence, and contemporary interest. Even so, I have had to omit several philosophers who may perhaps qualify for inclusion on all of these grounds, among them Schelling, Bentham, and F. H. Bradley. Had I included them, however, I would have had to omit someone else who, for one reason or another, it seemed to me unthinkable to omit. The reader is warned, however, that the nineteenth century is a period in philosophy so fertile that what glimpses of it are provided in these pages are nothing more than that.

The Age of Ideology is written for the thoughtful reader not likely to be interested in the learned debates of commentators, but searching for something that may have relevance to his own intellectual and spiritual perplexities or that sheds some light upon the ideological conflicts which our own age has inherited from its predecessor. I have tried to keep these legitimate demands constantly in view, without misrepresenting the philosophers with whom we are here concerned. In a word, my aim has been to write for those who think that philosophical reflection is not a dangerous luxury, but an indispensable adjunct of the conduct of life, and who at the same time believe, as I do, that it is impossible to adhere to the Socratic dictum,

"Know thyself!", if one knows nothing else. If a reader is hereby enabled to discover in the thought of a Kant or a Mill or a Nietzsche some clue to the solution of deep-lying problems of his own, or is stimulated to further reading in the works of these great men, I shall have accomplished all that I aspire to do.

Given the orientation of this book, it may be wondered why I have not chosen readings which are more obviously and explicitly ideological in character. Why, for example, include Mills' *Nature* rather than his *Liberty* or *Utilitarianism;* why Marx's *Theses on Feuerbach* rather than *The Communist Manifesto?* The answer to this question goes precisely to the heart of my conception of the nineteenth century as an age of ideology. No one doubts the patent ideological import of *Liberty* or *The Communist Manifesto.* They symbolize a vast ideological struggle which has reached its climax in our own time. What is perhaps not so clearly understood is that the more foundational doctrines of the nineteenth-century philosophers are also broadly ideological in character. By a strange paradox, Immanuel Kant, who thought that he had sounded the death knell to speculative metaphysics, initiated a great metaphysical revival in the absolute idealism of Fichte and Hegel. Yet, as we shall presently see, theirs was a form of metaphysics undreamed of by earlier philosophers. The difference between the metaphysics of a Fichte and that of a Descartes or a Leibniz is not, however, a theoretical difference, but a difference in regard to the very point and meaning of metaphysical theses. Essentially it is a difference between a form of inquiry which seeks theoretical knowledge of the most pervasive traits of being, and one which seeks to establish the basic commitments involved in being a man, being a person, being rational, or being civilized. Metaphysics was regarded by Descartes, and before him by Aristotle, as continuous with the inquiries of the special sciences, differing from them only in scope and primacy. For Fichte, on the contrary, its concern and its method essentially are practical, not theoretical; what it yields is not descriptions of matters of fact, but "posits" or commitments that are essential to the conduct of life.

My thesis, therefore, is not merely that the most salient and influential doctrines of the nineteenth-century philosophers are essentially ideological in character, but also that since Kant there has been an increasing awareness that the fundamental tasks of philosophical criticism belong not to "science" in any ordinary sense of that term, but to something for which there is no other word but "ideology."

So far as my characterizations of particular philosophers are concerned, my debts to dozens of commentators are heavy and far too numerous to be acknowledged in detail here. I thank them all for my borrowings, unconscious as well as conscious. To several persons, however, I should like to express a special indebtedness. First among them is my wife, Lillian Woodworth Aiken, who has read, wisely and most helpfully, every version of my working manuscript. My friend and colleague, Paul Ziff, has read considerable portions and has discussed with me at length several of the philosophers with whom I deal. I wish to thank him warmly for stimulus and encouragement. To two other colleagues, Morton White and W. V. Quine, it is a pleasure to express my gratitude for intellectual companionship and loyalty through many years in which I have groped toward philosophical perspectives which, I should like to think, are not wholly removed from their own. Upon the former's "historical consciousness," which is so much deeper than my own, I have relied more heavily than he knows. My greatest debt, however, is to Ralph Barton Perry, to whom this book is affectionately and respectfully dedicated, who has provided my chief standards of excellence during the years since I first came to Harvard as a graduate student.

Lexington, Mass.   HENRY DAVID AIKEN

Contents

CHAPTER I

Philosophy and Ideology
in the Nineteenth Century

THE PERIOD IN MODERN PHILOSOPHY BETWEEN IMMANUEL
Kant and Ernst Mach was a period in which metaphysics,
having lately been done in by David Hume and solemnly
pronounced dead by Kant, underwent a semi-miraculous
reincarnation in the absolute idealism of Fichte and Hegel,
lived a vigorous new life in the evolutionary naturalism of
Herbert Spencer, and, as some think, found its eternal
home in the dialectical materialism of Karl Marx. The Age
of Ideology was also a period in which the philosophy of
history, that gaudiest of metaphysical disciplines, came into
full flower, bringing with it a whole crop of grand theories
concerning the nature of historical development and the
destiny of man. At first glance, therefore, it would appear
that the nineteenth century, unlike its predecessor, was less
a century of social and political criticism which accepted
the principle that the proper study of philosophy, if not of
mankind itself, is man, than an age of uncritical and even
unbridled speculation about the nature of ultimate reality.

Even if such a description were allowed to pass without
qualification, a case might still be made for speaking of the
nineteenth century as an age of ideology. The term "ideology," in one of its several senses, means "ideal or abstract
speculation and visionary theorizing." Such a characteriza-
tion of nineteenth-century philosophy as a whole, however,
would be incomplete. What it misses is the fundamental
orientation and drift, even within metaphysics itself, of
nineteenth-century philosophical thought. If we revert to

13

Webster, we will find certain other senses of "ideology" which have greater relevance to what I have in mind in characterizing this period as The Age of Ideology. In one of these senses the term refers to "a system of ideas concerning phenomena, especially those of social life; the manner of thinking characteristic of a class or an individual." But the more closely one considers it, the more confused does this definition appear to become. For the first part of it suggests a theory about phenomena, especially social phenomena, while the second suggests, not a theory, but a way of thinking or a system of attitudes. The first calls to mind objective propositions that describe something existing in the world; the second suggests, not propositions which are true or false, but something more subjective which expresses the manner in which an individual or group views reality. This confusion, or ambiguity, is, I think, inherent in the ordinary use of "ideology." It is also an ambiguity which lies at the very heart of the philosophizing which is most characteristic of the period with which we are here concerned. Precisely because most nineteenth-century philosophers consider any proposition under the form of thought, as something conceived, posited, willed, or aspired to, one is never quite certain when they are talking about the mode of thought, and when they are talking about its object. Frequently they are talking about both at once, or, better, about a relation between them which they regard as fundamental to both. Why they talk in this way is a large part of our problem in this book. Right or wrong, however, this idea represents a departure from earlier philosophical speculation. In the end, it leads to a radically new conception of philosophical activity itself.

During the preceding period, philosophers were already much concerned with the problem of method. But they did not, on the whole, seriously doubt that there is a common, independent, and objective reality which can to some extent be understood. Nor did they question whether there is an objective way of thinking about reality, common to all rational animals, which does not radically modify or distort the thing known. Actually they did not deeply ponder the concept of objectivity itself; they merely used it to express a half-conscious conviction about the adequacy of the rational faculty to grasp its object and the correspondence between the thing itself and the thing-as-known. What they called "reason" was conceived both as the intellectual faculty by which the laws of nature are apprehended and as the principle of order or lawfulness within nature which the intellectual faculty apprehends. The relation between man's thinking about reality and reality itself was thus regarded as a non-distorting relation of "correspondence." It was also thought to be a purely "external" relation which in no way affects the inherent character of the thing known. The pre-established harmony of the knowing mind and the real object of knowledge, in such a view, is a divine miracle for which man can only express his gratitude.

From the time of Kant on, however, the assumption of a preordained correspondence between the mind and its object was regarded as dogmatic and uncritical. If the reason in things is the same as the reason which we acknowledge as the standard of valid thinking about any object, this is only because we ourselves have preordained what conditions any object must meet if it is to be counted by us as "real." In short, it is the thinking subject himself who establishes the standards of objectivity; if the world is not, as Schopenhauer misleadingly put it, "my idea," it is at any rate real for us only to the extent that it conforms to our own conception of what any real thing must be.

Every philosophical picture of reality, then, presupposes a way of thinking about it, a rule or principle of conceptual organization which must simply be accepted by its maker. Thus the element of subjectivity, however subtly disguised, can never be wholly eliminated from any philosophical system. Every such system, consciously or otherwise, presupposes certain ultimate commitments or "posits." These are made by the rational animal himself in order that he may live and do his work, and their validity has no higher court of appeal than his own determination to abide by them.

This radical subjectivism, however, was gradually modified by another factor which was even more pervasive in the thinking of most philosophers during the age of ideology. This is the so-called "historical consciousness." The philosopher who gave this way of thinking its greatest impetus was Hegel. And from the time of Hegel on, it became fashionable to think not only of human nature generally, but also of reason itself, as something developing within history, and hence as something continually affected by the changing conditions of individual and social life. This implied, or seemed to imply, that reason is not a constant, universal principle both of human understanding and of nature, but an historically evolving form of thought whose standards of validity are subject to change in accordance with the changing demands and opportunities of human life.

Webster lists a third sense of "ideology" which is also pertinent to our topic. In this, its original sense, the term refers to "the science of ideas; the study of the origin and nature of ideas; especially the system of Condillac, which derived all ideas exclusively from sensation."

The point of this historical allusion is not obvious, and some explanation of it is central to our problem. The word "ideology" was coined by a now forgotten French philosopher, Destutt de Tracy (1754-1836). Tracy used it to refer to the radically empirical analysis of the human mind, which had been most consistently formulated in the eighteenth century by Condillac and which derived ultimately from the "new way of ideas" that was first formulated by John Locke in his *Essay Concerning the Human Understanding*. This analysis, which claimed that sensation is the origin of all ideas, was adopted by the leaders of the French Revolution as an indispensable weapon for combating the authoritative political and religious dogmas by means of which the *ancien régime* had maintained its hold. In fact, the government of the Revolution recognized this analysis as the only philosophy, and during its reign the "ideologues," as they later came to be known, were the only acknowledged philosophers.

The word "ideology" has since lost this more limited connotation, but its associations with politically inspired and officially sanctioned doctrines remain. This sense of the term, however, was given still another twist during the

Napoleonic Era when "ideology" came to mean virtually any belief of a republican or revolutionary sort, that is to say, any belief hostile to Napoleon himself. These somewhat pejorative associations have never wholly disappeared from the use of this term. They were, on the contrary, reinforced and extended throughout the nineteenth century, especially in the writings of Karl Marx and his collaborator, Friedrich Engels. In their joint work, *German Ideology,* the meaning of the term is still closely identified with philosophy, particularly with those philosophies which they consider to be inimical to their own revolutionary philosophy of history. Thus they use it, not only in speaking of the "bourgeois" tradition of German idealism represented by Hegel and his followers, but also in referring to earlier "mechanistic" forms of materialism which, as they believe, cannot explain the nature of historical development.

There are several features of Marx and Engels' conception of ideology which require some mention here. In the first place, what they call "ideology" includes not only the theory of knowledge and politics, but also metaphysics, ethics, religion, and indeed any "form of consciousness" which expresses the basic attitudes or commitments of a social class. In *German Ideology* there are also a number of interesting passages in which Marx and Engels appear to be trying to make some sort of distinction between the "ideological" components of consciousness and what they variously refer to as "real knowledge" and "real positive science." What this distinction means is never made perfectly clear, but it at any rate suggests that ideologies, or the "reasons" which lead to their acceptance, are nonrational. It also raises difficult questions concerning the status of dialectical materialism itself, which Marx conceives to be not only the ideology of the revolutionary working classes but also a "scientific" philosophy which one can speak of as "true" with a straight face.

The relations of ideology to science and to knowledge have never been adequately formulated either by Marx and Engels or by their followers. Nevertheless, the associations of irrationality and of ulterior social or political interest which are still frequently attached to "ideological" doc-

trines have many of their roots in the Marxian theory that
the ideological, and hence philosophical, components of
consciousness belong exclusively to the "superstructure" of
culture. On this view, despite appearances, such doctrines
are without independent intellectual or "cognitive" content
and have no autonomous historical development.

Marx and Engels' account of the misleading "apparent"
meaning and the underlying "real" significance of ideological discourse has been more influential and has more profoundly permeated twentieth-century thinking than is commonly recognized. According to their view, when the relations of men and their "ideas" are formulated in ideological terms, they are thereby made to appear upside down
"as in a camera obscura." That is to say, ideology and
philosophy tend to present ideas themselves as determining
forces capable of guiding and controlling the political and
economic relations among men. To this tendency to ob-
jectify and personify what are in reality merely subjective
by-products of economic class struggle is due their hold
on those who believe them and who think that they make a
significant difference to their lives. All such impressions are
illusory. The form in which ideological theses are presented conceals their real content, and is indeed merely
an aspect of the necessary semantical mystification involved
in gaining acceptance for any ideological "theory." In fact,
according to Marx, ideologies are merely "reflexes" or
"echoes" of other determining forces that do the fundamental work in bringing about any real social change. Marx
calls such executive or efficient causes of social change
"material," and he does so to contrast them with their
ideological by-products.

This is not the place to undertake a full-dress analysis
or appraisal of Marx and Engels' not always consistent
statements about the relations between the ideological superstructure and its material economic foundation. But
the suggestion is always implicit in their theory that ideological doctrines are social myths or "opiates" of the people, and that the "reasons" for their acceptance have, at
bottom, nothing to do with considerations of evidence or

fact. This suggestion clings to the concept of ideology to this day.

In this book I wish to make use of some, but not all, of the complex meanings and historical associations of the term "ideology." I do wish to suggest that, in the nineteenth century, philosophy is no longer conceived, for the most part, as an extension or as part of science itself. This is true, as we shall see, even for those philosophers who are most friendly to science, such as Auguste Comte. But I do not use the term in a pejorative sense in order to insinuate that Hegel or Comte, or Marx himself for that matter, is merely using his philosophy, half-cynically, as a stalking-horse for his concealed political or social objectives. Neither idealism, positivism, or materialism, can be adequately understood or appraised if they are thought of merely as social myths or opiates. Nor do I wish to imply that all of the philosophical doctrines of the thinkers with whom we have to do in these pages are "irrational." My use of the term "ideology" is quite neutral in these respects. No doubt, the ideological commitments of the nineteenth-century philosophers can be contrasted with factual beliefs of the sort entertained by men of common sense or by men of science in their capacity as scientists. But this does not in the least imply that they are irrational or that they are proposed or accepted without reason. Hegel provides a case in point. He did not for a moment suppose that his philosophy of history belongs to positive science. But he did formulate it in a highly critical and self-conscious way, and he offers what Mill called "considerations to influence the intellect" which, in his judgment, should render it plausible and perhaps acceptable to any disinterested person. Moreover, even if most of the philosophical theses of the nineteenth-century philosophers are properly called "ideological," in contrast to the theories of empirical science, this by no means implies that there are no important relations, save those of contrast and or opposition, between them.

This brings us to a consideration which is fundamental to any proper estimate of the nineteenth-century philosophers. In marked contrast to those of their eighteenth-

century predecessors, their writings are usually difficult and
frequently obscure. But a principal reason for this is that
they were embarked upon an undertaking of which the
latter had, as yet, only caught the barest glimpses. Now,
it is easy to be clear and fluent, so long as one is content to use, without question, received concepts and methods that are already prescribed as "rational" or "valid."
But once one begins to question their eternal and universal
necessity, and, accordingly to doubt whether objective
standards and principles are inherent "in the nature of
things," the whole task of philosophical analysis and criticism begins to appear in another light. In the Age of
Reason, the appeal to reason, or to nature, remained uncritical, precisely because most philosophers shared the
same faith in reason and accepted essentially the same
body of "rational" principles. Such appeals were no longer
possible to Kant and his successors. And because of this
they were obliged to undertake that strangest and most
paradoxical of all philosophical tasks, the critique and justification of reason itself. These philosophers were not, in
any ordinary sense, skeptics; their skepticism was a limited
one, directed primarily against prevailing conceptions of
reason and against philosophical claims that were made,
uncritically, in its name.

Nor is it fair to dismiss them as Romantic irrationalists;
they were in revolt only against the Age of Reason and
against what may be called the hypertrophy of reason in
previous rationalistic philosophies. The fact is that the
concept of reason no longer seemed to be such a clear
and distinct idea as it had appeared to be to Descartes
or Spinoza; nor were its alleged laws so obviously self-
evident. These doubts, however, were merely one phase
of a general and progressively intense process of self-scru-
tiny that was going on throughout Western culture. The
political, social, and scientific revolutions that had been
going on since the Renaissance had now spread to the
heartland of philosophy itself, with the consequence that
the authority of the very implement of philosophical reflection, reason itself, was at last brought into question. Might
it not be true, perhaps, that reason, the supposed liberator

of the human mind, is no more than the repository of ancient prejudices and habits of mind that have no general validity whatever? But, then, what is "validity" anyway, and how are its standards to be determined or, if need be, to be revised? How, indeed, is a critique of reason even possible? Is there not something basically paradoxical in the very attempt to criticize the conditions and limits of all rational assertion and to evaluate the very undertaking of practical reason itself?

The answers provided by Kant and his successors to such questions as these are by no means as lucid as we could wish. But their comparative failure in this regard is due partly to the fact that they had not only to raise questions which had not been raised before, but virtually to invent a conceptual framework and a method for discussing them. In consequence, they made many mistakes, and frequently misled, not only their readers, but themselves, by the strange new language which they employed in trying to solve their problems. Sometimes they appeared to be doing something not unlike what earlier philosophers called "metaphysics" or "the science of knowledge." But in fact when one looks beneath the forms of words, one finds that what they were attempting, in effect, was a basic critique not only of reason, but of the entire system of norms and principles of Western culture. This task did not and could not be accomplished simply by using the "rational" methods which had been traditionally employed in philosophical speculation, for those methods themselves formed a principal part of the culture whose norms were being called in question.

In would be a mistake, however, to suppose that the nineteenth-century philosophers were "mere ideologists" or that the doctrines of their predecessors had no ideological aspects. Quite the contrary. Taken as a whole, what has gone under the name of "philosophy" has always included more than could be comprehended under any reasonable stretch of the meaning of "ideology." "Philosophy" suggests the love of knowledge as well as of practical wisdom, even if we stretch the latter phrase to include "world wisdom." Many philosophers, both before and after Kant,

believed that they were making contributions, not only
to the store of wisdom essential to the conduct of life, but
also to the store of man's theoretical knowledge or information about the world. Philosophy was and has remained
the mother, or at least the stepmother, of the sciences themselves. In the manner of all children, the sciences have
tended to reject their parent on arriving at the age of dis-
cretion, but philosophers have frequently raised questions
in speculative terms which the scientists have later an-
swered by experimental methods. In the nineteenth century, philosophy continued to be in part, a repository of
hitherto unsolved problems concerning the nature of things.
And particularly in the domains of social theory and
psychology, the nineteenth century philosophers made
many original and fruitful contributions. Hegel, for example, has had a profound influence upon subsequent
legal theory; Schopenhauer and Nietzsche made significant contributions to what is now called "depth psychology"; and Auguste Comte not only gave the science of
sociology its unfortunate name, but was perhaps the first
thinker to envisage a general science of society. These contributions were important, even if it remained for others
to clarify and confirm them.

The fact remains that the main efforts of the nineteenth-
century philosophers were directed to another end. Between, say, Spinoza's *Ethics* and Fichte's *Wissenschaftslehre* (or *Science of Knowledge* as it is usually and misleadingly translated) there lies an enormous gulf. The
difference lies, in part, in a radical shift in the very conception of what the basic philosophical disciplines of
epistemology, metaphysics, and ethics are or can be. Spinoza, whose writings provide a kind of paradigm of the
earlier conception of these disciplines, and hence of the
philosophical enterprise itself, aimed at nothing less than a
demonstration from self-evident axioms and definitions of
the basic necessary truths concerning God, man, and man's
well-being. He employed the same geometrical method
used by Euclid precisely because he believes it to be *the*
method by which scientific knowledge of any subject matter can be attained. And in the *Ethics* Spinoza sought to

convert the old informal wisdom of the prophets into moral science and the speculations of the ancients concerning nature into necessary metaphysical truth. From his point of view, the old Jewish and Christian philosophy of faith and revelation has at last been supplanted by a religion of reason whose only aim is to know what there is. As if to drive home the point that religion, philosophy, and science are essentially one in method, Spinoza placed a Q.E.D. (*quod erat demonstrandum*) at the end of the demonstration of each theorem of the *Ethics,* regardless of whether what the theorem asserted was that there is only one God, that there is no absolutely free will, or that the end of human life is the intellectual love of God.

All this is completely foreign to Fichte's conception of his subject. For him, metaphysics, theory of knowledge, and ethics, become essentially normative disciplines whose function it is to analyze, appraise, and reconstruct the basic principles by which we ought to think and live. And if he and his contemporaries talk a great deal about "reality," it is not everyday factual existence which they are talking about but only "ideal" reality. Fichte does not attempt to prove his basic metaphysical theses; rather does he simply "posit" them as inescapable demands of his own ego. Not many nineteenth-century philosophers accept— indeed few philosophers in any age have the courage to accept—the extreme subjectivism of Fichte's doctrine of knowledge. But most of them recognize, in one way or another, that their fundamental task, not only as ethicists, but also as metaphysicians, theologians, and epistemologists, has to do with questions of principle rather than of fact, with standards of validity or rationality in any domain rather than with the particular things that do or do not conform to those standards. Some of them, at least, come increasingly to recognize that objectivity is not so much a fact about the universe as it is a matter of common standards of judgment and criticism. Objectivity, in short, is now conceived as inter-subjectivity. Inter-subjective norms are not agreed to by the members of a society because they are objective, but, in effect, become objective because they are jointly accepted.

It is because they recognized, however obscurely, a difference in kind between normative questions and questions
of fact, and because they regarded their own distinctively
philosophical questions as normative, that most of the
nineteenth-century philosophers were gradually forced to
recognize that their own work as philosophers was not,
to that extent, a part of science. Nor could they use the
methods of science. This does not mean that they were,
as a whole, hostile to science. Some were; others were not.
But even those who were friendly to science were more or
less aware that the defense of science is not itself a part
of the corpus of accredited scientific theory. As philosophers, men like Comte and Mill were friends of the court,
rather than judges or members of the jury. Kant, with
whom our story opens, was himself a scientist and a friend
of science all his days. But his *Critique of Pure Reason,*
which seeks among other things to show how and on what
conditions scientific knowledge is possible, does not itself
belong to science. The same is true of the positive philosophy of Auguste Comte.

This is not to deny that some nineteenth-century philosophers, such as Herbert Spencer, believed that at least a
part of what they were asserting was scientifically justified.
Yet even with them one discerns that their philosophical
interest is not in the facts as such but in the basic attitudes
to which the facts, as they describe them, lend support.
They were not, like Charles Darwin, primarily scientific
inquirers, but attitudinizers who sought to draw the proper
moral from the findings of the evolutionary hypothesis.
As naturalists, they denied the existence of any transempirical entities. But they were far more concerned with the
use of such denials in raising practical doubts concerning
traditional religious and moral attitudes than with the bare
description of the pervasive traits of being, as such.

Nietzsche provides an excellent illustration of this point.
His work *The Genealogy of Morals* is, among other things,
an early forerunner of present-day historical and anthropo-
logical studies in the evolution of moral ideas and prac-
tices. From Nietzsche to Hobhouse, Westermarck, and
Malinowski, for example, there is a clear line of descent.

But although Nietzsche's conception of such a study is thoroughly empirical and naturalistic, his underlying interest is not scientific but ideological. That is to say, he uses his genealogy, and indeed even the idea that morality has a genealogy, as a device for the purpose of ridding his readers of their old uncritical commitments to a way of life which he regards as self-stultifying. For Nietzsche, the historical approach to the study of morals itself provides a main lever for his "transvaluation of values." In short, for him, as for Comte and Marx, history and science are themselves instruments of cultural change, to be used deliberately for the purpose of reconstituting Western man's attitudes toward his tradition and, hence, toward himself.

There is, however, a still broader sense in which philosophical reflection in the nineteenth century was "ideological" in character. From one point of view, the whole history of ideas in the modern age may be regarded as a history of the progressive breakdown of the medieval Christian synthesis which had been most powerfully articulated in the *Summas* of Thomas Aquinas and most movingly and persuasively expressed in Dante's *Divine Comedy*. Since the Renaissance, the primary and increasingly crucial "existential problem" of man has been the adjustment of the new attitudes and ideas to the orthodox values and the traditional conception of human destiny that are represented in the medieval synthesis. From the middle of the eighteenth century on, however, the very possibility of such an adjustment came increasingly into question, and on more and more fundamental cultural levels. In the nineteenth century, many philosophers can no longer credit such a possibility. They are determined, therefore, to reconstitute the ideals of Western culture on a radically secular and humanistic, that is to say, a radically non-Christian, basis. It is for this reason, in part, that the nineteenth-century philosophers are perhaps more concerned to question the meaning of religious symbols than the existence of God; and it is for this reason that, unlike the skeptics of the eighteenth century, who doubted whether there is a First Cause of things, they now begin to ask whether "God is

dead." For some of them, "God," the traditional symbol of
divinity, is indeed dead. What they suggest is that it no
longer has any relevant use for men in an age of science
and of secular political and social institutions. Others, no
less dubious of the meaningfulness to modern men of the
traditional theological question concerning God's existence, seek to reinterpret the basic symbols of Western
religion in such a way as to render them still expressive of
the predicaments of modern men. But the result, in either
case, is a profoundly revolutionary critique of religion
which is no longer satisfied with the answers either of rationalistic "natural" religion or of traditionally interpreted
revealed or Biblical religion. This critique often appears
"irrational," at least from the standpoint of earlier philosophical standards of rationality. Actually, it is but one
aspect of the continuing critique of reason itself.

Such considerations as these may help to explain how
it was that the nineteenth-century philosophers became involved in a gigantic task of ideological and cultural reconstruction which precluded the very possibility of doing
philosophy in the time-honored "rational" and "objective"
ways which had prevailed in Western philosophy since the
time of Plato and Aristotle. These philosophers could no
longer simply contemplate, speculate, or reason about the
nature of things, for the very framework within which traditional philosophical contemplation, speculation, and reasoning proceeded had now been shaken to its very foundations. They were involved, in short, in a prolonged crisis
of reason, more profound than any that had occurred in
Western culture since the original collision of paganism
with primitive Christianity.

CHAPTER II

The Transcendental Turn in
Modern Philosophy:
Immanuel Kant (1724-1804)

TO ANYONE WHO CASUALLY TURNS THE PAGES OF KANT'S *Critique of Pure Reason* for the first time, the reasons for his immense influence will not be immediately evident. His works bristle with highly abstract dilemmas and paradoxes that seem initially remote from the perplexities of ordinary mortals. They are written in a heavy academic style which is quite appalling to anyone who comes to them fresh from the reading of a Voltaire or a Hume. Nor is the absence in Kant's writing of that classical lucidity and wit which one associates with the Age of Enlightenment compensated for by any touch of the new enthusiasm and eloquence which that prince of Romantics, Rousseau, had recently introduced into philosophical prose. Yet Kant had one of the most daring and original minds in the history of human thought. And in his ponderous critiques of pure and practical reason, as some of his contemporaries knew, there occurred a profound philosophical revolution.

The poet Heine has given us a brief description of Kant which conveys his essential qualities better than a hundred pages of biography. "The history of the life of Immanuel Kant," said Heine, "is hard to write, inasmuch as he had neither life nor history, for he lived a mechanically ordered and abstract old bachelor life in a quiet retired street in Koenigsberg, an old town on the northeast border of Germany. I do not believe that the great clock of the cathedral there did its daily work more dispassionately and regularly

than its compatriot Immanuel Kant. Rising, coffee drink-
ing, writing, reading college lectures, eating, walking, all
had their fixed time, and the neighbors knew that it was
exactly half past three when Immanuel Kant in his grey
coat, with his bamboo cane in his hand, left his house door
and went to the Lime tree avenue, which is still called, in
memory of him, the Philosopher's Walk. . . . Strange
contrast between the external life of the man and his destroying, world-crushing thought! In very truth, if the
citizens of Koenigsberg had dreamed of the real meaning
of his thought, they would have experienced at his sight a
greater horror than they would on beholding an executioner
who only kills men. But the good people saw nothing in
him but a professor of philosophy, and when he at the
regular hour passed by, they greeted him as a friend, and
regulated their watches by him. But if Immanuel Kant, the
great destroyer in the world of thought, went far beyond
Maximilian Robespierre in terrorism, he had many points
of resemblance to him which challenge comparison between
the two. Firstly we find in both the same inexorable, cutting,
prosaic, sober sense of honor and integrity. Then we find in
them the same talent for mistrust, which the one showed as
regards thoughts and called it criticism, while the other
applied it to men and entitled it republican virtue. But there
was manifested in both, to the very highest degree, the type
of *bourgeoisie,* of the common citizen. Nature meant them
to weigh out coffee and sugar but destiny determined that
they should weigh other things; so one placed a king, and
the other a god in the scales—and they both gave exact
weight."*

Kant's intellectual development was unusually slow. As
a student he had been indoctrinated into the eminently respectable rationalism of Christian von Wolff, the uninspired
disciple of the great Leibniz. Only in middle age did Kant
manage to transcend that influence. He received help in this
respect primarily from the writings of Rousseau and Hume,
who, together with Leibniz, may be regarded as the three
major formative influences upon his mature thought. Some-

* Heinrich Heine, *Germany, Works,* V, pp. 136–37.

thing of the nature of these influences must be conveyed if Kant's own philosophy is to be understood.

From Descartes onward, the two major schools of philosophy, rationalism and empiricism, were much concerned with the problem of knowledge. It is this preoccupation, in fact, which is commonly said to distinguish the "modern" period in the history of philosophy from the ancient and medieval periods preceding it. Yet none of Kant's predecessors supposed for a moment that questions of method are the end-all of philosophy. Most of them considered the theory of knowledge, or epistemology, as it is called, merely a necessary preliminary to the proper business of philosophy, which is to characterize the fundamental nature of things and the conditions of man's well-being. Descartes's famous *Discourse on Method* was written, not merely to clarify what he took to be the method of science, which for him coincided with the way to knowledge generally, but also to apply his results toward the solution of the grand metaphysical questions concerning the nature and relations of mind and matter, and the cause of both, which he called God. Descartes and his successors in the rationalistic school, Spinoza and Leibniz, regarded themselves, in effect, as highly self-conscious scientists whose function it was to clarify and then apply the same methods that had recently achieved such astounding successes in the domains of mathematics and physics to the larger problems of existence with which philosophers had been concerned since before Plato. They conceived themselves, so to say, as super-geometers and super-physicists; nor did they doubt that their own metaphysical investigations were essentially continuous with those of the "special" sciences. For them, metaphysics, the science of being, is merely the "queen of the sciences," and for them, ethics is nothing but the system of "natural laws" that state the conditions under which men may realize their natures. Any sharp distinction between laws of nature and normative principles is entirely foreign to their thought. Such a distinction is fundamental to Kant's philosophy.

There are many anticipations of Kant in the writings

of the great opponents of rationalism, Locke, Berkeley, and Hume. But if Locke, in his famous *Essay,* was moving in a faltering way toward the Kantian problem of a critique of reason, his conception of that problem remained unclear. His analysis of the human understanding did not seriously impugn the basic methodological assumptions of Descartes. Nor did he envisage his own task of determining the "certainty and extent of human knowledge" as one which differs sharply from what we should think of as empirical psychology. His preoccupation with questions concerning the origins of our ideas and his adherence to what he called the "plain historical method" make it quite clear that he was aware of no fundamental cleavage between psychological investigations of the determining causes of our ideas and beliefs and philosophical analyses of the meaning of ideas and of the validity of beliefs.

Kant's whole philosophy, on the other hand, presupposes a radical distinction between *de facto* and *de jure* questions. Such a distinction, for him, is necessary, not merely in ethics, where a distinction must be made between the desired and the desirable, but also in logic and the theory of knowledge, where analogous distinctions must be drawn between the believed and the belief-worthy, the inferred and the validly inferred. It is significant that Kant, as a philosopher, did not write *A Treatise of Human Nature,* as Hume called his major work, but, rather a *Critique of Pure Reason* and a *Critique of Practical Reason.* For his purposes, evidently, Locke's "plain historical method" would not serve at all. He was obliged, therefore, to formulate a new "transcendental method" which alone could determine the grounds of rational belief and rational action.

Kant's use of the term "transcendental" has been frequently misunderstood. Observing its frequent occurrence in the pages of Kant's works, casual readers are sometimes led to suppose that he was attempting to provide a mode of access to things that are literally "out of this world." They are mistaken. Kant had, in fact, very stringent views about the possibility of our knowing any transcendent reality whatever. So far was he from desiring, like the character in Gilbert and Sullivan's *Patience,* to "get up all the germs of the transcendental terms, and plant them everywhere," that a very large part of his intellectual effort was spent in discrediting their metaphysical application beyond the bounds of possible experience.

Kant believed that what his critique of reason had effected was a virtual "Copernican Revolution" in philosophy. But the analogy thereby intended is ambiguous, and, like the use of the term "transcendental," has been much misunderstood. In order to grasp more fully what Kant himself meant by it we must turn again to the historical situation which confronted him when, as a follower of Leibniz, he read for the first time Hume's apparently skeptical analysis of causation.

As a rationalist, the young Kant had uncritically assumed that the principle of causality, that every event has a cause, is a necessary law of nature, written into the nature of things, the truth of which is discernible by pure reason without recourse to experience. He had taken for granted, also, that there are necessary connections in nature which are inherent in the objective order of reality. From such a point of view, the power of reason is nothing but the power to intuit such "real relations" and thereby to provide a kind of map or X ray of the inherent structure of being itself. The human mind thinks "cause-wise" precisely because the mind itself is, in effect, a mirror that reflects without distortion the indwelling structure of the external world. Reason knows such principles to be true "self-evidently" because it "sees," through an act of intellectual intuition, that they are necessarily true of the nature of things. From this standpoint, reason is not merely a faculty of abstraction and inference but also one of discovery which enables us to discern the most general traits of things as they are in themselves.

Hume's reply to all this is quite simple. How, he asked, can we know that every event has and must have a cause independently of experience? Hume was ready to admit that some propositions are necessarily true. Among them he included the truths of mathematics and logic, and such "verbal" propositions as "Every dog is a dog" and "Every colored thing is extended." Such truths, however, express "relations of ideas"; they tell us nothing about matters of fact or existence. The sole criterion of necessary truth, according to Hume, is the law of non-contradiction. If a proposition cannot be denied without contradiction, it is necessarily true. But by the same token, it tells us nothing beyond what is implied by the concepts which it contains. Any proposition that can be denied without contradiction is not necessarily true. In that case, if it means anything at all, the evidence for it can be acquired only by experience,

What, then, about the law of causality? Is there any contradiction in denying that something may exist without a cause? According to Hume, the answer must be an unqualified "No." The Law of universal causation, so far as it is a law of nature, cannot be known to be true a priori in advance of experience.

The issue here is fundamental. For if the principle of causality is uncertain, then it would appear that the whole enterprise of science has no more secure foundation than revealed religion. Is there, then, no justification of the scientist's belief in the uniformity of nature? Is is merely another act of faith that has no more rational foundation than the commitments of the priest, the prophet, or the medicine man?

It was to such momentous questions as these that Kant addressed himself in the *Critique of Pure Reason*. And his answers to them constitute the greater part of his Copernican Revolution in philosophy. Kant accepts Hume's analysis on its negative side. He agrees that the rationalists have been uncritical in supposing that the law of universal causation is a necessary truth intuited by reason as true of all things as they are in themselves. The law is not, as Kant puts it, "analytic." Hume is entirely right in denying that it follows from the very meaning of a "thing" that it must have a cause. The principle, therefore, must be "synthetic." But Kant refuses to regard it as merely a contingent statement of fact such as "All swans are white" or "All philosophers are neurotic." What sort of proposition, then, is the law of causality?

Kant's reply is that it is neither a factual statement which is true only a posteriori, nor an "analytic" explication of the meanings already contained in a concept. Rather is it a regulative principle which expresses a universal rule of all rational inquiry. All principles of this sort are a priori, but they are also synthetic. They are, that is to say, absolutely universal and necessary, and their validity, therefore, does not await the confirmation of experience. On the contrary, their validity is presupposed by all judgments which purport to give us knowledge of phenomena. But they apply, nevertheless, to our conception of things as existing, and not merely to what Hume called relations of ideas.

For Kant, then, the fundamental question of the critique of reason is simply, "How are a priori synthetic judgments possible?" In the space here available, Kant's answer to this question can be indicated only in a general way. His premise is that the human understanding can no longer be conceived as a passive mirror which reflects intuitively the patterns, the *logos,* of things in themselves. What we call the "mind" must be regarded as an active agency which itself composes the raw material of sense experience into a world order of conceptualized phenomena. Kant is not, however, an "idealist." He does not hold, that is to say, that mind itself is the only reality, nor that mind creates its world. The data of sense experience are "given" willy-nilly; we simply find them to be there when we open our eyes and ears. Nor does Kant doubt that in some sense there are "things in themselves," "outside" the mind, which are independently real. This assumption, in fact, is a central thesis of his whole philosophy. But things in themselves are not, according to Kant, objects of knowledge, and about them the understanding has properly nothing whatever to say. The function of the understanding is rather to legislate the rules of inquiry by which the brute facts of sense may come to live together in a civil society of law-abiding objects.

Such an analogy must not be pressed too far. It is not, in Kant's view, as if the legislating mind, if it so elected, could establish other rules than those actually employed in common-sense and scientific thinking about phenomena. In this respect, Kant remains bound to his own rationalistic heritage. What he calls the "forms of intuition," space and time, although subjective, are inherent in all human perception. To imagine an object which is not in space and time is, for him, impossible. Moreover, Kant thinks of the Euclidean geometry, which in his time was the only geometry that had yet been constructed by mathematicians, as stating the necessary and universal relations of all objects that can appear to us in space. It never occurs to him that other geometrical systems might be devised that might be more useful than Euclid's for certain scientific purposes. He also thinks of such categories as cause and substance as essential to all rational thinking about phenomena. The possibility of a science which might dispense with such categories did not so much as enter his mind.

What he did clearly understand, however, is that all such categories as "cause" and "substance" do not represent real relations or entities. And he is the progenitor of the view, later expressed in many different ways, that the methodological concepts and principles of inquiry are not reflections of a "logos," resident in the nature of things, but rather procedural ideas and rules that are adopted "pragmatically" for the purpose of controlling the world in which we live.

On the whole, the negative side of Kant's doctrine has had the greatest historical influence. As we have seen, it is essential to his position that the forms of intuition, space and time, and the categories of the understanding, such as substance and cause, have no proper application beyond what is given in sense experience. For the possibility of a priori synthetic principles, such as the law of causality, we must pay the price of restricting their application to the world of experiencable phenomena. Within that world we may continue to make distinctions between the "real" and the "illusory," but such distinctions have no application to things in themselves. When we try to extend the application of such notions as cause or substance to things in themselves or try to reason "realistically" concerning the "cause" of the phenomenal universe as a whole, we land

inevitably in imponderable paradoxes which are wholly
beyond the power of the human understanding to resolve.
Such an unbridled "speculative" use of reason is characteristic of the previous uncritical and dogmatic assertions
of the rationalists concerning the ultimate nature and cause
of things. In every case, Kant holds, the speculative use
of reason results in metaphysical theses whose very meaningfulness is doubtful. For all propositions such as the
thesis that the universe as a whole has a cause, there is
an equally plausible antithesis which can be demonstrated
with the same finality, and whose meaning, therefore, is
equally dubious. You demonstrate, by purely rational
means, that the world must have a beginning in time; but
I can prove, with an equal show of necessity, that it can
have no such beginning. You argue, with what seems to
be complete cogency, that matter is composed of simple,
indivisible atoms; but I can as convincingly prove that
matter is infinitely divisible. You argue that if anything
at all exists, yourself for example, there must be a necessary
beginning for its cause; but when you do, I can as well
"demonstrate" the antithesis that there is and can be no
such necessary being.

In all such cases, what happens is that we uncritically
extend the application of the categories of the understanding to suppositious entities that lie entirely beyond the
range of possible experience. In doing so we lose our
logical bearings, and are left with imponderable antithetical
claims whose validity is equally doubtful. Superficially it
seems sensible to ask whether the universe as a whole has
a cause or a beginning in time. But on closer examination
we find that we cannot answer such questions at all, not,
however, because we lack sufficient evidence, but because
the questions themselves are wrongheaded. If the universe
as a whole is to be thought of as the effect of some outsized
cause, we are obliged to think of the universe as a gigantic
physical object which stands to that "cause" in the same
sort of relation as that which holds between ordinary
phenomena. But the universe as a whole is not a phenomenon and cannot properly be thought of as such. In all metaphysical thinking of this sort we are compelled to apply

concepts so far beyond their normal ranges of application that we no longer know what we appear to be saying. The consequence is an interminable vacillation between theses and antitheses which are equally plausible and, by the same token, of equally doubtful intelligibility. Better, thinks Kant, to give up the whole wretched game of speculative metaphysics, lest the very categories themselves fall into disrepute and the human understanding become frozen in the grip of skepticism.

Kant's refutations of the traditional proofs for the existence of God, which have so important a place in rationalistic metaphysics and theology, are based upon similar considerations. It must suffice to say here that, in Kant's opinion, all such proofs rest upon the so-called "ontological argument," according to which the existence of God cannot be denied without contradiction: By definition, the concept of God is that of an absolutely perfect being; but an absolutely perfect being must have existence as one of its attributes, since otherwise it would be imperfect; hence God, as the absolutely perfect being, must exist. This argument is fallacious precisely because it requires us to regard "existence" as a predicate which names an attribute on all fours with the other attributes, such as omniscience, that are traditionally assigned to God. But "existence" is not a predicate, and does not name an attribute or characteristic of the things to which it is ascribed. To illustrate his point, Kant gives the example of the difference between a hundred real dollars and a hundred possible dollars. The only difference lies in the fact that the former exist, and the latter do not. The concept of a hundred dollars is precisely the same in both cases.

The point that Kant is making here is that the logical function of the term "existence" is subverted when it is construed, as the traditional proofs of God's existence require, as a predicate term which designates a property. The only conclusion to be drawn from this, as Hume had argued earlier, is that the very notion of God, when conceived as a "necessary being," is an impossible idea. Kant adds the important point that even if these proofs of God's existence were valid, it would still not follow that such a "necessary being" is identical with the providential deity who is taken by many to be the proper subject of human worship and piety.

It might be inferred from all this that Kant's devastating critique of speculative metaphysics is an anticipation of the later positivistic theory that all metaphysical and theological propositions are strictly meaningless. This would be a mistake. For while he bitterly opposes all pretentions to metaphysical knowledge of reality, Kant does think that certain metaphysical or theological convictions have a certain point as "postulates" of *practical* reason. In order, therefore, to gain a more correct picture of Kant's teaching in this regard, it is essential to say something about his moral philosophy.

The business of morality or practical reason, according to Kant, is never to describe or predict matters of fact. Its concern is merely to tell us how we ought to live and what we ought to do. The judgments of practical reason thus yield no knowledge in the theoretical sense; they are, rather, practical imperatives whose function it is to guide us in making decisions. Practical or moral reasoning is not addressed to the resolution of intellectual doubts concerning what exists, but, rather, to the removal of irresolutions of the will. Such indecisions, Kant thinks, are of two main sorts: (a) those which arise from ordinary conflicts of desire or inclination, and (b) those which arise from conflicts between natural desires or inclinations and our sense of duty. Answering to these two very different types of practical indecision, there are two main types of imperative: (a) "hypothetical imperatives" which tell us what we must do if we wish to satisfy our desires, and (b) "categorical imperatives," which tell us what, as moral beings, we ought to do. If I wish to keep my health, then I ought not to worry. But in this case nothing supports the "ought" save my natural desire to be healthy. In such an example, therefore, we are faced with a hypothetical imperative whose only practical necessity derives from our desire to achieve the end to which it expresses the necessary means. Categorical imperatives, however, demand that we perform the acts which they enjoin regardless of our per-

sonal inclinations. They ask no questions about preference
or taste, and are addressed to us unconditionally and impersonally as rational moral beings.

The key to a correct understanding of categorical or
moral imperatives, according to Kant, is the concept of
law, that is to say, a principle which is valid without exception. But moral laws, unlike the laws of nature which
science describes, do not tell us what is the case; they
tell us, rather, what ought to be the case, what, in the circumstances, any rational being ought to do. The categorical imperative, whose similarity to the Golden Rule
has often been noted, is, therefore, that we ought to adopt
as our rules of conduct in any practical situation only those
maxims that we could consistently will to be universal
laws of nature. Such rules, again, are not natural laws,
and those who treat them as such misconceive their function. But they are not moral rules unless we would, if we
could, make them such.

Kant's theory has frequently been criticized. What concerns us here is the important consequence of his sharp
distinction between pure or theoretical reason and practical
reason, between science and ethics. For anyone who accepts Kant's doctrine of "the two reasons," as it has been
called, and who, like him, holds that the foundation of all
practical reason lies in the will rather than in the intellect
alone, a whole major domain of philosophical reflection is
removed, at a single stroke, from the exclusive jurisdiction
of the scientific method. Ethics, and whatever else resembles it in this respect, may still be, in an important
sense, "rational"; but in that case reason itself can no
longer be regarded as a purely theoretical faculty. Moreover, if, as Kant holds, the only legitimate theological or
metaphysical convictions are those which are based, finally,
upon the demands of the moral will, then two other
crucially important branches of philosophical inquiry are
also removed from the domain which, however liberally
construed, may be called "science." In this historically
important part of Kant's philosophy, one can, in short, see
philosophy itself gradually shifting from the status of superscience to that of ideology. What is crucially significant,

however, is that Kant himself can at once acknowledge this move in the case of ethics and still insist that it is a form of rational activity.

In order to complete our picture it is necessary to follow Kant's analysis of the conditions of the moral life one step further. The imperatives of morality, as we have seen, are categorical. Yet, for Kant, they make sense only if we make certain assumptions. For example, unless the moral will is free either to do or not to do what the moral law prescribes, morality itself will be regarded as an illusion. But nothing, says Kant, is more inescapably real to us than the deliverances of conscience. So far, however, as we conceive ourselves as physical organisms, there is no way of conceiving ourselves as free; our behavior, like that of any organism, is so far subject to the determination of natural causes. In short, so far as we can *know* by scientific means, our bodies are phenomena operating in space and time and hence entirely subject to the laws of physics and physiology. But Kant's doctrine regarding things in themselves, or noumena, as he also calls them, provides him with an escape clause. It is not necessary to suppose that the category of cause and effect applies beyond the domain of spatio-temporal phenomena. Hence, since we are bound to believe that the will is free in order to give reality to the moral life, we can consistently believe that we belong to a moral realm "outside" the phenomenal order of space and time. The "metaphysical" presuppositions of morality are thus entirely compatible with the rules of scientific inquiry.

By a series of arguments which need not detain us here, Kant endeavors in this way to show, on moral grounds. that we must believe that we are the free members of a rational, spiritual order, and that, as such, we are also immortal. He also argues that, as a practical necessity, we must believe in a Being or God who alone can guarantee our immortality, and thus give substance to the moral life. Such beliefs or acts of faith, however, are merely postulates of practical reason. They can never be known to be true, and any theoretical attempt to prove them to be such inevitably lands us in the antinomies and paradoxes of pure reason. In a word, Kant regards religion (and, in effect, metaphysics) as an adjunct of the moral life; we accept its "truths," in the last analysis, not because we have any evidence for them, but because, as moral agents, we must do so.

The details of Kant's argument have not convinced many of his successors. But its essential thesis has been of lasting importance. For what he is virtually saying is that the whole enterprise of traditional theology is misconceived: The essence of religion, like that of morality, does not consist in superscientific hypotheses concerning the nature and origins of the "created" world, but rather in the support it gives to moral experience and conduct. Perhaps this is why, in English, we speak of the articles of any religious creed as articles of "faith" rather than of belief. In so doing, we are acknowledging, in effect, Kant's point that the meaning of a religious creed does not lie in the evidences of the human understanding.

The philosophy of Kant is a bridge between the Enlightenment, with its faith in science as the know-all and cure-all for every human perplexity, and the age of Romanticism, in which an entirely different basis is sought for morality, religion, and philosophy itself. Kant himself repudiated some of the later philosophical implications which his younger contemporary, Fichte, saw in his doctrine of the two reasons. Yet that doctrine, together with his conception of philosophy as essentially "critique," was itself responsible, in considerable degree, for the most important philosophical developments in the period which followed.

The following is a selection from Sections 50-54 of Kant's *The Prolegomena to Any Future Metaphysics.** These sections are entitled "The Cosmological Ideas."

[This product of pure reason in its transcendent use is its most remarkable phenomenon. It serves as a very powerful agent to rouse philosophy from its dogmatic slumber

* *The Prolegomena to Any Future Metaphysics,* edited by Lewis W. Beck, Library of Liberal Arts Edition, New York; The Liberal Arts Press, 1951, pp. 86–95. The original appeared under the title *Prolegomena zu einer jeden kunftigen Metaphysic,* 1783.

and to stimulate it to the arduous task of undertaking a critical examination of reason itself.

I term this Idea cosmological because it always takes its object only in the sensible world and does not need any other world than one whose object is given to sense; consequently it remains in this respect in its native home, does not become transcendent, and is therefore so far not an Idea; whereas to conceive the soul as a simple substance, on the contrary, means to conceive such an object (the simple) as cannot be presented to the senses. Yet, in spite of this, the cosmological idea extends the connection of the conditioned with its condition (whether this is mathematical or dynamical) so far that experience never can keep up with it. It is therefore with regard to this point always an Idea, whose object never can be adequately given in any experience.

In the first place, the use of a system of categories becomes here so obvious and unmistakable that, even if there were not several other proofs of it, this alone would sufficiently prove it indispensable in the system of pure reason. There are only four such transcendent Ideas, as many as there are classes of categories; in each of which, however, they refer only to the absolute completeness of the series of the conditions for a given conditioned. In accordance with these cosmological Ideas, there are only four kinds of dialectical assertions of pure reason, which, being dialectical, prove that to each of them, on equally specious principles of pure reason, a contradictory assertion stands opposed. As all the metaphysical art of the most subtle distinction cannot prevent this opposition, it compels the philosopher to recur to the first sources of pure reason itself. This antinomy, not arbitrarily invented but founded in the nature of human reason, and hence unavoidable and never ceasing, contains the following four theses together with their antitheses:

1

Thesis: The world has, as to time and space, a beginning (limit).

Antithesis: The world is, as to time and space, infinite.

2

Thesis: Everything in the world consists of [elements that are] simple.

Antithesis: There is nothing simple, but everything is composite.

3

Thesis: There are in the world causes through freedom.

Antithesis: There is no freedom, but all is nature.

4

Thesis: In the series of the world-causes there is some necessary being.

Antithesis: There is nothing necessary in the world, but in this series all is contingent.

Here is the most singular phenomenon of human reason, no other instance of which can be shown in any other use of reason. If we, as is commonly done, represent to ourselves the appearances of the sensible world as things in themselves, if we assume the principles of their combination as principles universally valid of things in themselves and not merely of experience, as is usually, nay, without our *Critique* unavoidably, done, there arises an unexpected conflict which never can be removed in the common dogmatic way; because the thesis, as well as the antithesis, can be shown by equally clear, evident, and irresistible proofs—for I pledge myself as to the correctness of all these proofs—and reason therefore perceives that it is divided against itself, a state at which the skeptic rejoices, but which must make the critical philosopher pause and feel ill at ease.

We may blunder in various ways in metaphysics without any fear of being detected in falsehood. If we but avoid self-contradiction, which in synthetical though purely fictitious propositions is quite possible, then whenever the concepts which we connect are mere Ideas that cannot be given (with respect to their whole content) in experience, we cannot be refuted by experience. For how can we make out by experience whether the world is from eternity or had a beginning, whether matter is infinitely divisible or consists of simple parts? Such concepts cannot be given in any experience, however extensive, and consequently the falsehood either of the affirmative or the negative proposition cannot be discovered by this touchstone.

The only possible way in which reason could have revealed unintentionally its secret dialectic, falsely announced as its dogmatics, would be when it were made to ground an assertion upon a universally admitted principle and to deduce the exact contrary with the greatest accuracy of inference from another which is equally granted. This is actually here the case with regard to four natural Ideas of reason, whence four assertions on the one side and as many counterassertions on the other arise, each consistently following from universally acknowledged principles. Thus they reveal, by the use of these principles, the dialectical illusion of pure reason, which would otherwise forever remain concealed.

This is therefore a decisive experiment, which must necessarily expose any error lying hidden in the assumptions of reason.* Contradictory propositions cannot both be false, except the concept on which each is founded is self-contradictory; for example, the propositions, "A square circle is round," and "A square circle is not round," are both false. For as to the former, it is false that the circle is round because it is quadrangular; and it is likewise false that it is not round, that is, angular, because it is a circle. For the logical criterion of the impossibility of a concept consists in this that, if we presuppose it, two contradictory propositions both become false; consequently, as no middle

* I therefore would be pleased to have the critical reader to devote to this antinomy of pure reason his chief attention, because nature itself seems to have established it with a view to stagger reason in its daring pretensions and to force it to self-examination. For every proof which I have given of both thesis and antithesis I undertake to be responsible, and thereby to show the certainty of the inevitable antinomy of reason. When the reader is brought by this curious phenomenon to fall back upon the proof of the presumption upon which it rests, he will feel himself obliged to investigate the ultimate foundation of all knowledge by pure reason with me more thoroughly.

between them is conceivable, nothing at all is thought by that concept.

The first two antinomies, which I call mathematical because they are concerned with the addition or division of the homogeneous, are founded on such a contradictory concept; and hence I explain how it happens that both the thesis and antithesis of the two are false.

When I speak of objects in time and in space, it is not of things in themselves, of which I know nothing, but of things in appearance, that is, of experience, as the particular way of knowing objects which is afforded to man. I must not say of what I think in time or in space, that in itself, and independent of these my thoughts, it exists in space and in time, for in that case I should contradict myself; because space and time together with the appearances in them, are nothing existing in themselves and outside of my representations, but are themselves only modes of representation, and it is palpably contradictory to say that a mere mode of representation exists without our representation. Objects of the senses therefore exist only in experience, whereas to give them a self-subsisting existence apart from experience or before it is merely to represent to ourselves that experience actually exists apart from experience or before it.

Now if I inquire into the magnitude of the world, as to space and time, it is equally impossible, as regards all my concepts, to declare it infinite or to declare it finite. For neither assertion can be contained in experience, because experience either of an infinite space or of an infinite elapsed time, or again, of the boundary of the world by a void space or by an antecedent void time, is impossible; these are mere Ideas. The magnitude of the world, decided either way, would therefore have to exist in the world itself apart from all experience. But this contradicts the concept of a world of sense, which is merely a complex of the appearances whose existence and connection occur only in our representations, that is, in experience; since this latter is not an object in itself but a mere mode of representation. Hence it follows that, as the concept of an absolutely existing world of sense is self-contradictory, the solution of the problem concerning its magnitude, whether attempted affirmatively or negatively, is always false.

The same holds of the second antinomy, which relates to the division of appearances. For these are mere representations; and the parts exist merely in their representation, consequently in the division—that is, in a possible experience in which they are given—and the division reaches only as far as the possible experience reaches. To assume that an appearance, for example, that of body, contains in itself before all experience all the parts which any possible experience can ever reach is to impute to a mere appearance, which can exist only in experience, an existence previous to experience. In other words, it would mean that mere representations exist before they can be found in our faculty of representation. Such an assertion is self-contradictory, as also every solution of our misunderstood problem, whether we maintain that bodies in themselves consist of an infinite number of parts or of a finite number of simple parts.

In the first (the mathematical) class of antinomies the falsehood of the presupposition consists in representing in one concept something self-contradictory as if it were compatible (that is, an appearance as a thing in itself). But, as to the second (the dynamical) class of antinomies, the falsehood of the presupposition consists in representing as contradictory what is compatible; so that while in the former case the opposed assertions were both false, in this case, on the other hand, where they are opposed to one another by mere misunderstanding, they may both be true.

Any mathematical connection necessarily presupposes homogeneity of what is connected (in the concept of magnitude), while the dynamical one by no means requires this. When we have to deal with extended magnitudes all the parts must be homogeneous with one another and with the whole, whereas in the connection of cause and effect homogeneity may indeed likewise be found but is not necessary; for the concept of causality (by means of which something is posited through something else quite different from it) does not in the least require it.

If the objects of the world of sense are taken for things

in themselves and the above laws of nature for laws of things in themselves, the contradiction would be unavoidable. So also, if the subject of freedom were, like other objects, represented as mere appearance, the contradiction would be just as unavoidable; for the same predicate would at once be affirmed and denied of the same kind of object in the same sense. But if natural necessity is referred merely to appearances and freedom merely to things in themselves, no contradiction arises if we at the same time assume or admit both kinds of causality, however difficult or impossible it may be to make the latter kind conceivable.

In appearance every effect is an event, or something that happens in time; it must, according to the universal law of nature, be preceded by a determination of the causal act of its cause [*Kausalität ihrer Ursache*]—this determination being a state of the cause—which it follows according to a constant law. But this determination of the cause to a causal act [*Ursache zur Kausalität*] must likewise be something that takes place or happens; the cause must have begun to act, otherwise no succession between it and the effect could be conceived. Otherwise the effect, as well as the causal act of the cause, would have always existed. Therefore the determination of the cause to act must also have originated among appearances and must consequently, like its effect, be an event, which must again have its cause, and so on; hence natural necessity must be the condition on which efficient causes are determined. Whereas if freedom is to be a property of certain causes of appearances, it must, as regards these, which are events, be a faculty of starting them spontaneously. That is, it would not require that the causal act of the cause should itself begin [in time], and hence it would not require any other ground to determine its start. But then the cause, as to its causal act, could not rank under time-determinations of its state; that is, it could not be an appearance, but would have to be considered a thing in itself, while only its effects would be appearances.* If

* The Idea of freedom occurs only in the relation of the intellectual, as cause, to the appearance, as effect. Hence we cannot attribute freedom to matter in regard to the incessant action by

without contradiction we can think of the beings of understanding as exercising such an influence on appearances, then natural necessity will attach to all connections of cause and effect in the sensuous world; though, on the other hand, freedom can be granted to the cause which is itself not an appearance (but the foundation of appearance). Nature and freedom therefore can without contradiction be attributed to the very same thing, but in different relations—on one side as an appearance, on the other as a thing in itself. . . .

We have in us a faculty which not only stands in connection with its subjective determining grounds [motives] which are the natural causes of its actions and is so far the faculty of a being that itself belongs to appearances, but is also related to objective grounds which are only Ideas so far as they can determine this faculty. This connection is expressed by the word *ought*. This faculty is called "reason," and, so far as we consider a being (man) entirely according to this objectively determinable reason, he cannot be considered as a being of sense; this property is a property of a thing in itself, a property whose possibility we cannot comprehend. I mean we cannot comprehend how the *ought* should determine (even if it never has actually determined) its activity and could become the cause of actions whose effect is an appearance in the sensible world. Yet the causality of reason would be free-

---

which it fills its space, though this action takes place from an internal principle. We can likewise find no notion of freedom suitable to purely rational beings, for instance, to God, so far as his action is immanent. For his action, though independent of external determining causes, is determined in his eternal reason, that is, in the divine *nature*. It is only if *something is to start* by an action, and so the effect occurs in the sequence of time, or in the world of sense (for example, the beginning of the world), that we can put the question whether the causal act of the cause must in its turn have been started or whether the cause can originate an effect without its causal act itself beginning. In the former case, the concept of this activity is a concept of natural necessity; in the latter, that of freedom. From this the reader will see that as I explained freedom to be the faculty of starting an event spontaneously, I have exactly hit the concept which is the problem of metaphysics.

dom with regard to the effects in the sensuous world, so
far as we can consider *objective grounds,* which are themselves Ideas, as their determinants. For its action in that
case would not depend upon subjective conditions, consequently not upon those of time, and of course not upon
the law of nature which serves to determine them, because
grounds of reason give the rule universally to actions,
according to principles, without influence of the circumstances of either time or place.

Now I may say without contradiction that all the actions
of rational beings, so far as they are appearances (met
with in any experience), are subject to the necessity of
nature, but the very same actions, as regards merely the
rational subject and its faculty of acting according to
mere reason, are free. For what is required for the necessity of nature? Nothing more than the determinability of
every event in the world of sense according to constant
laws, that is, a reference to cause in the [world of] appearance; in this process the thing in itself at its foundation
and its causality remains unknown. But, I say, the law of
nature remains, whether the rational being is the cause of
the effects in the sensuous world from reason—that is,
through freedom—or whether it does not determine them
on grounds of reason. For if the former is the case, the
action is performed according to maxims, the effect of
which as appearance is always conformable to constant
laws; if the latter is the case, and the action not performed
on principles of reason, it is subjected to the empirical
laws of the sensibility, and in both cases the effects are
connected according to constant laws; more than this we
do not require or know concerning natural necessity.
But in the former case reason is the cause of these laws
of nature, and therefore free; in the latter, the effects
follow according to mere natural laws of sensibility, because reason does not influence it. But reason itself is not
determined on that account by the sensibility (which is
impossible) and is therefore free in this case too. Freedom
is therefore no hindrance to natural law in appearances;
neither does this law abrogate the freedom of the practical

use of reason, which is connected with things in themselves, as determining grounds.

Thus practical freedom, namely, the freedom in which reason possesses causality according to objectively determining grounds, is rescued; and yet natural necessity is not in the least curtailed with regard to the very same effects, as appearances. The same remarks will serve to explain what we had to say concerning transcendental freedom and its compatibility with natural necessity in the same subject, but not taken in the same context. For, as to this, every beginning of the action of a being from objective causes regarded as determining grounds is always a *first beginning,* though the same action is in the series of appearances only a *subordinate beginning,* which must be preceded by a state of the cause which determines it and is itself determined in the same manner by another immediately preceding. Thus we are able, in rational beings, or in beings generally so far as their causality is determined in them as things in themselves, to think of a faculty of beginning from themselves a series of states without falling into contradiction with the laws of nature. For the relation of the action to objective grounds of reason is not a time relation; in this case that which determines the causality does not precede in time the action, because such determining grounds represent, not a reference to objects of sense, for example, to causes in the appearances, but to determining causes as things in themselves, which do not fall under conditions of time. And in this way the action, with regard to the causality of reason, can be considered as a first beginning, while in respect to the series of appearances as merely a subordinate beginning. We may therefore without contradiction consider it in the former aspect as free, but in the latter (as it is merely appearance) as subject to natural necessity.

As to the fourth antinomy, it is solved in the same way as the conflict of reason with itself in the third. For, provided the cause *in* the appearance is distinguished from the cause *of* the appearances (so far as it can be thought as a thing in itself), both propositions are perfectly reconcilable: the one, that there is nowhere in the sensuous world a cause (according to similar laws of causality) whose existence is absolutely necessary; the other, that this world is nevertheless connected with a necessary being as its cause (but of another kind and according to another law). The incompatibility of these propositions rests entirely upon the mistake of extending what is valid merely of appearances to things in themselves and in confusing both in one concept.]

CHAPTER III

Egoism in German Philosophy:
Johann Gottlieb Fichte (1762-1814)

ALTHOUGH MANY OF THE SEEDS OF THE ROMANTIC REVOLT
against the Age of Reason were already germinating in
Kant's philosophy, most of his own substantive attitudes
are characteristic of that age. His insistence upon the
moral autonomy of the individual is characteristic of a
period in which most reflective men denied the independent
spiritual authority of any institution. Kant was an individualist, for whom the basic moral obligation is respect
for the integrity of every person as an end. He was not,
however, a Romantic individualist. He would doubtless
have been horrified by Nietzsche's assertion of the right of
superior men to "transvalue" all values or to regard their
own personal aspirations as laws unto themselves. Kant
remained a universalist: any moral order is an order for
men and not merely for Germans, Christians, or white
people. And his tendency to place questions both of individual happiness and of social welfare in a subordinate
position is symptomatic of a period in which the problem
of common human rights was still the paramount social
issue.

Kant took over from Rousseau, the true father of Romanticism, the thesis regarding the moral primacy of will.
Unlike Rousseau, however, he was always careful to qualify
this by insisting that the moral will is at the same time a
rational will for which the concept of law is fundamental.
Nor did he share Rousseau's fear or hatred of theoretical

reason, or Rousseau's desire to subordinate intellectual to moral or religious standards. It might be true, in one sense, that, as Pascal had claimed, the heart has "reasons" which the intellect knows not of. But for Kant this would never justify us in abandoning the laws of logic at the behest of conscience or faith; nor would it entitle us to believe that the moon is made of green cheese if morality or religion seemed to require it.

It is where Kant stops short in following the lead of Rousseau that is essential for a correct understanding of his philosophical temper. Any attempt to push him, as some commentators have tried to do, beyond the threshold of the Romantic Age invariably results in egregious misconceptions of his teaching. With Fichte, his first important and self-constituted follower, no such push is required. He passes over that threshold naturally, by inclination and temperament as well as by conviction. In him the constraints that prevented Kant from glorifying will at the expense of the understanding are no longer firm. And in him the transformation of the concept of reason, which had already begun in Kant, is now virtually complete. Kant conceived the laws of rationality, not as a reflection of the structure of things in themselves, but as forms of the human understanding. But he did not suppose that any featherless biped might, at its pleasure, choose to reject them. No doubt the human understanding imposes upon itself the rules by which the game of knowledge is to be played. But the understanding legislates rules of inquiry which are essentially the same for all men. Fichte, at least initially, construes the point of Kant's Copernican Revolution in a much more personal sense. At the outset, he adopts the view that just as no moral law can bind me unless I myself elect to be bound by it, so no supposedly impersonal laws of the human understanding can legislate how I must play the game of knowledge unless I am prepared to make those laws my own. Any "reason" to which I am to be held responsible must be *my* reason. In short, Fichte takes the point of the "critical" philosophy to be that the demands of the individual Self, or Ego, are the starting point of all philosophical reflection. The fundamental problem is to understand these demands.

Thus Fichte turns the Kantian critique of reason into an affair of life or death for Johann Gottlieb Fichte himself. If the conclusions he arrives at are also acceptable to other individuals, that is their affair. To be sure, no man can or should remain an island, but philosophically he must begin as one. No one will grasp the fundamental human crisis implicit in the Kantian critique of reason unless he recognizes that no other philosophical beginning is possible. Or, to vary the figure, no man may leave the island of his own ego save by bridges of his own choice. In a practical sense, he also *must* build them. But the only "necessity" lies in his own volition. In the end, Fichte fudges a bit, and we find him talking, especially in his later period, of an Absolute Spirit of which my finite ego is only a manifestation. But even if Fichte himself seems only half-serious in construing Kant's transcendental turn in purely personal terms, we at least must take him seriously if his philosophy is to have any point for us.

Fichte's philosophical development was the diametrical opposite of Kant's. Kant began as a dogmatic rationalist who achieved the new perspective of his critical philosophy only in his advanced middle age. Fichte began as a disciple of Kant who thought of himself as merely carrying out, in a more thoroughgoing way, the program of the *Critiques*. He ended up as a dogmatic idealist for whom "spirit" is the only reality. Kant himself was finally obliged to repudiate Fichte's philosophy as an essential perversion of his own teaching.

Fichte's best work is to be found in his earlier writings when he is still under Kant's influence; his later writings are less stimulating and much less attractive. At first he vigorously defended the ideals which inspired the French Revolution, insisting with characteristic vigor upon the absolutely inalienable rights of the individual, upon freedom of speech and of thought, and upon the moral right of any people to revolt against any form of government which suppresses their liberties. Later, as a fanatical

German patriot, angered by the Napoleonic invasion of his fatherland, he delivered his famous *Addresses to the German Nation,* in which are plainly visible the violent racism and nationalism that have caused some of his critics to regard him as a direct ancestor of Nazism. In his last period, his earlier individualism is gradually replaced by an historically oriented statism in which the freedom of the individual ego is increasingly subordinated to, and perhaps even identified with, the Self-development of the Absolute Spirit as that manifests itself historically in the life of a community. In this respect, Fichte's career is like those of many other Romantics of his age who begin as rebels and end as conservatives—or worse.

There are two ways of approaching Fichte's philosophy, which, finally, come to much the same thing. The first approach would normally be called "ethical," the second "metaphysical." They come to the same thing precisely because, for Fichte, metaphysics is not superscience but a system of "posits" or affirmations of the will. As he understands it "reality" is not coextensive with what, in any ordinary sense, would be said to "exist," but rather with what the will takes to be necessary to the realization of its own ends. In his philosophy any distinction between what ought to be and what is real finally breaks down altogether. It is for this reason that there is no radical distinction for him between ethics or basic ideology and metaphysics. From Fichte's standpoint, it is pointless to ask, in the manner of a scientist, whether there is an external world beyond experience or whether there is a God. Such a way of putting these questions entirely misrepresents their significance, which is practical, not theoretical. The person who doubts whether there is an external world does not need proof; what he needs is a cure. It is the sincerity of my effort, the seriousness of my work, that alone makes or can make the external world a reality to me. And it is my Self and its demands which provide the only possible warrant for believing in God. In fact, there is for Fichte no essential difference, so far as metaphysical questions are concerned, between "believing that" and "believing in." Anything is metaphysically real if we must or will believe in it, even though we have no reason in the ordinary sense, for saying that it exists.

All this will sound wildly fanciful unless one constantly bears in mind the Kantian teaching which underlies it. But if one follows Fichte's tortured argument with this perspective constantly in view, his doctrine becomes somewhat more plausible. Fichte contrasts, at the outset, two antithetical philosophies, which he calls "dogmatism" and "idealism." One can finally choose between them, he contends, on no other basis than that the one adopted suits "the kind of man one is." Fichte is saying, in effect, what many believe but few admit, that ultimate philosophical commitments are made, in the last analysis, on temperamental rather than evidential grounds. He is also saying, which is more important, that such commitments are prerational, since it is only in relation to them that judgments concerning what is rational or valid can be understood. The philosophical realist uncritically holds that there is a world of independently real things by which alone the truth or adequacy of our ideas may be tested. He forgets that even to say that such a world exists is already to adopt a philosophical position with respect to which the data of experience are completely neutral.

Dogmatism is a philosophy for those who require an external authority, even if it be only the authority of an impersonal "objective" reason in whose laws or rules one dutifully aquiesces as a "rational being." Such rationalistic philosophers as Descartes and Spinoza are dogmatists. Their dogmatism, however, is self-stifling, for it cannot resolve their own residual philosophical doubts. They talk, to be sure, as though knowledge were the fundamental goal of the philosophical life, but as it turns out "knowledge" means for them nothing more than passive intuition. Thus the rationalists wind up, in effect, by identifying cognition with aesthetic contemplation, which notoriously makes no distinction between the "real" and the "unreal" and is as well satisfied by imaginary fictions as it is by apprehensions of what exists. Any serious distinction between the self and the not-self can be made only by an active ego which goes beyond what is "given" in intuition to *assert* that it is either appearance or reality. Idealism, on the other hand, is an activistic philosophy, which self-consciously makes its own assumptions and refuses to be bound by any external authority, even when it is asserted, impersonally, in the name of Reason itself. Any authoritative reason, so far as the idealist is concerned, must be his reason, and its laws are binding upon him only because they express the demands of his own ego. The rationalist uncritically presupposes an external world of things in themselves to which our ideas are supposed to correspond. The idealist refuses to be bound, a priori, by any such presupposition. At the outset, he accepts only the reality of ideas as they are given in experience. If he then asserts the reality of a world beyond his ideas, this must be understood merely as a consequence of what he chooses to make of them.

There is, of course, no doubt what sort of man Fichte himself is. He accepts idealism, not so much because he takes it to be "truer" to the nature of things, but rather because it accords better with his conception of himself as a freely willing agent. If he accepts the reality of nature, as he does, then it must be on his own terms, and not because some impersonal principle of reason compels him to do so. Fichte is no skeptic, nor is he preaching solipsism. That there is something else in reality besides himself and his ideas he does not deny; but, for him, it is "real" only because it provides grist for his will.

The first step of Fichte's idealistic philosophy is thus to reject that remnant of rationalistic dogmatism in Kant's theory of knowledge, the "thing in itself." According to Fichte, any talk of "things in themselves" is, from the standpoint of a truly critical philosophy, pointless. What we call "the world order" is the world of our assertions. Reality, in fact, is just what we make it, and the only reason for positing anything beyond our immediate impressions as real is a practical one. The rationalist merely conceals this fact from himself by impersonal locutions such as "reason," "intuition," or "self-evident truth."

Fichte's point of departure, then, is the conclusion at which Kant eventually arrived in his doctrine of practical reason. Kant himself acknowledged that our only access to the transempirical world of things in themselves is through the postulates of practical reason. Fichte goes beyond Kant to assert that our only access to any world, transempirical or empirical, is through the posits which the active self is obliged to make in order to do its business. On Kant's own showing, the objects of scientific inquiry are not "given." Fichte maintains that even their empirical reality depends upon the fact that we find it necessary, for the purposes of knowledge, to posit them. In fact, any "object" in which we are obliged to believe, whether it be the God, free will, and immortal soul which Kant thinks necessary for the moral life, or the empirical objects of science and common sense, is itself only an objective which satisfies some serious demand of the self.

The spirit of Fichte's doctrine may be conveyed in the following way. Imagine an ordinary, down-to-earth fellow who is at first stimulated but then increasingly perplexed by metaphysical controversies over the question whether there is an external world. At last he bursts out with the apparently unphilosophical question, "What does it *matter,* after all, whether there is an external world or not?" Such a question is precisely in the spirit of Fichte's philosophy. The philosophical question, for Fichte, is not so much whether something is "there," but whether there is any practical point in saying so.

Although he insists that all human activity, scientific or otherwise, begins with certain posits, and that what we call the "objective" not-self is itself not given independently of the activity of will, Fichte does not maintain that nothing is given in experience. The materials of sense are not created by the knowing mind. We may regard them or disregard them as we will, but we do not decide whether they will appear before us when we open our eyes. They are given, but they are not given as objects, and the fact that they are given does not of itself make them real. Put in another way, sensation, as such, contains no element of assertion or judgment. No sensation comes tagged as "real" or "apparent," any more than it comes tagged as "blue" or "hard." Before the mind acts upon it in any

way, any sensory presentation is an unclassified, unin-
terpreted *x,* about which there is nothing to say except
that it is presented. What the senses disclose becomes data
or evidence for any belief only when we take them to be
such in accordance with rules of inquiry which we ourselves have laid down. The scientific method itself is thus
not something which is self-evidently revealed or presented
to us as "valid" or "true." As a method, it is something
which we must adopt in the service of our own interests.
There is nothing, finally, but the seriousness of our own
commitments and our loyalty to our own ends to guarantee
any procedure or rule as a standard of validity or justification. The concept of validity, like that of obligation, does
not point to certain "real relations" inherent in an independently given reality; what it signifies is only certain
conditions of credibility through which we prescribe in
advance the terms on which anything, as we think, ought
to be believed.

Fichte thus wholly rejects the old, uncritical "correspondence theory" of truth. What he replaces it with verges
on what later idealists call a "coherence theory," according
to which the truth of any assertion is to be tested by its
compatibility with the totality of other assertions which we
are obliged to make. The final aim of knowledge is simply
the most consistent and comprehensive organization of
posits that is required for the fulfillment of our selves as
active beings. And the only "proof" of the validity of
such a system is our willingness to adhere to it.

There is much in Fichte's philosophy that anticipates the
philosophical temper of the pragmatists of the next century.
One of them, C. I. Lewis, is fully aware of the resemblance,
and on more than one occasion has indicated the influence
of Fichte upon his own thought. The sensory "given," for
the pragmatist, is not knowledge. Experience is not a mirror of an ulterior reality which, by an odd circumstance,
we cannot directly apprehend. Ideas are guides to action,
whose significance can only be appraised by envisaging
the consequences which would ensue if we acted upon
them. Standards of rationality, in any domain, are not written into the heavens, but are adopted by active beings as

practical necessities. Properly understood, all thought is an anticipation of experience, the "correctness" of which is finally established by its capacity to serve our needs. The highest achievement of the intellect, therefore, is not "contemplation" but practical problem-solving. The "real," so to say, is not an object contemplated, but that which we finally accept as the satisfactory solution to our problems.

Fichte's manner of expression is, of course, very far removed from that of the "tough-minded" pragmatists, who will have nothing to do with his animistic manner of speech. Because of Fichte's curious propensity to talk as though something called "freedom" posits itself and realizes itself in action, much that he says inevitably strikes the unsympathetic reader as the most errant sort of metaphysical mystification. Nor can it be denied that, especially in his own later "dogmatic" phase, Fichte falls into the very traps which the critical philosophy seeks to expose. He is taken in, at last, by his tendency to personify concepts and to treat them as though it is they, rather than ourselves, that will and act. And he winds up, depressingly, as an "absolute idealist" for whom the individual self, together with the "not-self" which it posits for practical reasons, are aspects or manifestations of an Absolute Spirit or Great Self which is alleged to encompass all reality.

Fichte ends by trying to have his cake and eat it. Beginning with a particular, finite ego which posits a world for action, he ends by assimilating both to an absolute ego which posits both. Thus Kant's thing in itself, which Fichte so unceremoniously rejects as the last vestigial remnant of dogmatism, finally comes home to haunt him. The consequence is that he himself gives dogmatic metaphysics a new lease on life which defeats the whole point of his doctrine regarding the primacy of practical reason. Obliterating Kant's distinction between the transcendental and the transcendent, he thereby converts what began as legitimate self-criticism into a monstrous Higher Criticism which he now confuses with reality itself.

Yet even here, if we follow the lead of Josiah Royce, his most sympathetic interpreter, something may still be salvaged which is more and less than metaphysical extravaganza. For all his "egoism," Fichte is profoundly aware of the social and even institutional character of all human activity. What we call "rational" in any sphere is, as Kant saw, conceived as something which is common to others like ourselves. We don't think of ourselves, in practice, as working alone, nor do we regard our standards as peculiar to ourselves. In short, in any enterprise in which we engage, whether it be something we call moral action or scientific inquiry, we think of ourselves as bound by "objective" or interpersonal criteria, to which others, like ourselves, are also committed. If we did not presuppose that others, like ourselves, exist, there would be no point in talking about objective criteria at all. And if we did not presuppose that there is a community of beings like ourselves who are willing to live by them there would be no point to the claim that any rational being ought to acknowledge them. What would be the point of talking about "rights" and "duties," indeed what would be the point of talking at all, if I did not assume that my world is a common world of action in which others, like myself, are also implicated and for essentially the same reasons? In this way, although no one else can do my positing for me, I am still obliged to regard the rules by which I choose to live as interpersonal or intersubjective.

No one can escape thinking of his world as a social world, of his ego as belonging to a wider community of egos. This is not, perhaps, a "datum," like the color yellow or the taste of garlic, but it is none the less an inescapable dimension of our thought and action as social beings. Dropping all pretense, then, what we call a common world is, or involves, a plurality of egos, like ourselves, that make common posits and hold themselves responsible to common rules of thought and action. From Fichte's standpoint, it is but a step from this to the further supposition of a Great Ego which wills this common world and common life through us. We are not, of course, bound to take this step, but it is one which many men in all ages have taken. For them it seems to be necessary in order to give "reality" to the common principles to which *we* hold ourselves responsible.

The following selection is from the first three sections of Fichte's *The Science of Knowledge*.*

{ I. — FIRST AND ABSOLUTELY UNCONDITIONED FUNDA-MENTAL PRINCIPLE.

We must *search for* the absolute, first, and unconditioned fundamental principle of human knowledge. It can not be *proven* nor *determined* if it is to be absolute first principle.

This principle is to express that *deed-act* which does not occur among the empirical determinations of our consciousness, nor can so occur, since it is rather the basis of all consciousness, and first and alone makes consciousness possible. In representing this deed-act it is not so much to be feared that my readers will *not* think what they ought to think, as that they will think what they ought not to think. This renders necessary a *reflection* on what may perhaps for the present be taken for that deed-act, and an *abstraction* from all that does not really belong to it.

Even by means of this abstracting reflection, that deed-act, which is not empirical *fact* of consciousness, can not become fact of consciousness; but by means of this abstracting reflection we may recognize so much: that this deed-act must necessarily be *thought* as the basis of all consciousness.

The laws **according to which this deed-act must necessarily be thought as basis of human knowledge, or, which is the same, the rules according to which that abstracting reflection proceeds, have not yet been proven as valid, but are for the present tacitly presupposed as well-known and agreed upon. As we proceed we shall deduce them from that fundamental principle, the establishment whereof is correct only if they are correct. This is a circle, but an unavoidable circle. And since it is unavoidable and freely admitted, it is also allowable to appeal to all the laws of general logic in establishing this highest fundamental principle.

In undertaking this abstracting reflection we must start

---

* *The Science of Knowledge*, translated by A. E. Kroeger, London; Trubner and Co., 1889, pp. 63–73, 75–78, 79–84. The original appeared under the title *Grundlage der gesammten Wissenschaftslehre*, 1794.

** The laws of general logic.

from some proposition which everyone will admit without
dispute. Doubtless there are many such. We choose the one
which seems to us to open the shortest road to our purpose.

In admitting this proposition, the deed-act, which we intend to make the basis of our whole science of knowledge,
must be admitted; and the reflection must show *that* this
deed-act is admitted the moment that proposition is admitted.

Our course of proceeding in this reflection is as follows:
Any fact of empirical consciousness, admitted as such valid
proposition, is taken hold of, and from it we separate one
of its empirical determinations after the other, until only
that remains, which can no longer be separated and abstracted from.

As such admitted proposition we take this one: A is A.

Every one admits this proposition, and without the least
hesitation. It is recognized by all as completely certain and
evident.

If any one should ask a proof of its certainty, no one
would enter upon such a proof, but would say: This
proposition is *absolutely* (that is, *without any further
ground*) *certain;* and by saying this would ascribe to himself the power of *absolutely positing something.*

In insisting on the in itself certainty of the above proposition, you posit *not* that A *is.* The proposition A is A is by
no means equivalent to A *is.* (*Being* when posited without
predicate is something quite different from being when
posited with a predicate.) Let us suppose A to signify a
space inclosed within two straight lines, then the proposition A is A would still be correct; although the proposition
A *is* would be false, since such a space is impossible.

But you posit by that proposition: *If* A is, *then* A is.
The question *whether* A is at all or not, does not, therefore,
occur in it. The *content* of the proposition is not regarded
at all: merely its *form.* The question is not whereof you
know, but *what* you know of any given subject. The only
thing posited, therefore, by that proposition is the *absolutely* necessary connection between the two As. This connection we will call X.

In regard to A itself nothing has as yet been posited. The
question, therefore, arises: Under what condition *is* A?

X at least is in the Ego, and posited *through* the Ego, for it is the Ego which asserts the above proposition, and so asserts it by virtue of X as a law, which X or law must, therefore, be given to the Ego; and, since it is asserted absolutely, and without further ground, must be given to the Ego through itself.

Whether and *how* A is posited we do not know; but since X is to designate a connection between an unknown positing of A (of the first A in the proposition A is A) and a positing of the same A, which latter positing is absolute on condition of the first positing, it follows that A, *at least in so far as that connection is posited,* is posited *in* and *through* the Ego, like X. Proof: X is only possible in relation to an A; now X is really posited in the Ego; hence, also, A must be posited in the Ego, in so far as X is related to it.

X is related to that A, in the above proposition, which occupies the logical position of subject, and also to that A which is the predicate, for both are united by X. Both, therefore, are posited in the Ego, in so far as they are posited; and the A of the predicate is posited *absolutely* if the first one is posited. Hence, the above proposition may be also expressed: If A is posited *in the Ego,* then *it is posited,* or then it *is.*

Hence, by means of X, the Ego posits: that A *is* absolutely for the asserting Ego, and *is* simply because it is posited in the Ego; or that there is something in the Ego which always remains the same, and is thus able to connect or posit; and hence the absolutely posited X may also be expressed, Ego = Ego, or I am I.

Thus we have already arrived at the proposition *I am;* not as expression of a deed-act, it is true, but, at least, as expression of a *fact.*

For X is absolutely posited; this is a fact of empirical consciousness, as shown by the admitted proposition. Now, X signifies the same as I am I; hence, this proposition is also absolutely posited.

But Ego is Ego, or I am I, has quite another significance than A is A. For the latter proposition had content only on a certain condition, namely, *if* A is posited. But the proposition I am I is unconditionally and absolutely valid, since it is the same as X; it is valid not only in form, but also in content. In it the Ego is posited not on condition, but absolutely, with the predicate of self-equality; hence, it is posited, and the proposition may also be expressed, *I am*.

This proposition, *I am,* is as yet only founded upon a fact, and has no other validity than that of a fact. If "A = A" (or X) is to be certain, then "I am" must also be certain. Now, it is fact of empirical consciousness that we are compelled to regard X as absolutely certain; hence, also, "I am" is certain, since it is the ground of the X. It follows from this, that the *ground of explanation of all facts of empirical consciousness is this: before all positing, the Ego must be posited through itself*.

*   *   *   *   *   *   *   *   *

The proposition A = A is *asserted*. But all asserting is an act of the human mind; for it has all the conditions of such an act in empirical consciousness, which must be presupposed as well known and admitted in order to advance our reflection. Now, this act is based on something which has no higher ground, namely, X or I am.

Hence, that which is *absolutely posited and in itself grounded* is the ground of *a certain* (we shall see hereafter of *all*) acting of the human mind; hence its pure character; the pure character of activity in itself, altogether abstracting from its particular empirical conditions.

The positing of the Ego through itself is, therefore, the pure activity of the Ego. The Ego *posits itself;* and the Ego is by virtue of this its mere self-positing. Again, *vice versa:* the Ego *is* and *posits* its being, by virtue of its mere being. It is both the acting and the product of the act; the active and the result of the activity; deed and act in one; and hence the *I am* is expressive of a deed-act; and of the *only possible* deed-act, as our science of knowledge must show.

*   *   *   *   *   *   *   *   *

§ 2.—SECOND, AND IN REGARD TO ITS CONTENT, CONDITIONED FUNDAMENTAL PRINCIPLE.

For the same reason why the first fundamental principle could not be proven or deduced, the second, also, can not be proven. Hence, we here, also, proceed from a fact of empirical consciousness in the same manner.

The proposition not A is not A will doubtless be recognized by everyone as certain, and it is scarcely to be expected that anyone will ask for its proof.

If, however, such a proof were possible, it must in our system be deduced from the proposition A=A.

But such a proof is impossible. For let us assume, at the utmost, that the above proposition is the same as —A is —A (and hence that —A is equal to some Y posited in the Ego), and that for this reason our proposition signifies now: *if* the opposite of A is posited, *then* it is posited; still we should only have the same connection posited (X) which we obtained in our § 1, and our proposition, —A is not A, instead of being derived from A=A, would, after all, be only the very same proposition. The chief question, *Is* the opposite of A posited, and under what condition *of form of mere acting* is it posited? is altogether ignored. If our second proposition were a derived one, then this condition of the form of acting would have to be derived from the proposition A=A. But how can the proposition A=A, which involves only the form of positing, also involve the form of oppositing? Hence, that form of acting, the oppositing, is posited absolutely, and with no attached condition. —A is posited *as* such simply *because* it is posited.

Hence, as sure as the proposition —A not =A occurs among the facts of empirical consciousness, there occurs among the acts of the Ego an *oppositing;* and this oppositing, as far as its *form* is concerned, is absolutely and unconditionally possible, and is an acting which has no higher ground.

Through this absolute act the opposite, *as mere* opposite, is posited. Every opposite, in so far as it is merely opposite, is simply by virtue of an absolute act of the Ego, and has no other ground. Opposition generally is simply posited through the Ego.

But if any —A is to be posited, an A must be posited. Hence, the act of oppositing is also, in another respect, conditioned. Whether the act at all is possible depends upon another act; hence, the act in its *content,* as acting generally, is conditioned; it is an acting in relation to another acting. The *form* of the act, however (the How? namely, that it is not an act of positing, but of oppositing), is unconditioned.

(Opposition is only possible on condition of the unity of consciousness of the positing and the oppositing. For if the consciousness of the first act were not connected with that of the second, then the second positing would not be an *op*-positing, but an absolute positing. Oppositing it becomes only through its relation to a positing.)

As yet we have only spoken of the act, as mere act, of the *manner* of acting. Let us now examine its product, = —A.

In —A we can again distinguish *form* and *content*. Through the form is determined, that it is an *opposite;* the content determines that it is an opposite of a determined something (of A), that it is *not* this something.

The *form* of —A is determined simply through the act; it is an opposite because it is product of an oppositing; the *content* is determined through A: it is *not* what A is, and its whole essence consists in this, that it is not what A is. I know of —A simply *that* it is the opposite of A. But *what* that is *whereof* I know this, I can only know by knowing A.

Originally only the Ego is posited, and this alone is absolutely posited. (§ 1.) Hence, an absolute oppositing can only refer to the Ego. The opposite of the Ego we call *Non-Ego*.

As sure as the proposition —A is not A is unconditionally admitted as fact of empirical consciousness, a *non-Ego is absolutely opposed to the Ego*. All we have said above in reference to oppositing generally, is deduced from this original oppositing, and hence is valid for it; it is, therefore, unconditioned in form, but conditioned in content. And thus we have also found the second principle of all human knowledge.

Whatsoever appertains to the Ego, of that the opposite must appertain to the non-Ego.

*   *   *   *   *   *   *   *   *

By undertaking the same abstraction with this proposition, which we undertook with the first, we obtain the logical proposition —A is not A, which I should call the proposition of *oppositing*. In the present place, this proposition can not yet be properly determined, or expressed in a formula, the reason whereof will appear in the following section.

By abstracting from the determined act of asserting this proposition, and looking merely to the form of drawing a conclusion from the being opposited of something to its being, we obtain the *category of negation*. This also can not be clearly developed till in the following section.

§ 3.—THIRD, IN ITS FORM CONDITIONED FUNDAMENTAL PRINCIPLE.

Every step we take in our science brings us nearer to the point where everything can be proven. In the first principle, nothing could be nor was to be proven; in the second, only the *act of oppositing* was not provable; but, this act once admitted, it was strictly shown that the opposite must be a Non-Ego. The third principle is almost throughout capable of proof, since it is not, like the second, conditioned in content, but only in form, and, moreover, conditioned in form by the *two* foregoing propositions.

It is conditioned in form signifies, the *problem of the act* it establishes is given by the two foregoing propositions, but not the *solution* of the problem. The solution is the result of an unconditioned and absolute act of reason.

We therefore commence with a deduction, and proceed as far as we can go. When we can go no further, we shall have to appeal to this absolute act.

1. In so far as the Non-Ego is posited, the Ego is not posited; for the Non-Ego completely cancels the Ego.

Now, the Non-Ego is posited *in* the Ego, for it is opposited; and all oppositing presupposes the identity of the Ego.

Hence, the Ego is not posited in the Ego in so far as the Non-Ego is posited in it.

2. But the Non-Ego can only be posited in so far as an Ego is posited in the Ego (in the identical consciousness), as the opposite of which it is posited.

Hence, in so far as the Non-Ego is posited in the Ego, the Ego also must be posited in it.

3. The conclusions of our 1st and 2d are opposed to each other; yet both are developed from the second fundamental principle; hence, that second principle is opposed to itself and cancels itself.

4. But it cancels itself only in so far as the posited is canceled by the opposited, hence in so far as itself is valid.

Hence, it does not cancel itself. The second fundamental principle cancels itself and does not cancel itself.

5. If this is the case with the second principle, it must also be with the first principle. That first principle cancels itself and does not cancel itself. For,

If Ego is = Ego, then all is posited, which is posited in the Ego.

Now, the second principle is to be posited and not to be posited in the Ego.

Hence, Ego is not = Ego, but Ego is = to the Non-Ego, and Non-Ego = Ego.

All these results have been deduced from the established principles according to the laws of reflection presupposed as valid; they must be correct, therefore. But if they are correct, the identity of consciousness, the only absolute foundation of our knowledge, is canceled. This determines our problem. We must find an X by means of which all these results may be correct, without destroying the identity of consciousness.

1. The opposites, to be united, are in the Ego as consciousness. Hence, X must also be in consciousness.

2. Both the Ego and Non-Ego are products of original acts of the Ego, and consciousness itself is such a product of the first original act of the Ego, of the positing of the Ego through itself.

3. But our above results show that the act of which the Non-Ego is the product, that is, the oppositing, is not at all possible without X. Hence, X itself must be a product of an original act of the Ego. There must be, accordingly, an act of the human mind = Y, the product of which is X.

4. The form of this act Y is determined by the above problem. It is to be a uniting of the opposites (the Ego and

the Non-Ego) without their mutually canceling each other. The opposites are to be taken up into the identity of consciousness.

5. But the problem does not determine the How, or the manner of this uniting, nor even suggests it at all. We must, therefore, make an experiment, and ask: How can A and —A, being and not being, reality and negation, be thought together, without their mutually canceling each other?

6. It is not to be expected that anyone will reply otherwise but: They must mutually *limit* each other. If this answer is correct, the act Y is a *limiting* of both opposites through each other, and X would signify the *limits*.

*   *   *   *   *   *   *   *   *

7. The conception of limits, however, involves more than the required X; for it involves also the conceptions of reality and negation, which are to be united. Hence, to get X pure, we must undertake another abstraction.

8. To *limit* something signifies to cancel the reality thereof not *altogether,* but only *in part.* Hence the conception of limits involves, besides the conceptions of reality and negation, that of *divisibility,* (of *quantitability generally,* not of a *determined* quantity). This conception is the required X, and hence, through the act Y, *the Ego as well as the Non-Ego is posited divisible.*

9. *The Ego as well as the Non-Ego are posited divisible;* for the act Y can not *succeed* the act of oppositing, for in itself the act of oppositing has shown itself impossible; nor can it *precede* that act, for the act Y occurs merely to make the act of oppositing possible; and divisibility is nothing but a divisible. Hence, the act Y and the act of oppositing occur in and with each other; both are one and the same, and are only distinguished in reflection. By oppositing, therefore, a Non-Ego to the Ego, both the Ego and the Non-Ego are posited divisible.

Let us now see whether the here established act has really solved the problem and united the opposites.

The first result is now determined as follows. The Ego is not posited in the Ego in so far, that is, with those parts of reality wherewith the Non-Ego is posited. That part of reality which is ascribed to the Non-Ego, is canceled in the Ego.

This proposition at present does not contradict the second result: in so far as the Non-Ego is posited, the Ego also must be posited; for both are posited as divisible in regard to their reality.

And only now can you say of either, it is *something*. For the absolute Ego of the first fundamental principle is not *something* (has no predicate and can have none); it is simply *what* it is. But now *all* reality is in consciousness, and of this reality that part is to be ascribed to the Non-Ego which is not to be ascribed to the Ego, and *vice versa*. Both are something. The Non-Ego is what the Ego is *not,* and *vice versa*. Opposed to the absolute Ego, the Non-Ego is *absolutely nothing* (but it can be opposed to the absolute Ego only in so far as it is an object of representation, as we shall see hereafter); opposed to the divisible Ego, the Non-Ego is a *negative quantity*.

The Ego is to be = Ego, and yet it is also to be opposed to itself. But it is self-equal in regard to consciousness; and in this consciousness the absolute Ego is posited as indivisible, and the Ego, to which the Non-Ego is opposed, as divisible. Hence, in the unity of consciousness, all the opposites are united; for in it even the Ego, in so far as a Non-Ego is opposed to it, is opposed to the absolute Ego; and this is, as it were, the test that the established conception of divisibility was the correct one.

According to our presupposition, which can be proven only through the completion of the science of knowledge, only one absolute unconditioned, one in its content conditioned, and one in its form conditioned principle is possible. Hence, no further principle can be possible. All that is unconditionally and absolutely certain has been exhausted, and I might express the total in this formula:

The Ego opposits in the Ego a divisible Non-Ego to a divisible Ego.

Beyond this cognition no philosophy can go; but every thorough philosophy ought to go to it, and by doing so will become science of knowledge. Whatsoever is hereafter to occur in the system of the human mind must be deducible from what we have here established.]

CHAPTER IV

Dialectics and History:
G. W. F. Hegel (1770-1831)

HEGEL'S PHILOSOPHY IS GENERALLY REGARDED AS THE culminating point in the development of post-Kantian idealism in Germany. It is unquestionably one of the most influential systems of thought in the nineteenth century. Without Hegel, Marxism would be unthinkable; without him, therefore, the ideological conflicts of our own age would be hard to imagine. But Hegel has had many other far-reaching effects upon modern thought, including not only philosophy itself, but also social theory, history, and jurisprudence. The only area, I was about to say, in which Hegel's thought has had no effect is that of physical science; but this would be mistaken, for in Russia even physical scientists are obliged to do homage to Marx's version of the Hegelian dialectic.

It is not easy to do justice to Hegel's philosophy. Concerning no other major philosopher is opinion so divided. Some regard him, as Thomas Aquinas regarded Aristotle, as "The Philosopher," in whose commodious system all of the chickens of earlier philosophies have at last come home to roost. Others consider him to be "the greatest mistake" in the history of philosophy. In a way this is odd, since Hegel's writing is as coldly impersonal as *The World Almanac*. As a human being Hegel is uninteresting; he lived, apparently, for no other purpose than that of playing secretary to the Absolute. But if there is little about the man himself which greatly attracts or greatly repels, there can be no doubt of his enormous influence. One may dislike his philosophy, but it cannot be ignored.

Hegel described his writings as "an attempt to teach philosophy to speak in German." If so, it was a German that no one had ever spoken before. Hegel's writing has been called "pregnant." This is not a bad description: With Hegel, one is never presented with the finished result; always there remains some further qualification to be made, some new perspective from which any idea must be viewed. The result does not make for easy reading. Hegel's prose is dense, elaborate, and laborious. He rarely says what he means, or means what he seems to be saying. For him qualification is the essence of truth. The consequence is that the harassed critic finally despairs of saying anything about him which is not false, or, which for Hegel comes to much the same thing, misleading. Nevertheless the "gray on gray" of his prose is strangely fascinating, and when we are through he has somehow managed to give us a philosophical world. If things do not move in that world in their accustomed ways, they nevertheless do move; the trick is to learn to see them.

In Hegel's philosophy we find, for the first time, a thoroughgoing attempt to view all philosophical problems and concepts, including the concept of reason itself, in essentially historical terms. No idea, for Hegel, has a fixed meaning, no form of understanding an eternal, unchanging validity. Most earlier philosophers, including Kant, had viewed both nature and mind from the standpoint of static categories and laws which are eternally imposed and reimposed upon the changing manifold of particular things. Kant conceives the mind as an active, formative agency, but the categories of the understanding and the imperatives of practical reason are not, for him, subject to change. Hegel, on the contrary, views everything—save perhaps his own philosophy—under the form of history. For earlier philosophers, the particular, as such, eludes comprehension; they conceive all knowledge to be concerned with universals, and philosophical knowledge to be the most universal of all. For Hegel, it is the particular alone which requires to be understood, even though, in his view, it cannot be fully understood save as it is seen in its relations to everything else. Apart from its relations, every particular is a "bare particular" and hence merely another abstraction; viewed concretely as it really is, any particular "exists" only in its relations to its total environment. So conceived, it ceases to be thought of as a "substance" or "thing" and becomes a continuously changing process of events. For this reason it is the "historical consciousness" which alone grasps reality as it is, that is to say, as a process of becoming.

Hegel's philosophy is, then, a philosophy of change, like that of the ancient pre-Socratic philosopher, Heraclitus, whom Hegel much admired. There are, however, important differences between them. For Heraclitus "Whirl is king," but, as the metaphor suggests, Heraclitus, like most other Greek philosophers, believed that change is subject to an eternal "logos" or law, which is itself unchanging. For Hegel, history means development; every historical process is something new under the sun, and nothing is ever precisely like anything before it. Any true law of historical change must conceive it, not as a succession of eternally recurrent cycles of change, but rather as a progressive development in which every stage, or "moment," as Hegel calls it, is viewed both as a necessary consequence of its predecessor and as radically different from it.

Hegel's theory of historical development, unfortunately, cannot be fully understood without some reference to his notorious dialectic or "logic." It will be remembered that, according to Kant, pure reason, when it tries to extend the application of such categories as cause and effect beyond experience, invariably becomes involved in insoluble contradictions. For this reason, Kant maintained that metaphysical speculation about the ultimate cause of things is completely sterile. He might, however, have taken the bolder, and, as most philosophers would think, rasher, course of accepting such contradictions as themselves indicative of the nature of things. This, in effect, is Hegel's ploy. With some assistance from Fichte, Hegel transforms Kant's doctrine regarding the inescapable dialectical conflict of metaphysical theses, which for Kant was an infallible sign of metaphysical illusion, into a new logic of philo-

sophical truth. According to Hegel, dialectical opposition is
characteristic of all valid thinking about reality. Every
"thesis," as Kant saw, generates its own contradictory
antithesis. What Kant did not see is that the thesis and its
antithesis may both be regarded as true if both are understood, in a new light, as imperfect expressions of a higher,
more inclusive proposition which contains what is significant in both of them. Such a proposition Hegel calls a
"synthesis."

More technically, every contradiction, for Hegel, is
really a disguised relation. Any contradiction may thus be
viewed as merely an abstract and hence imperfect description of a more inclusive and more concretely understood
reality. According to the traditional logic of Aristotle, which
Hegel regards as useless for the purpose of understanding
change, the contradictory of any "A" is always treated as
a "not-A" which totally excludes it. And according to the
traditional law of non-contradiction, every A is always not
not-A. Hegel claims, however, that any not-A, considered
merely as such, is a complete nonentity, a bare abstraction
which is indistinguishable from nothing at all. Hence, if
any contradiction is to have any positive meaning, the
not-A must be understood as a "B," that is, as something
positive with a definite character of its own. But in so conceiving it, we at once remove the contradiction and replace
it with a relational synthesis which may now be symbolized
as "A r B." All valid thinking about reality thus involves
a triadic movement from a thesis, A, to its antithesis, not-A,
which in turn gives way to a synthesis which transforms
our conceptions of both A and not-A. This synthesis, however, is bound to generate a new antithesis which can be
removed only by a still higher synthesis. Then the dialectic
breaks out once more. According to Hegel, there is no end
to this sort of thing.

It will perhaps not come as a shock to the reader to learn,
after all this, that Hegel is frequently charged with contra-
dicting himself at every turn. No doubt he does, but he can
at least claim the quality of his defects. For him, contradiction is not a sign of intellectual incoherence, but rather of
creativity and insight. The true philosopher will welcome it

as a challenge to the formation of a new synthesis which more adequately represents its object. For human beings, there is no end whatever to self-contradiction and, hence, to intellectual development. And if there is no final resting place for the human mind, we may at least console ourselves with the thought that our ideas are always getting bigger and better. There is, of course, the Absolute, which, in his paradoxical way, Hegel regards as the only concrete reality. But we cannot grasp it save, abstractly, as an unattainable ideal.

Hegel makes no distinction between his logic and his metaphysics. The dialectic, as he conceives it, is at once a law of thought and a law of being. Superficially, the thing that appears most real to us is the individual thing or substance. But this, when considered in itself, always turns out to be a bare abstraction, a mere "being" which is so far distinguishable from nothing at all. Anything becomes real, so to say, only in so far as it ceases to be a bare particular, just as any human being, for Hegel, becomes a person only in so far as he gives up his claim to individual uniqueness and is content to be regarded as an aspect of the large social whole to which he belongs. Concreteness and particularity, in this philosophy, are not only not the same, but actually contrary ideas. The bare particular is abstract; only the concrete universal is fully real. The only completely concrete or real entity is that unenvisageable totality, the Absolute itself. Everything else—if there were anything else—is merely a "moment" in the Absolute. Thus, by a paradox to end all paradoxes, the only concrete reality, in Hegel's view, remains for us an ideal of reason which is always being realized by particular processes that never "really" are.

It is easy, in the midst of such obscurities, to lose sight of the underlying human significance of Hegel's philosophy. Hegel is frequently charged with willful perversity, but he would doubtless reply that only so can he represent a reality which is still more perverse. Throughout his philosophy one is aware of a brooding sense of the mutability of all things, and a Romantic obsession with the imperfections inherent in every human activity and institution. There is in him a curious combination of restlessness and resignation, of extreme intellectual ambition and well-concealed humility. Again and again, in reading him, one is reminded of Faust's eternal "ever not quite." His philosophy, from one point of view, is a logician's nightmare, a veritable debauch of reason. Yet the Absolute, which for Hegel is alone fully rational and real, remains an unattainable ideal of reason which the finite, dialectical consciousness of man can grasp only as a goal endlessly to be striven for, yet never reached or even comprehended. Hegel's system, if that is what it is, has been called a philosophical Divine Comedy. It has its comic aspect, no doubt, but, from the human perspective, what it presents is closer to tragedy than to comedy. It is no accident, indeed, that in his own monumental philosophy of art, Hegel has probed the meaning of tragedy more profoundly than any other modern philosopher. For him, tragedy is at once intellectual, ethical, and metaphysical, an inescapable feature of our particular, finite, changing, and self-divided lives.

We must now return to Hegel's philosophy of history. Briefly put, Hegel regards all change as historical, and history itself as the dialectic deployed in time. As such, it is, in effect, a great waltz-like movement, from thesis through antithesis to synthesis, with each step representing a still higher stage in the self-development of the Absolute. In the dialectical development of ideas which Hegel calls "logic" no proposition is ever wholly and finally denied, and in the same way, in the dialectic of history, no star is ever completely lost. Each historical moment, in negating its antecedent, at the same time "takes up" whatever is significant in it and preserves it as the aspect of a richer, more comprehensive, social reality. Thus, from Hegel's standpoint, each successive generation may regard itself as at once the destroyer, preserver, and improver of the culture which it has inherited from its predecessor. Our own Western European culture is, in part, a new thing under the sun. But whatever was vital in the cultures of Greece, Rome, Judea, and medieval Christendom, although transmuted and, in part, transcended, has not been "really" lost. In fact, for Hegel, the inner significance of these cultures is known to us as it could not have been known to the ancient Greeks, Romans, Jews, and Christians themselves. It is for this reason that Hegel can claim to understand Christianity better than the Church Fathers, and the implications of Greek philosophy more accurately than Plato or Aristotle.

But there is another side of the coin. For if in one way we can understand the "Idea" of Greece or of Christianity better than the ancient Greeks and Christians themselves (because of our own place in history), we cannot relive their lives, nor reinstitute the cultural conditions of the societies in which they lived. Much as he admired Greece, Hegel is thus free of any touch of the "archaistic mentality," as the historian Toynbee calls it, which is always characteristic of those who look back to some previous culture as a Golden Age. Hegel also regarded himself as a "Christian," but there is little trace in his philosophy of the medievalism of so many other Romantics of his age.

For Hegel, history is both a dialectical and a spiritual process. He thus conceives it as the dialectical unfolding or self-development of that which is completely unconditioned, namely, the Absolute itself. More concretely this means that historical change must be read as a continuous struggle toward the spiritual freedom of mankind. Every stage in this process is, relatively to what went before, a "higher" stage, just as, relatively to what follows, it is also a "lower" stage. From the standpoint of what is to come, whatever appears to resist change is so far evil; but as an achievement and fulfillment of what precedes it it is so far good. Hegel is commonly regarded as an extreme conservative, and in his later years he increasingly stressed the importance of tradition and stable institutions, as carriers of culture. But his thought, as Marx later discerned, has also its revolutionary aspect, and on his own ground the inevitable transitoriness of all traditions and institutions is simply a fact of life. In fact Hegel's philosophy is at once conservative and revolutionary. Hegel himself tended, personally, to stand for tradition; but he was aware, at the same time, that the age whose spirit he represents was drawing to a close.

At bottom, Hegel's *Philosophy of History* is a theodicy,

like St. Augustine's *City of God,* which, in many respects,
it closely resembles. He is not interested in history as a
mere chronology of events following one upon the other in
time. The description of any culture, for him, is merely
incidental to a determination of its spiritual significance for
the present age. By viewing our own culture as the inevitable historical outcome of a continuous development
of society, our social thinking acquires a determinateness
and solidity which it would lack if we tried to work out our
problems "from scratch." In this way also we may over-
come the sense of spiritual isolation which is the bane of
modern life. We may discover through the philosophical
study of history a continuity of purpose and aspiration
between ourselves and our ancestors. Yet if we grasp the
dialectical character of historical development, this historical consciousness will not deprive us of the sense of
our own individuality or of the differences between our
own predicament and that of our predecessors. The spiritual significances of the historical record is not something
"given" but the product of philosophical insight. Similarly
the "necessity" ascribed to the dialectical progress of mankind through the ages is not just another "arbitrary" fact
which we find there in the way that we discover that
Caesar was bald. On the contrary, it is quite impossible,
when we read history "mechanistically" as a bare sequence
of particular occurrences, to discern any necessity in it
whatever. "Necessity," as Kant saw, is a concept of reason
which we ourselves must read into that record. As Fichte
would put it, it is only because we *will* view history under
the form of spirit or reason that any purpose or any necessity can be ascribed to it. And if we ascribe "reality" to such
a spiritual reading, then it must be remembered that reality,
for Hegel, is not a thing in itself which we find simply by
looking, but an ideal construction of the spirit itself.

The "metaphysics" of history is thus not an inevitable
by-product of purely historical examinations of the record
of past events; it is something which is arrived at only by
reflection upon that record when it is conceived dialectically
under the form of spirit—only, that is to say, when we
ourselves impute to what has happened a direction or a

goal. What Hegel perhaps did not so clearly see is that his is not the only form which such a spiritualization of history might take, and that someone else might with equal propriety view history, as the Manicheans did, as an endless struggle between opposing forces which leaves the spiritual issue finally in doubt, or even as the systematic frustration by "reality" of all human aspirations. Why Hegel's own reading is more "rational" than the rest we are not told, although on his own grounds it would not be easy to see how he could deny "validity" to such other readings since, from their own point of view they might reflect an even "higher" stage in the development of the human spirit. A more sardonic Hegel, indeed, might find in the pessimism of Hegel's own antithesis, Schopenhauer, a more perfect spirituality than Hegel's own.

Two other important ideas of Hegel's require mention here. One is his conception of freedom. Hegel is frequently criticized for making the concept of freedom walk the plank, and it is true that when he is through very little of its ordinary meaning remains. But that is the consequence of his dialectical treatment of this concept, as of others, according to which any notion, adequately understood, tends to pass over into its opposite. Hegel views the matter in the following way: Initially one thinks of freedom as doing just as one pleases. Such a notion of freedom, Hegel thinks, is the barest of abstractions, completely devoid of ethical significance. Freedom, for him, is the power to realize one's self. The self is not a pure ego; it is concretely a personality invested with determinate tendencies and capacities. What these will be depends entirely upon the training and education which the individual receives from the society in which he lives. The first step toward self-knowledge and self-culture, therefore, is the recognition of one's membership within an historically-evolving community. Thus only does one find oneself as an integral human being. The free person is he who is able to identify himself with the duties and responsibilities invested in him by the State, which, for Hegel, is the highest of all social institutions.

There are evidences in Hegel's philosophy of a pro-

foundly bureaucratic mentality. But his doctrine of freedom is not quite so anti-individualistic and illiberal, nor
is his statism so unqualified, as his more hostile critics
have alleged it to be. It is true that Hegel regards the State
as "the embodiment of rational freedom, realizing and recognizing itself in an objective form." "The State," he says,
"is the Idea of Spirit in the external manifestation of human Will and its Freedom." Such "objective" forms of
freedom are not, however, its only forms. The highest
stages of human culture are reached only in art, religion,
and philosophy, which Hegel speaks of as human manifestations of "absolute spirit." Here are domains of the
spiritual life which are laws unto themselves. Concerning
their own internal development, no purely political institution has anything properly to say.

Hegel's philosophy of freedom thus exhibits that paradoxical combination of outward subservience or even ser-
vility toward the state and inner spiritual freedom which
is so frequently to be found among German intellectuals.
Similar traits may also be discerned in such other representatives of Germany's golden age as Leibniz, Goethe,
and even Kant. In Hegel's case, it is only fair to say that
he regards conformity to the institutionalized duties imposed by society as merely one aspect of self-culture. Like
most traditionalists, however, he does not always remember that the "objective reason" which is embodied in social
institutions may sometimes be only a dead weight of accumulated customs and rules that no longer serve the underlying "spiritual" functions. His own unseemly glorification
of the Prussian state ill becomes a philosopher who conceives his whole philosophy, in one sense, as a meditation
on the problem of human freedom.

A word remains to be said about Hegel's philosophy of
religion. Hegel was born a Lutheran, and, as he himself
once said, "proposed to die one." But his Christianity has
nothing to do with fundamentalism. Like many later "liberal" Christians, upon whom his influence has been very
great, Hegel regards the Bible, not as a record of historical
truth, but as a book of symbols whose inner meaning can
be properly understood only after a great deal of philo-

sophical interpretation. The question of God's existence as usually understood, is not an issue for him. This does not imply, however, that the rational mind must renounce religion in general or Christianity in particular. "Religion," according to Hegel, "anticipates philosophy; philosophy is nothing but conscious religion." Accordingly, he regards the Christian doctrine of the Incarnation as an early mythic expression of his own philosophy, which conceives history as the progressive incarnation of the Absolute Spirit. What the Bible presents in figurative terms as a "revelation" he himself professes to justify in more critical or rational terms. Common to both is the religious need to justify human history as a whole, and to see in it something more than a "tale told by an idiot, signifying nothing."

Other Christian philosophers in the nineteenth century, as we shall see presently, were unable to follow Hegel's lead. Some of them in fact considered his rationalized reconstruction of the idea of Christ in the Gospels to be merely another step toward the secularization and hence eventual supersession of Christian culture. In their view, Hegel's way of reading the Bible completely by-passes the serious existential claims that are made within that book. Hegel's great opponent, Kierkegaard, bluntly charged that he was, at bottom, merely an atheist who hid his unbelief behind a mask of symbols. According to Kierkegaard, Hegel's "Christianity" is typical of the bourgeois worldling who seeks to enjoy a vaguely Christian unction while at the same time refusing to make any of the commitments of the Christian faith.

It may be said, in Hegel's defense, that the world-view of primitive Christianity is, in his judgment, no longer a live option for reflective men who come after the Ages of Reason and Enlightenment. The only possibility, for them, of remaining Christians at all is on such terms as his philosophy of religion provides. From Hegel's point of view, there is no more chance of regaining the religious perspective of the early Christians than there is of reviving political institutions of ancient Greece. For all his talk about the Absolute, Hegel's own profoundly historical and therefore relativizing consciousness is as responsible as any other one thing in the nineteenth century for the decline of religious and philosophical absolutism. By an irony after his own heart, the fall of the Absolute, is very largely Hegel's own doing.

The following selection is from the Introduction to Hegel's *The Philosophy of History*.*

[III. The third kind of history—the *Philosophical*. No explanation was needed of the two previous classes; their nature was self-evident. It is otherwise with this last, which certainly seems to require an exposition or justification. The most general definition that can be given, is, that the Philosophy of History means nothing but the *thoughtful consideration of it*. Thought is, indeed, essential to humanity. It is this that distinguishes us from the brutes. In sensation, cognition, and intellection; in our instincts and volitions, as far as they are truly human, Thought is an invariable element. To insist upon Thought in this connection with history may, however, appear unsatisfactory. In this science it would seem as if Thought must be subordinate to what is given, to the realities of fact; that this is its basis and guide: while Philosophy dwells in the region of self-produced ideas, without reference to actuality. Approaching history thus prepossessed, Speculation might be expected to treat it as a mere passive material; and, so far from leaving it in its native truth, to force it into conformity with a tyrannous idea, and to construe it, as the phrase is, "*à priori*." But as it is the business of history simply to adopt into its records what is and has been, actual occurrences and transactions; and since it remains true to its character in proportion as it strictly adheres to its data, we seem to have in Philosophy, a process diametrically opposed to that of the historiographer. This contradiction, and the charge consequently brought against speculation, shall be explained and confuted. We do not, however, propose to correct the innumerable special mis-

* *The Philosophy of History*, translated by J. Sibree, New York; The Willey Book Co., 1944, pp. 8–26; London: W. H. Allen & Co., Ltd. This work was published after Hegel's death by his students, from notes taken at his lectures. Its original title was *Die Philosophie der Geschichte*. Its date of publication was 1832.

representations, trite or novel, that are current respecting the aims, the interests, and the modes of treating history, and its relation to Philosophy.

The only Thought which Philosophy brings with it to the contemplation of History, is the simple conception of *Reason;* that Reason is the Sovereign of the World; that the history of the world, therefore, presents us with a rational process. This conviction and intuition is a hypothesis in the domain of history as such. In that of Philosophy it is no hypothesis. It is there proved by speculative cognition, that Reason—and this term may here suffice us, without investigating the relation sustained by the Universe to the Divine Being—is *Substance,* as well as *Infinite Power;* its own *Infinite Material* underlying all the natural and spiritual life which it originates, as also the *Infinite Form*—that which sets this Material in motion. On the one hand, Reason is the *substance* of the Universe; viz., that by which and in which all reality has its being and subsistence. On the other hand, it is the *Infinite Energy* of the Universe; since Reason is not so powerless as to be incapable of producing anything but a mere ideal, a mere intention—having its place outside reality, nobody knows where; something separate and abstract, in the heads of certain human beings. It is *the infinite complex of things,* their entire Essence and Truth. It is its own material which it commits to its own Active Energy to work up; not needing, as finite action does, the condition of an external material of given means from which it may obtain its support, and the objects of its activity. It supplies its own nourishment, and is the object of its own operations. While it is exclusively its own basis of existence, and absolute final aim, it is also the energizing power realizing this aim; developing it not only in the phenomena of the Natural, but also of the Spiritual Universe—the History of the World. That this "Idea" or "Reason" is the *True,* the *Eternal,* the absolutely *powerful* essence; that it reveals itself in the World, and that in that World nothing else is revealed but this and its honor and glory—is the thesis which, as we have said, has been proved in Philosophy, and is here regarded as demonstrated.

*   *   *   *   *   *   *   *   *

I will only mention two phases and points of view that concern the generally diffused conviction that Reason has ruled, and is still ruling the world, and consequently in the world's history; because they give us, at the same time, an opportunity for more closely investigating the question that presents the greatest difficulty, and for indicating a branch of the subject, which will have to be enlarged on in the sequel.

I. One of these points is, that passage in history, which informs us that the Greek Anaxagoras was the first to enunciate the doctrine that νοῦς, Understanding generally, or Reason, governs the world. It is not intelligence as self-conscious Reason—not a Spirit as such that is meant; and we must clearly distinguish these from each other. The movement of the solar system takes place according to unchangeable laws. These laws are Reason, implicit in the phenomena in question. But neither the sun nor the planets, which revolve around it according to these laws, can be said to have any consciousness of them.

*   *   *   *   *   *   *   *   *

We have next to notice the rise of this idea—that Reason directs the World—in connection with a further application of it, well known to us—in the form, viz., of the *religious truth,* that the world is not abandoned to chance and external contingent causes, but that a *Providence* controls it. I stated above that I would not make a demand on your faith, in regard to the principle announced. Yet I might appeal to your belief in it, *in this religious aspect,* if, as a general rule, the nature of philosophical science allowed it to attach authority to presuppositions. To put it in another shape—this appeal is forbidden, because the science of which we have to treat, proposes itself to furnish the proof (not indeed of the abstract *Truth* of the doctrine, but) of its correctness as compared with facts. The truth, then, that a Providence (that of God) presides over the events of the World—consorts with the proposition in question; for *Divine* Providence is Wisdom, endowed with an infinite Power, which realizes its aim, viz., the absolute rational design of the world. Reason is Thought conditioning itself with perfect freedom. But a difference—rather a contradiction—will manifest itself, between this belief and our principle . . . For that belief is similarly indefinite; it is what is called a belief in a general Providence, and is not followed out into definite application, or displayed in its bearing on the grand total—the entire course of human history. But to *explain* History is to depict the passions of mankind, the genius, the active powers, that play their part on the great stage; and the providentially determined process which these exhibit, constitutes what is generally called the "plan" of Providence. Yet it is this very plan which is supposed to be concealed from our view: which it is deemed presumption, even to wish to recognize.

*   *   *   *   *   *   *   *   *

But in the history of the World, the *Individuals* we have to do with are *Peoples;* Totalities that are States. We cannot, therefore, be satisfied with what we may call this "peddling" view of Providence, to which the belief alluded to limits itself. Equally unsatisfactory is the merely abstract, undefined belief in a Providence, when that belief is not brought to bear upon the details of the process which it conducts. On the contrary our earnest endeavor must be directed to the recognition of the ways of Providence, the means it uses, and the historical phenomena in which it manifests itself; and we must show their connection with the general principle above mentioned. But in noticing the recognition of the plan of Divine Providence generally, I have implicitly touched upon a prominent question of the day; viz., that of the possibility of knowing God: or rather —since public opinion has ceased to allow it to be a matter of *question*—the *doctrine* that it is impossible to know God. In direct contravention of what is commanded in holy Scripture as the highest duty—that we should not merely love, but *know* God—the prevalent dogma involves the denial of what is there said; viz., that it is the Spirit [*der Geist*] that leads into Truth, knows all things, penetrates even into the deep things of the Godhead. While the Divine Being is thus placed beyond our knowledge, and outside the limit of all human things, we have the convenient

license of wandering as far as we list, in the direction of
our own fancies. We are freed from the obligation to refer
our knowledge to the Divine and True. On the other hand,
the vanity and egotism which characterize it, find, in this
false position, ample justification; and the pious modesty
which puts far from it the knowledge of God, can well estimate how much furtherance thereby accrues to its own
wayward and vain strivings. I have been unwilling to leave
out of sight the connection between our thesis—that Reason governs and has governed the World—and the question
of the possibility of a knowledge of God, chiefly that I
might not lose the opportunity of mentioning the imputation against Philosophy of being shy of noticing religious
truths, or of having occasion to be so; in which is insinu-
ated the suspicion that it has anything but a clear conscience in the presence of these truths. So far from this
being the case, the fact is, that in recent times Philosophy
has been obliged to defend the domain of religion against
the attacks of several theological systems. In the Christian
religion God has revealed Himself—that is, he has given
us to understand what He is; so that He is no longer a concealed or secret existence. And this possibility of knowing
Him, thus afforded us, renders such knowledge a duty.
God wishes no narrow-hearted souls or empty heads for
his children; but those whose spirit is of itself indeed, poor,
but rich in the knowledge of Him; and who regard this
knowledge of God as the only valuable possession. That
development of the thinking spirit, which has resulted from
the revelation of the Divine Being as its original basis,
must ultimately advance to the *intellectual* comprehension
of what was presented in the first instance, to *feeling* and
imagination. The time must eventually come for understanding that rich product of active Reason, which the
History of the World offers to us. It was for awhile the
fashion to profess admiration for the wisdom of God, as
displayed in animals, plants, and isolated occurrences. But,
if it be allowed that Providence manifests itself in such
objects and forms of existence, why not also in Universal
History? This is deemed too great a matter to be thus re-

garded. But Divine Wisdom, *i.e.,* Reason, is one and the
same in the great as in the little; and we must not imagine
God to be too weak to exercise his wisdom on the grand
scale. Our intellectual striving aims at realizing the conviction that what was *intended* by eternal wisdom, is actually *accomplished* in the domain of existent, active Spirit,
as well as in that of mere Nature. Our mode of treating the
subject is, in this aspect, a Theodicæa—a justification of
the ways of God—which Leibnitz attempted metaphysically, in his method, *i.e.,* in indefinite abstract categories—
so that the ill that is found in the World may be comprehended, and the thinking Spirit reconciled with the fact
of the existence of evil. Indeed, nowhere is such a harmo-
nizing view more pressingly demanded than in Universal
History; and it can be attained only by recognizing the
positive existence, in which that negative element is a subordinate, and vanquished nullity. On the one hand, the
ultimate design of the World must be perceived; and, on
the other hand, the fact that this design has been actually
realized in it, and that evil has not been able permanently
to assert a competing position. . . .

II. The inquiry into the *essential destiny* of Reason—
as far as it is considered in reference to the World—is
identical with the question, *what is the ultimate design of
the World?* And the expression implies that that design is
destined to be realized. Two points of consideration suggest themselves; first, the *import* of this design—its abstract definition; and secondly, its *realization.*

It must be observed at the outset, that the phenomenon
we investigate—Universal History—belongs to the realm
of *Spirit.* The term *"World,"* includes both physical and
psychical Nature. Physical Nature also plays its part in the
World's History, and attention will have to be paid to the
fundamental natural relations thus involved. But Spirit, and
the course of its development, is our substantial object. Our
task does not require us to contemplate Nature as a Rational System in itself—though in its own proper domain
it proves itself such—but simply in its relation to *Spirit.*
On the stage on which we are observing it—Universal

History—Spirit displays itself in its most concrete reality. Notwithstanding this (or rather for the very purpose of comprehending the *general* principles which this, its form of *concrete reality,* embodies) we must premise some abstract characteristics of the *nature of Spirit.* Such an explanation, however, cannot be given here under any other form than that of bare assertion. The present is not the occasion for unfolding the idea of Spirit speculatively; for whatever has a place in an Introduction, must, as already observed, be taken as simply historical; something assumed as having been explained and proved elsewhere; or whose demonstration awaits the sequel of the Science of History itself.

We have therefore to mention here:

(1) The abstract characteristics of the nature of Spirit.
(2) What means Spirit uses in order to realize its idea.
(3) Lastly, we must consider the shape which the perfect embodiment of Spirit assumes—the State.

(1) The nature of Spirit may be understood by a glance at its direct opposite—*Matter.* As the essence of Matter is Gravity, so, on the other hand, we may affirm that the substance, the essence, of Spirit is Freedom. All will readily assent to the doctrine that Spirit, among other properties, is also endowed with Freedom; but philosophy teaches that all the qualities of Spirit exist only through Freedom; that all are but means for attaining Freedom; that all seek and produce this and this alone. It is a result of speculative Philosophy, that Freedom is the sole truth of Spirit. Matter possesses gravity in virtue of its tendency toward a central point. It is essentially composite; consisting of parts that *exclude* each other. It seeks its Unity; and therefore exhibits itself as self-destructive, as verging toward its opposite [an indivisible point]. If it could attain this, it would be Matter no longer, it would have perished. It strives after the realization of its Idea; for in Unity it exists *ideally.* Spirit, on the contrary, may be defined as that which has its center in itself. It has not a unity outside itself, but has already

found it; it exists *in* and *with itself*. Matter has its essence
out of itself; Spirit is *self-contained existence* [Bei-sich-
selbst-seyn]. Now this is Freedom, exactly. For if I am
dependent, my being is referred to something else which I
am not; I cannot exist independently of something external.
I am free, on the contrary, when my existence depends
upon myself. This self-contained existence of Spirit is none
other than self-consciousness—consciousness of one's own
being. Two things must be distinguished in consciousness;
first, the fact *that I know;* secondly, *what I know.* In *self*
consciousness these are merged in one; for Spirit *knows
itself.* It involves an appreciation of its own nature, as also
an energy enabling it to realize itself; to make itself *actually*
that which it is *potentially.* According to this abstract definition it may be said of Universal History, that it is the
exhibition of Spirit in the process of working out the
knowledge of that which it is potentially. And as the germ
bears in itself the whole nature of the tree, and the taste
and form of its fruits, so do the first traces of Spirit virtually contain the whole of that History. The Orientals have
not attained the knowledge that Spirit—Man *as such*—is
free; and because they do not know this, they are not free.
They only know that *one is free.* But on this very account,
the freedom of that one is only caprice; ferocity—brutal
recklessness of passion, or a mildness and tameness of the
desires, which is itself only an accident of Nature—mere
caprice like the former.—That *one* is therefore only a Des-
pot; not a *free man.* The consciousness of Freedom first
arose among the Greeks, and therefore they were free; but
they, and the Romans likewise, knew only that *some* are
free—not man as such. Even Plato and Aristotle did not
know this. The Greeks, therefore, had slaves; and their
whole life and the maintenance of their splendid liberty,
was implicated with the institution of slavery: a fact moreover, which made that liberty on the one hand only an accidental, transient and limited growth; on the other hand,
constituted it a rigorous thraldom of our common nature—
of the Human. The German nations, under the influence
of Christianity, were the first to attain the consciousness,
that man, as man, is free: that it is the *freedom* of Spirit

which constitutes its essence. This consciousness arose first in religion, the inmost region of Spirit; but to introduce the principle into the various relations of the actual world, involves a more extensive problem than its simple implantation; a problem whose solution and application require a severe and lengthened process of culture. In proof of this, we may note that slavery did not cease immediately on the reception of Christianity. Still less did liberty predominate in States; or Governments and Constitutions adopt a rational organization, or recognize freedom as their basis. That application of the principle to political relations; the thorough moulding and interpenetration of the constitution of society by it, is a process identical with history itself. I have already directed attention to the distinction here involved, between a principle as such, and its *application; i.e.,* its introduction and carrying out in the actual phenomena of Spirit and Life. This is a point of fundamental importance in our science, and one which must be constantly respected as essential. And in the same way as this distinction has attracted attention in view of the *Christian* principle of self-consciousness—Freedom; it also shows itself as an essential one, in view of the principle of Freedom *generally.* The History of the world is none other than the progress of the consciousness of Freedom; a progress whose development according to the necessity of its nature, it is our business to investigate.

*   *   *   *   *   *   *   *   *

The destiny of the spiritual World, and—since this is the *substantial World,* while the physical remains subordinate to it, or, in the language of speculation, has no truth *as against* the spiritual—*the final cause of the World at large,* we allege to be the *consciousness* of its own freedom on the part of Spirit, and *ipso facto,* the *reality* of that freedom. But that this term "Freedom," without further qualification, is an indefinite, and incalculable ambiguous term; and that while that which it represents is the *ne plus ultra* of attainment, it is liable to an infinity of misunderstandings, confusions and errors, and to become the occasion for all imaginable excesses—has never been more clearly known and felt than in modern times. Yet, for the present, we must content ourselves with the term itself without further definition. Attention was also directed to the importance of the infinite difference between a principle in the abstract, and its realization in the concrete. In the process before us, the essential nature of freedom—which involves in it absolute necessity—is to be displayed as coming to a consciousness of itself (for it is in its very nature, self-consciousness) and thereby realizing its existence. Itself is its own object of attainment, and the sole aim of Spirit. This result it is, at which the process of the World's History has been continually aiming; and to which the sacrifices that have ever and anon been laid on the vast altar of the earth, through the long lapse of ages, have been offered. This is the only aim that sees itself realized and fulfilled; the only pole of repose amid the ceaseless change of events and conditions, and the sole efficient principle that pervades them. This final aim is God's purpose with the world; but God is the absolutely perfect Being, and can, therefore, will nothing other than himself—his own Will. The Nature of His Will —that is, His Nature itself—is what we here call the Idea of Freedom; translating the language of Religion into that of Thought. The question, then, which we may next put, is: What means does this principle of Freedom use for its realization? This is the second point we have to consider.

(2) The question of the *means* by which Freedom develops itself to a World, conducts us to the phenomenon of History itself. Although Freedom is, primarily, an undeveloped idea, the means it uses are external and phenomenal; presenting themselves in History to our sensuous vision. The first glance at History convinces us that the actions of men proceed from their needs, their passions, their characters and talents; and impresses us with the belief that such needs, passions and interests are the sole springs of action—the efficient agents in this scene of activity. Among these may, perhaps, be found aims of a liberal or universal kind— benevolence it may be, or noble patriotism; but such virtues and general views are but insignificant as compared with the World and its doings. We may perhaps see the Ideal of Reason actualized in those who adopt such aims, and within the sphere of their in-

fluence; but they bear only a trifling proportion to the mass of the human race; and the extent of that influence is limited accordingly. Passions, private aims, and the satisfaction of selfish desires, are, on the other hand, most effective springs of action. Their power lies in the fact that they respect none of the limitations which justice and morality would impose on them; and that these natural impulses have a more direct influence over man than the artificial and tedious discipline that tends to order and self-restraint, law and morality. When we look at this display of passions, and the consequences of their violence; the Unreason which is associated not only with them, but even (rather we might say *especially*) with *good* designs and righteous aims; when we see the evil, the vice, the ruin that has befallen the most flourishing kingdoms which the mind of man ever created; we can scarce avoid being filled with sorrow at this universal taint of corruption: and, since this decay is not the work of mere Nature, but of the Human Will—a moral embitterment—a revolt of the Good Spirit (if it have a place within us) may well be the result of our reflections. Without rhetorical exaggeration, a simply truthful combination of the miseries that have overwhelmed the noblest of nations and polities, and the finest exemplars of private virtue—forms a picture of most fearful aspect, and excites emotions of the profoundest and most hopeless sadness, counterbalanced by no consolatory result. We endure in beholding it a mental torture, allowing no defense or escape but the consideration that what has happened could not be otherwise; that it is a fatality which no intervention could alter. And at last we draw back from the intolerable disgust with which these sorrowful reflections threaten us, into the more agreeable environment of our individual life—the Present formed by our private aims and interests. . . . But even regarding History as the slaughter-bench at which the happiness of peoples, the wisdom of States, and the virtue of individuals have been victimized—the question involuntarily arises—to what principle, to what final aim, these enormous sacrifices have been offered. From this point the investigation usually proceeds to that which we have made the general commencement of our inquiry. Starting from this we pointed out those phenomena which made up a picture so suggestive of gloomy emotions and thoughtful reflections—as *the very field* which we, for our part, regard as exhibiting only the means for realizing what we assert to be the essential destiny —the absolute aim, or—which comes to the same thing— the true *result* of the World's History. We have all along purposely eschewed "moral reflections" as a method of rising from the scene of historical specialties to the general principles which they embody. Besides, it is not the interest of such sentimentalities, really to rise above those depressing emotions; and to solve the enigmas of Providence which the considerations that occasioned them, present. It is essential to their character to find a gloomy satisfaction in the empty and fruitless sublimities of that negative result. We return them to the point of view which we have adopted; observing that the successive steps [*Momente*] of the analysis to which it will lead us, will also evolve the conditions requisite for answering the inquiries suggested by the panorama of sin and suffering that history unfolds.

The *first* remark we have to make, and which—though already presented more than once—cannot be too often repeated when the occasion seems to call for it—is that what we call *principle, aim, destiny,* or the nature and idea of Spirit, is something merely general and abstract. Principle—Plan of Existence—Law—is a hidden, undeveloped essence, which *as such*—however true in itself—is not completely real. Aims, principles, etc., have a place in our thoughts, in our subjective design only; but not yet in the sphere of reality. That which exists for itself only, is a possibility, a potentiality; but has not yet emerged into Existence. A *second* element must be introduced in order to produce actuality—viz., actuation, realization; and whose motive power is the Will—the activity of man in the widest sense. It is only by this activity that that Idea as well as abstract characteristics generally, are realized, actualized; for of themselves they are powerless. The motive power that puts them in operation, and gives them determinate existence, is the need, instinct, inclination, and passion of man. That some conception of mine should be developed into act and existence, is my earnest desire: I wish to assert my personality in connection with it: I wish to be satisfied by its execution. If I am to exert myself for any object, it must in some way or other be *my* object. In the accomplishment of such or such designs I must at the same time find *my* satisfaction; although the purpose for which I exert myself includes a complication of results, many of which have no interest for me. This is the absolute right of personal existence—to find *itself* satisfied in its activity and labor. If men are to interest themselves for anything, they must (so to speak) have part of their existence involved in it; find their individuality gratified by its attainment. Here a mistake must be avoided. We intend blame, and justly impute it as a fault, when we say of an individual, that he is "interested" (in taking part in such or such transactions), that is, seeks only his private advantage. In reprehending this we find fault with him for furthering his personal aims without any regard to a more comprehensive design; of which he takes advantage to promote his own interest, or which he even sacrifices with this view. But he who is active in *promoting an object,* is not simply "interested," but interested in that object itself. Language faithfully expresses this distinction.—Nothing therefore happens, nothing is accomplished, unless the individuals concerned, seek their own satisfaction in the issue. They are particular units of society; *i.e.,* they have special needs, instincts, and interests generally, peculiar to themselves. Among these needs are not only such as we usually call necessities—the stimuli of individual desire and volition—but also those connected with individual views and convictions; or—to use a term expressing less decision—leanings of opinion; supposing the impulses of reflection, understanding, and reason, to have been awakened. In these cases people demand, if they are to exert themselves in any direction, that the object should commend itself to them; that in point of opinion—whether as to its goodness, justice, advantage, profit—they should be able to "enter into it" [*dabei seyn*]. . . .

We assert then that nothing has been accomplished without interest on the part of the actors; and—if interest

be called passion, inasmuch as the whole individuality, to
the neglect of all other actual or possible interests and
claims, is devoted to an object with every fiber of volition,
concentrating all its desires and powers upon it—we may
affirm absolutely that *nothing great in the World* has been
accomplished without *passion*. Two elements, therefore,
enter into the object of our investigation; the first the Idea,
the second the complex of human passions; the one the
warp, the other the woof of the vast arras-web of Universal
History. The concrete mean and union of the two is Liberty,
under the conditions of morality in a State. We have spoken
of the Idea of Freedom as the nature of Spirit, and the
absolute goal of History. Passion is regarded as a thing of
sinister aspect, as more or less immoral. Man is required
to have no passions. Passion, it is true, is not quite the suitable word for what I wish to express. I mean here nothing
more than the human activity as resulting from private interests—special, or if you will, self-seeking designs—with
this qualification, that the whole energy of will and character is devoted to their attainment; that other interests
(which would in themselves constitute attractive aims) or
rather all things else, are sacrificed to them. The object in
question is so bound up with the man's will, that it entirely
and alone determines the "hue of resolution," and is inseparable from it. It has become the very essence of his
volition. For a person is a specific existence; not man in
general (a term to which no real existence corresponds)
but a particular human being. . . .

From this comment on the second essential element in
the historical embodiment of an aim, we infer—glancing at
the institution of the State in passing—that a State is then
well constituted and internally powerful, when the private
interest of its citizens is one with the common interest of
the State; when the one finds its gratification and realization in the other—a proposition in itself very important.
But in a State many institutions must be adopted, much
political machinery invented, accompanied by appropriate
political arrangements—necessitating long struggles of the
understanding before what is really appropriate can be discovered—involving, moreover, contentions with private

interest and passions, and a tedious discipline of these latter, in order to bring about the desired harmony. The epoch
when a State attains this harmonious condition, marks the
period of its bloom, its virtue, its vigor, and its prosperity.
But the history of mankind does not begin with a *conscious*
aim of any kind, as is the case with the particular circles
into which men form themselves of set purpose. The mere
social instinct implies a conscious purpose of security for
life and property; and when society has been constituted,
this purpose becomes more comprehensive. The History
of the World begins with its general aim—the realization of
the Idea of Spirit—only in an *implicit* form [*an sich*] that
is, as Nature; a hidden, most profoundly hidden, unconscious instinct; and the whole process of History (as already observed), is directed to rendering this unconscious
impulse a conscious one. Thus appearing in the form of
merely natural existence, natural will—that which has been
called the subjective side—physical craving, instinct, passion, private interest, as also opinion and subjective conception—spontaneously present themselves at the very
commencement. This vast congeries of volitions, interests
and activities, constitute the instruments and means of the
World-Spirit for attaining its object; bringing it to consciousness, and realizing it. And this aim is none other than
finding itself—coming to itself—and contemplating itself in
concrete actuality. But that those manifestations of vitality
on the part of individuals and peoples, in which they seek
and satisfy their own purposes, are, at the same time, the
means and instruments of a higher and broader purpose of
which they know nothing—which they realize unconsciously—might be made a matter of question; rather has been
questioned, and in every variety of form negatived, decried
and contemned as mere dreaming and "Philosophy." But
on this point I announced my view at the very outset, and
asserted our hypothesis—which, however, will appear in
the sequel, in the form of a legitimate inference—and our
belief, that Reason governs the world, and has consequently governed its history. In relation to this independently
universal and substantial existence—all else is subordinate,

subservient to it, and the means for its development.——The Union of Universal Abstract Existence generally with the Individual——the Subjective——that this alone is Truth, belongs to the department of speculation, and is treated in this general form in Logic.——But in the process of the World's History itself——as still incomplete——the abstract final aim of history is not yet made the distinct object of desire and interest. While these limited sentiments are still unconscious of the purpose they are fulfilling, the universal principle is implicit in them, and is realizing itself through them. The question also assumes the form of the union of *Freedom* and *Necessity;* the *latent* abstract process of Spirit being regarded as *Necessity;* while that which exhibits itself in the conscious will of men, as their interest, belongs to the domain of *Freedom.*}

CHAPTER V

The World as Will and Idea:
Arthur Schopenhauer (1788-1860)

AS ONE PLOWS ONE'S WAY THROUGH HEGEL'S PONDEROUS tomes, it is sometimes hard to avoid the impression that he regards himself, with becoming modesty, merely as a medium through which the Absolute itself has unaccountably elected to speak. It is with a sense of relief, therefore, that one turns at last to the writings of his archenemy, Schopenhauer, whose philosophy impresses one at once as one particular human being's highly unedifying idea of a world he never made and little admired.

Schopenhauer's personality was the reverse of saintly. As a brash and highly egotistical young *Privatdocent* at the University of Berlin, he characteristically chose to lecture at the same hour as the great Hegel himself—needless to say, to an empty room. He was rejected by his mother, and became, almost as a matter of course, a misogynist. A prudent sensualist who always took his pleasures in smallish doses, Schopenhauer distinguished himself as a man only by becoming one of the world's great haters. It is understandable, therefore, that he is not generally regarded as one of the nineteenth century's cultural heroes. But there is something not wholly unattractive about this crotchety, self-absorbed old bachelor who preferred his cat to any human being. His pessimism is authentic. Nor is it peculiar to himself; like the Italian poet, Leopardi, Schopenhauer represents the world-weariness and loneliness which are implicit in so much of the Romantic movement and are, indeed, never far beneath the surface even of such official optimists as Hegel. But Schopenhauer resolutely refused to make use of the ideological props employed by most of his contemporaries. He is entirely free, for example, of the nationalistic mania that afflicted Fichte and Hegel. Nor is there in his writing any trace of their tiresome, self-congratulatory unction. He does not strike official poses, and never permits himself to be used as a mouthpiece for the Spirit of the Age. In the last analysis his philosophy is a kind of inverted theodicy which serves to justify his conviction that reality is inherently malignant and that the only way out for ordinary men lies in the world of self-less contemplation. But it is refreshing to read a younger contemporary of Hegel who can call a pain a misery and who does not feel impelled to view the history of mankind as an inevitable march of progress. His cultivation and sense of form, his instinctive secularism, his wit, and the elegance of his literary style all remind one of the Age of Enlightenment.

With his usual perspicacity, Schopenhauer saw at once the fundamental ideological point of Hegel's and Fichte's philosophies. These are the words he uses to describe the political and social import of Hegelianism: "Philosophy, brought afresh to repute by Kant . . . had soon to become a tool of interests; of state interests from above, of personal interests from below. . . . The driving forces of this movement are, contrary to all these solemn airs and assertions, not ideas; they are very real purposes indeed, namely personal, official, clerical, political, in short, material interests. . . . Party interests are vehemently agitating the pens of so many pure lovers of wisdom. . . . Truth is certainly the last thing they have in mind. . . . Philosophy is misused, from the side of the state as a tool, from the other side as a means of gain. . . . Who can really believe that truth also will come to light, just as a by-product?" If Karl Marx, instead of trying to stand Hegel's dialectic on its head, had fully understood the drift of Schopenhauer's criticism, the history of mankind in the past hundred years might well have been very different.

One of the reasons for Schopenhauer's detestation of

Fichte and Hegel was his conviction that they had subverted what is true and profound in the philosophy of Kant.
He is one of the first in a long line of philosophers who,
in an age of Hegelianism, adopted the slogan "Back to
Kant!" as a protest against prevailing tendencies. What this
means, in Schopenhauer's case, is that he regards himself
essentially as a "critical" philosopher for whom, therefore,
the philosophical use of reason must await its critique.
Schopenhauer is not famous for his contributions to the
theory of knowledge, but his greatest work, *The World as
Will and Idea,* begins, not dogmatically with a statement
of metaphysical principles, but with an appraisal of the nature and limits of the understanding. Like Kant, Schopenhauer thinks that reason cannot know what things are in
themselves. According to him, our ideas provide no access
to a world beyond our sense perceptions. To a considerable
extent, in fact, Schopenhauer reads like a Lockean empiricist who insists on deriving all concepts from what is
found in experience. He holds, however, that we have another, non-intellectual, access to reality which is provided
by the will. How far he diverges from Kant in this regard
may be measured by the difference between their interpretations of this concept. Kant undoubtedly is the historical
progenitor of those voluntaristic philosophies which crop
up again and again in the nineteenth century. But he conceives will primarily in ethical terms. For Schopenhauer,
on the other hand, will is the basic metaphysical category,
the root of all that we regard as "real." According to him,
it is only in our acts of will that we realize ourselves as existing beings; and it is only in our sense of ourselves as willing something that we are aware of reality as something
more than a system of coherent ideas.

For all his antipathy to Fichte, it is evident that at least
in this part of his philosophy there is a close affinity between Schopenhauer and his predecessor. The primary difference between them in this regard, is not so much theoretical as temperamental. Fichte, in the end, glorifies will;
Schopenhauer, although he also tends to personify it, regards it as a malignant force which at every turn frustrates
the spiritual life of man.

Schopenhauer is not, however, merely a satanic metaphysician who subverts the "reality" which his contemporaries identify as "rational" and "real." He is also something of a naturalist whose conception of the conscious life of man as a by-product of will is plainly anticipatory of Freud. Schopenhauer makes constant use of empirical biological and historical data in order to illustrate his thesis that the will to live is the fundamental law of life itself. And if he also stretches the notion of will beyond endurance and invests it with quasi-demonic attributes with which empirical science itself has nothing to do, several of Schopenhauer's commentators have remarked upon the depths of his psychological insight.

In one sense Schopenhauer's informally empirical descriptions of will are a major source of embarrassment for a philosopher whose starting point is Kant's Copernican Revolution in philosophy. For so closely does he tie his account of will to descriptions of the observable behavior of organisms that it becomes a principal problem for him to preserve his essential distinction between will as a transempirical thing in itself and the human body as a phenomenal "objectification" or idea. For all his Kantianism, Schopenhauer has not fully learned the lesson of the critical philosophy. For in describing the will, or its manifestations, in such detail, he appears to transform it into merely another "idea," which, according to his own premises, has no greater claim to reality than any other idea gained from experience. Schopenhauer, in short, cannot have it both ways: he cannot regard the observable behavior of human organisms as evidence of the underlying reality of will as a thing in itself and still maintain that the domain of empirical observation is entirely divorced from things as they are in reality.

The solution to this problem, if such it is to be called, does not lie in any theoretical argument or logical analysis. It is to be found, rather, within the ideological sphere, in Schopenhauer's prevailing attitudes toward the conduct of life, and in his ironical use of such golden words as "reality." Where Fichte and, later, Nietzsche construe the unqualified reality of will as a sign of its fundamental positive value, Schopenhauer uses the same words to express his profound disdain. "This," he seems to say, "is *really* real," as if there were no more impressive way to express his loathing. It is his misanthropic manner of expressing his distaste for the whole distracted, busy, bourgeois activism which underlies the whole idealist movement. Is the "will" now regarded by his contemporaries as synonymous with "reality?", he seems to ask. Reality then is something to be withdrawn from at all costs, even, if need be, into a "world" of illusion. So far, indeed, does Schopenhauer go in his repudiation of the active, "moral" life which is glorified by Fichte and, in part, by Hegel, that he refuses to accord to will, the "ultimate reality," even that natural piety which the godly normally pay to the devil. In itself will is altogether evil, and he turns his face against it altogether, and "uses" it, in his ironical way, to subvert and destroy it.

There are some critics of Schopenhauer who profess to find something "insincere" in Schopenhauer's pessimistic unworldliness. What they miss is the irony implicit in Schopenhauer's way of doing metaphysics. From the standpoint of the worldlings for whom "reality" is identified with their own frantic strivings Schopenhauer is indeed a pessimist. Let them, if they so choose, call will "rational" and its "objective" manifestations in the historical institutions of the state and church objectifications of "spirit"; they testify only to their own modes of self-identification. In such a "reality," according to Schopenhauer, there is no peace or happiness for man. Look at the "spiritual" reality which Hegel himself describes: What is the dialectic of history but a record of endless conflict in which each "moment" is destined to be betrayed by the fatal opposition which it breeds within itself? If this be "reality," says Schopenhauer in effect, then Hegel is welcome to it; and if the alternative is pessimism, then why not pessimism?

But what if the will, the source of all our miseries, can be turned against itself? If volition is evil, then the cure should be its extinction. The obvious answer, here, might seem to be suicide. But Schopenhauer rejects suicide as only the last, most desperate of all acts of will. Suicide destroys the phenomenal body; it does not destroy will itself. The only alternative, according to him, is to turn the will against itself, and, by a series of renunciations, to extinguish our particular desires. The result for him is, then, not death, but contemplation.

It has frequently been said that Schopenhauer's philosophy is influenced both by Plato and by the Hindu mystics. This is true, but his own conception of the life of contemplation is somewhat different from theirs. For Schopenhauer, release from volition comes through aesthetic contemplation, and in particular through the contemplation of art. In the response to great art, and particularly to music, there is, for the nonce, a characteristic disinterestedness, a suspension of belief and disbelief, of hope and despair, which leaves us free to contemplate the forms of things without concern and even the manifestations of will itself without personal involvement or care.

Schopenhauer's critics have not neglected to point out a formal inconsistency in this aspect of his doctrine. For if the will *is* the real, and if it is manifested in every form of life, then contemplation cannot be supposed to "destroy" it. It is not *willing* as such which Schopenhauer's contemplative life removes, but only the predatory, competitive willing of ordinary life. But this inconsistency is not serious, if we view Schopenhauer's metaphysics, not as an essay in logical construction, but as a personal *Weltanschauung* which is his answer to the "objective" ideologies of his predecessors. The more serious question is not whether the life of contemplation gets rid of will, but whether it provides an adequate solution to the spiritual problems of anxiety and disillusionment, self-estrangement and isolation that are such frequent characteristic by-products of modern life. At least one twentieth-century philosopher, Santayana, has virtually reaffirmed the aestheticism of Schopenhauer, and many other philosophers, for whom a *life* of contemplation is not a viable ideal, have nevertheless insisted that aesthetic contemplation must form a large part of what we understand by "the good life."

It would be a mistake to regard Schopenhauer's philosophy as merely the expression of his own highly idiosyncratic and neurotic personality. It represents, in one form, the perennial disillusionment of sensitive men with the forms of collective salvation that are offered by the institutions of society. Moreover, in his recognition of the depths of human "irrationality," Schopenhauer was prophetic. Again and again in his writings one finds an amazing grasp of the subrational and unconscious volitional life which the followers of Freud have dramatized for our own age. Schopenhauer understands the precariousness of reason and the futility of opposing the will with mere "ideas." But unlike many other "irrationalists," Schopenhauer never glorifies irrationality. Like Freud, he acknowledges the full range of the animality in human nature without deifying it. Nor, in the end, is he really frightened by it. For he knows that there is a way out, through understanding, through artistic creativity, and through aesthetic contemplation. There is much that is wise in the philosophy of this great pessimist. He is not a mere "episode" in the history of nineteenth-century thought; on the contrary, he stands to Hegel, in certain ways, much as Freud stands to Karl Marx. To ignore him is to ignore the fact that the age which worshipped progress was also a century of individual despair.

The following selections are from the First Book (Sections 1-2) and from the Second Book (Sections 17-19) of Schopenhauer's *The World as Will and Idea*.* The First Book is entitled "The World as Idea—First Aspect. The Idea Subordinated to the Principle of Sufficient Reason: The Object of Experience and Science." The Second Book is entitled "The World as Will—First Aspect. The Objectification of the Will."

〔 1. "The world is my idea:"—this is a truth which holds good for everything that lives and knows, though man alone can bring it into reflective and abstract consciousness. If he really does this, he has attained to philosophical wisdom.

---

* *The World as Will and Idea*, translated by R. B. Haldane and J. Kemp. London: Kegan Paul, Trench, Trubner and Co., Ltd., 1907, pp. 3–6, 127–36. The original work appeared in 1819 under the title *Die Welt als Wille und Verstellung*.

It then becomes clear and certain to him that what he knows is not a sun and an earth, but only an eye that sees a sun, a hand that feels an earth; that the world which surrounds him is there only as idea, *i.e.,* only in relation to something else, the consciousness, which is himself. If any truth can be asserted *a priori,* it is this: for it is the expression of the most general form of all possible and thinkable experience: a form which is more general than time, or space, or causality, for they all presuppose it; and each of these, which we have seen to be just so many modes of the principle of sufficient reason, is valid only for a particular class of ideas; whereas the antithesis of object and subject is the common form of all these classes, is that form under which alone any idea of whatever kind it may be, abstract or intuitive, pure or empirical, is possible and thinkable. No truth therefore is more certain, more independent of all others, and less in need of proof than this, that all that exists for knowledge, and therefore this whole world is only object in relation to subject, perception of a perceiver, in a word, idea. This is obviously true of the past and the future, as well as of the present, of what is farthest off, as of what is near; for it is true of time and space themselves, in which alone these distinctions arise. All that in any way belongs or can belong to the world is inevitably thus conditioned through the subject, and exists only for the subject. The world is idea.

*　　*　　*　　*　　*　　*　　*　　*　　*

In this first book, then, we consider the world only from this side, only so far as it is idea. The inward reluctance with which any one accepts the world as merely his idea, warns him that this view of it, however true it may be, is nevertheless one-sided, adopted in consequence of some arbitrary abstraction. And yet it is a conception from which he can never free himself. The defectiveness of this view will be corrected in the next book by means of a truth which is not so immediately certain as that from which we start here; a truth at which we can arrive only by deeper research and more severe abstraction, by the separation of what is different and the union of what is identical. This truth, which must be very serious and impressive if not awful to every one, is that a man can also say and must say, "the world is my will."

In this book, however, we must consider separately that aspect of the world from which we start, its aspect as knowable, and therefore, in the meantime, we must, without reserve, regard all presented objects, even our own bodies (as we shall presently show more fully), merely as ideas, and call them merely ideas. By so doing we always abstract from will (as we hope to make clear to every one further on), which by itself constitutes the other aspect of the world. For as the world is in one aspect entirely *idea,* so in another it is entirely *will.* A reality which is neither of these two, but an object in itself (into which the thing in itself has unfortunately dwindled in the hands of Kant), is the phantom of a dream, and its acceptance is an *ignis fatuus* in philosophy.

§ 2. That which knows all things and is known by none is the subject. Thus it is the supporter of the world, that condition of all phenomena, of all objects, which is always presupposed throughout experience; for all that exists, exists only for the subject. Every one finds himself to be subject, yet only in so far as he knows, not in so far as he is an object of knowledge. But his body is object, and therefore from this point of view we call it idea. For the body is an object among objects, and is conditioned by the laws of objects, although it is an immediate object. Like all objects of perception, it lies within the universal forms of knowledge, time and space, which are the conditions of multiplicity. The subject, on the contrary, which is always the knower, never the known, does not come under these forms, but is presupposed by them; it has therefore neither multiplicity nor its opposite, unity. We never know it, but it is always the knower wherever there is knowledge.

*   *   *   *   *   *   *   *   *

[*From* BOOK II, § 17] But what now impels us to inquiry is just that we are not satisfied with knowing that we have ideas, that they are such and such, and that they are connected according to certain laws, the general expression of which is the principle of sufficient reason. We wish to know the significance of these ideas; we ask whether this world is merely idea; in which case it would pass by us like an empty dream or a baseless vision, not worth our notice; or whether it is also something else, something more than idea, and if so, what. Thus much is certain, that this something we seek for must be completely and in its whole nature different from the idea; that the forms and laws of the idea must therefore be completely foreign to it; further, that we cannot arrive at it from the idea under the guidance of the laws which merely combine objects, ideas, among themselves, and which are the forms of the principle of sufficient reason.

Thus we see already that we can never arrive at the real nature of things from without. However much we investigate, we can never reach anything but images and names. We are like a man who goes round a castle seeking in vain for an entrance, and sometimes sketching the façades. And yet this is the method that has been followed by all philosophers before me.

§ 18. In fact, the meaning for which we seek of that world which is present to us only as our idea, or the transition from the world as mere idea of the knowing subject to whatever it may be besides this, would never be found if the investigator himself were nothing more than the pure knowing subject (a winged cherub without a body). But he is himself rooted in that world; he finds himself in it as an *individual,* that is to say, his knowledge, which is the necessary supporter of the whole world as idea, is yet always given through the medium of a body, whose affections are, as we have shown, the starting-point for the understanding in the perception of that world. His body is, for the pure knowing subject, an idea like every other idea, an object among objects. Its movements and actions are so far known to him in precisely the same way as the changes of all other perceived objects, and would be just as strange and incomprehensible to him if their meaning were not explained for him in an entirely different way. Otherwise he would see his actions follow upon given motives with the constancy of a law of nature, just as the changes of other objects follow upon causes, stimuli, or motives. But he would not understand the influence of the motives any more than the connection between every other effect which he sees and its cause. He would then call the inner nature of these manifestations and actions of his body which he did not understand a force, a quality, or a character, as he pleased, but he would have no further insight into it. But all this is not the case; indeed the answer to the riddle is given to the subject of knowledge who appears as an individual, and the answer is *will*. This and this alone gives him the key to his own existence, reveals to him the significance, shows him the inner mechanism of his being, of his action, of his movements. The body is given in two entirely different ways to the subject of knowledge, who becomes an individual only through his identity with it. It is given as an idea in intelligent perception, as an object among objects and subject to the laws of objects. And it is also given in quite a different way as that which is immediately known to every one, and is signified by the word *will*. Every true act of his will is also at once and without exception a movement of his body. The act of will and the movement of the body are not two different things objectively known, which the bond of causality unites; they do not stand in the relation of cause and effect; they are one and the same, but they are given in entirely different ways—immediately, and again in perception for the understanding. The action of the body is nothing but the act of the will objectified, *i.e.*, passed into perception. It will appear later that this is true of every movement of the body, not merely those which follow upon motives, but also involuntary movements which follow upon mere stimuli, and, indeed, that the whole body is nothing but objectified will, *i.e.*, will become idea. All this will be proved and made quite clear in the course of this work. In one respect, therefore, I shall call the body the *objectivity of will;* as in the previous book, and in the essay on the principle of sufficient reason, in accordance with the one-sided point of view intentionally adopted there (that of the idea), I called it *the immediate object*. Thus in a certain sense we may also say that will is the knowledge *a priori* of the body, and the body is the knowledge *a posteriori* of the will. Resolutions of the will which relate to the future are merely deliberations of the reason about what we shall will at a particular time, not real acts of will. Only the carrying out of the resolve stamps it as will, for till then it is never more than an intention that may be changed, and that exists only in the reason *in abstracto*. *It is only in reflection that to will and to act are different; in reality they are one.* Every true, genuine, immediate act of will is also, at once and immediately, a visible act of the body. And, corresponding to this, every impression upon the body is also, on the other hand, at once and immediately an impression upon the will. As such it is called pain when it is opposed to the will; gratification or pleasure when it is in accordance with it. The degrees of both are widely different. It is quite wrong, however, to call pain and pleasure ideas, for they are by no means ideas, but immediate affections of the will in its manifestation, the body; compulsory, instantaneous willing or not-willing of the impression which the body sustains. There are only a few impressions of the body which do not touch the will, and it is through these alone that the body is an immediate object of knowledge, for, as perceived by the understanding, it is already an indirect object like all others. These impressions are, therefore, to be treated directly as merely ideas, and excepted from what has been said. The impressions we refer to are the affections of the purely objective senses of sight, hearing, and touch, though only so far as these organs are affected in the way which is specifically peculiar to their specific nature. This affection of them is so excessively weak an excitement of the heightened and specifically modified sensibility of these parts that it does not affect the will, but only furnishes the understanding with the data out of which the perception arises, undisturbed by any excitement of the will. But every stronger or different kind of affection of these organs of sense is painful, that is to say, against the will, and thus they also belong to its objectivity. Weakness of the nerves shows itself in this, that the impressions which have only such a degree of strength as would usually be sufficient to make them data for the understanding reach the higher degree at which they influence the will, that is to say, give pain or pleasure, though more often pain, which is, however, to some extent deadened and inarticulate, so that not only particular tones and strong light are painful to us, but there ensues a generally unhealthy and hypochondriacal disposition which is not distinctly understood. The identity of the body and the will shows itself further, among other ways, in the circumstance that every vehement and excessive movement of the will, *i.e.*, every emotion, agitates the body and its inner constitution directly, and disturbs the course of its vital functions. . . .

Lastly, the knowledge which I have of my will, though it is immediate, cannot be separated from that which I have of my body. I know my will, not as a whole, not as a unity, not completely, according to its nature, but I know it only in its particular acts, and therefore in time, which is the form of the phenomenal aspect of my body, as of every object. Therefore the body is a condition of the knowledge of my will. Thus, I cannot really imagine this will apart from my body. In the essay on the principle of sufficient reason, the will, or rather the subject of willing, is treated as a special class of ideas or objects. But even there we saw this object become one with the subject; that is, we saw it cease to be an object. . . . So far as I know my will specially as object, I know it as body. But then I am again at the first class of ideas laid down in that essey, *i.e.*, real objects. As we proceed we shall see always more clearly that these ideas of the first class obtain their explanation and solution from those of the fourth class given in the essay, which could no longer be properly opposed to the subject as object, and that, therefore, we must learn to understand the inner nature of the law of causality which is valid in the first class, and of all that happens in accordance with it from the law of motivation which governs the fourth class.

The identity of the will and the body, of which we have now given a cursory explanation, can only be proved in the manner we have adopted here. We have proved this identity for the first time, and shall do so more and more fully in the course of this work. By "proved" we mean raised from the immediate consciousness, from knowledge of the reason, or carried over into abstract knowledge. On the other hand, from its very nature it can never be demonstrated, that is, deduced as indirect knowledge from some other more direct knowledge, just because it is itself the most direct knowledge; and if we do not apprehend it and stick to it as such, we shall expect in vain to receive it again in some indirect way as derivative knowledge. It is knowledge of quite a special kind, whose truth cannot therefore properly be brought under any of the four rubrics under which I have classified all truth in the essay on the principle of sufficient reason, the logical, the empirical, the metaphysical, and the metalogical, for it is not, like all these, the relation of an abstract idea to another idea, or to the necessary form of perceptive or of abstract ideation, but it is the relation of a judgment to the connection which an idea of perception, the body, has to that which is not an idea at all, but something *toto genere* different, will. . . .

§ 19. In the first book we were reluctantly driven to explain the human body as merely idea of the subject which knows it, like all the other objects of this world of perception. But it has now become clear that what enables us consciously to distinguish our own body from all other objects which in other respects are precisely the same, is that our body appears in consciousness in quite another way *toto genere* different from idea, and this we denote by the word *will;* and that it is just this double knowledge which we have of our own body that affords us information about it, about its action and movement following on motives, and also about what it experiences by means of external impressions; in a word, about what it is, not as idea, but as more than idea; that is to say, what it is *in itself*. None of this information have we got directly with regard to the nature, action, and experience of other real objects.

It is just because of this special relation to one body that the knowing subject is an individual. For, regarded apart from this relation, his body is for him only an idea like all other ideas. But the relation through which the know-

ing subject is an *individual,* is just on that account a relation which subsists only between him and one particular
idea of all those which he has. Therefore he is conscious
of this one idea, not merely as an idea, but in quite a different way as a will. If, however, he abstracts from that special relation, from that twofold and completely heterogeneous knowledge of what is one and the same, then that
one, the body, is an idea like all other ideas. Therefore, in
order to understand the matter, the individual who knows
must either assume that what distinguishes that one idea
from others is merely the fact that his knowledge stands in
this double relation to it alone; that insight in two ways at
the same time is open to him only in the case of this one
object of perception, and that this is to be explained not
by the difference of this object from all others, but only
by the difference between the relation of his knowledge
to this one object, and its relation to all other objects. Or
else he must assume that this object is essentially different
from all others; that it alone of all objects is at once both
will and idea, while the rest are only ideas, *i.e.,* only phantoms. Thus he must assume that his body is the only real
individual in the world, *i.e.,* the only phenomenon of will
and the only immediate object of the subject. That other
objects, considered merely as *ideas,* are like his body, that
is, like it, fill space (which itself can only be present as
idea), and also, like it, are causally active in space, is
indeed demonstrably certain from the law of causality
which is *a priori* valid for ideas, and which admits of no
effect without a cause; but apart from the fact that we can
only reason from an effect to a cause generally, and not to
a similar cause, we are still in the sphere of mere ideas,
in which alone the law of causality is valid, and beyond
which it can never take us. But whether the objects known
to the individual only as ideas are yet, like his own body,
manifestations of a will, is, as was said in the First Book,
the proper meaning of the question as to the reality of the
external world. To deny this is *theoretical egoism,* which
on that account regards all phenomena that are outside its
own will as phantoms, just as in a practical reference ex-

actly the same thing is done by practical egoism. For in it a man regards and treats himself alone as a person, and all other persons as mere phantoms. Theoretical egoism can never be demonstrably refuted, yet in philosophy it has never been used otherwise than as a sceptical sophism, *i.e.,* a pretence. As a serious conviction, on the other hand, it could only be found in a madhouse, and as such it stands in need of a cure rather than a refutation. We do not therefore combat it any further in this regard, but treat it as merely the last stronghold of scepticism, which is always polemical. Thus our knowledge, which is always bound to individuality and is limited by this circumstance, brings with it the necessity that each of us can only *be one,* while, on the other hand, each of us can *know all;* and it is this limitation that creates the need for philosophy. We therefore who, for this very reason, are striving to extend the limits of our knowledge through philosophy, will treat this sceptical argument of theoretical egoism which meets us, as an army would treat a small frontier fortress. The fortress cannot indeed be taken, but the garrison can never sally forth from it, and therefore we pass it by without danger, and are not afraid to have it in our rear.

The double knowledge which each of us has of the nature and activity of his own body, and which is given in two completely different ways, has now been clearly brought out. We shall accordingly make further use of it as a key to the nature of every phenomenon in nature, and shall judge of all objects which are not our own bodies, and are consequently not given to our consciousness in a double way but only as ideas, according to the analogy of our own bodies, and shall therefore assume that as in one aspect they are idea, just like our bodies, and in this respect are analogous to them, so in another aspect, what remains of objects when we set aside their existence as idea of the subject, must in its inner nature be the same as that in us which we call *will.* For what other kind of existence or reality should we attribute to the rest of the material world? Whence should we take the elements out of which we construct such a world? Besides will and idea nothing is known to us or thinkable. If we wish to attribute the greatest known reality to the material world which exists immediately only in our idea, we give it the reality which our own body has for each of us; for that is the most real thing for every one. But if we now analyse the reality of this body and its actions, beyond the fact that it is idea, we find nothing in it except the will; with this its reality is exhausted. Therefore we can nowhere find another kind of reality which we can attribute to the material world. Thus if we hold that the material world is something more than merely our idea, we must say that besides being idea, that is, in itself and according to its inmost nature, it is that which we find immediately in ourselves as *will*.]

CHAPTER VI

The Father of Positivism:
Auguste Comte (1798-1857)

AUGUSTE COMTE IS THE FIRST MAJOR NINETEENTH-CEN-
tury philosopher whose ideas do not stem directly from
Kant. He is also the first non-German thinker with whom
we have to do in this book. Superficially his thought stands
in the sharpest contrast to the new idealistic metaphysics
of Fichte and Hegel. But there are many concealed affinities between Comte and his German contemporaries.
Comte professes to reject metaphysics altogether. Yet he
is not unspeculative. And, beneath the terminological differences, what passes for metaphysics among the idealists
is not so far removed from what Comte does under the
guise of "positive philosophy." Such resemblances between
the two philosophies will seem less fanciful if it is not
forgotten that for the idealists "metaphysics" is not "super-
physics" but basic ideology or *Weltanschauung,* and if it
is also borne in mind that Comte does not think of positive
philosophy as a part of empirical science itself. The most
serious differences between idealism and positivism, are,
in large part, ideological. The idealists were ideological
conservatives who sought to preserve, although on a modified basis, what they took to be the primary values of the
Christian tradition. In the meantime, however, the intransigent secularistic spirit of the Enlightenment still remained
alive, and in the age which followed there were many
philosophers who were opposed to even such attenuated
reinterpretations of the Christian world-view as the idealists had proposed. There were many philosophers, par-

ticularly in France and England, who continued to insist upon a more radical break with the tradition than the idealists were prepared to countenance, and they sought to provide the basis for a new scientifically oriented ideology which would replace altogether what remained of the outlook of medieval Christendom. What they aspired to was a completely humanistic culture, securely based on the foundation of modern science, and purged of the double-talking equivocations and evasions of idealism. Among them Auguste Comte occupies a place of pre-eminence.

The best way of understanding the standpoint of Comte's positive philosophy is to compare it with Kant's critical philosophy. Kant is no less opposed to speculative metaphysics and theology than Comte. But he never denies that it is in some sense meaningful to speak of things in themselves which are beyond the reach of the scientific understanding. Nor does he deny that there are forms of rational activity other than those which conform to the procedures of empirical science. His critique of reason, in short, does not fundamentally challenge the traditional view that the life of reason is not exhausted in scientific endeavor; for him, ethics, religion, and art also have a rationale, even if it is no longer possible to speak of their achievements as "knowledge."

Comte, on the other hand, refuses to go outside science in order to provide it with a critical justification as the only form of human knowledge. His only standard of rationality, from the outset, is that of science, and his refusal to regard theology or metaphysics as domains of knowledge is based merely on the fact that their cognitive claims cannot be justified by scientific methods of inquiry. Comte adopts, in brief, not a critical but a "positive" attitude toward science; the world which it describes is *the* world, and its method is *the* method of knowledge itself. This does not mean, as we shall see, that Comte is completely hostile to ethics or religion. It does mean, however, that they must no longer be thought of as competing with science in its own sphere, and that they must go to science for any cognitive claims which they may be obliged to make.

Comte's critics have frequently alleged that his philosophy is wholly derivative. This is a mistake which becomes clear when one compares him with such predecessors as Locke or Hume. The British empiricists all attempt to justify their empiricism by showing that the "origins" of all our ideas may be traced to impressions of sensation and reflection or feeling. Comte refuses any such psychologistic justification and simply announces, in effect, his determination not to accept any statement as worthy of belief which cannot be verified by the methods of empirical science. His empiricism in short is "positivistic," and he employs it flatly and explicitly as an ideological tool for destroying all unscientific modes of thought. His aim, as a philosopher, is to inculcate a mentality which simply will not think in unscientific terms, and which will reject the propositions of traditional theology and metaphysics simply on the ground that they are unscientific.

This hard-boiled attitude seems and in many ways is extremely remote from the patiently critical philosophy of Kant and the tender-minded transcendentalism of Fichte and Hegel. Yet Kant, as sternly as Comte himself, rejects the possibility of speculative metaphysics and in the end their opposition to rationalistic metaphysics and theology comes to much the same thing. Comte's philosophy, like Hegel's, is profoundly impregnated with the concept of historical development. His famous "law" of the "three stages" of human intellectual development has an authentically Hegelian ring and he uses it, in Hegel's own fashion, as a device for subtly undermining all points of view previous to his own. Is the law itself an empirical hypothesis? Yes and no. Superficially it is no more than an historical description of the development of the human mind; more profoundly, it is a law of intellectual progress and freedom which prescribes, synoptically, the direction which a progressively enlightened mankind ought to take. Like Hegel, Comte affects a rather avuncular attitude toward all religious and philosophical outlooks before his own. Like Hegel, Comte treats them as inescapable "moments" in the historical development of human thought toward its ideal consummation in the positive philosophy. Moreover, Comte also makes it quite clear that his philosophy not merely transcends all earlier and lower forms of thought, but also transmutes what is really significant in them.

So far as it competes or interferes with the progress of science, Comte is radically opposed to the mythical thinking which he thinks is characteristic of traditional religion. But once one has been fortified by the positive philosophy against the illusions which are generated by that way of thinking, it is then possible to return to religious myths for whatever poetry or moral edification they may contain. Indeed, there is a sense in which a positivist might even "accept" the dogmas of the Church, although, of course, such an acceptance would have, for him, nothing to do with rational belief. In this way some of the subtly ambivalent attitudes toward Christianity that we found in Hegel crop out again in Comte. They are ambivalences, I may add, which may still be found in most of the "liberal" theologies of our own day.

According to Comte the first or theological stage of development is distinguished by a mentality which thinks of other things largely in terms of analogies with the human mind itself, and which therefore ascribes to natural phenomena the feelings and volitions that are characteristic of our own responses to them. At this stage all thought tends to be animistic and anthropomorphic, viewing everything under the categories of purpose, will, and spirit, and conceiving the explanation of the existence of anything entirely in terms of the indwelling purpose or spirit which is imputed to it. It is thus characteristic of the theological consciousness that it is aware of no sharp distinction between the questions "How?" and "Why?", and accordingly makes no clear distinction between what we would call "explanation" and "justification." From this standpoint, the world is conceived mythically as a spiritual order in which the animating purposes of things are also thought of as effective agencies which "cause" them to behave as they do. Stated in other terms, all phenomena tend, at this stage, to be personified, and every process is regarded as an action. What happens not merely happens; it is something done, something suffered, or something achieved.

The theological stage, as Comte describes it, has its own important subdivisions. Its own first stage is the "fetishistic" one in which physical objects are themselves treated as though they were alive and had feelings and purposes of their own. At the second or polytheistic stage, there occurs a gradual simplification of this radically pluralistic animism. Now "gods" are conceived as invisible or quasi-invisible powers which preside over whole classes of phenomena. Finally, however, a third or monotheistic stage is reached at which there is effected a further consolidation of powers in the form of a unified godhead, which is thought of as creating the whole universe and as governing it either directly or through lesser agencies that do its bidding.

The second great stage of intellectual progress Comte calls "metaphysical." Here the tendency to think animistically begins for the first time to disappear. The metaphysician no longer conceives nature as the divine creation of a providential god, but as a first principle or cause which it is necessary to assume in order to account for the order of the universe. Traces of animism no doubt remain, but the idea of purpose or will is now, as Arnold Toynbee might say, "etherialized" until it becomes hardly more than an intellectual abstraction. No longer is it the animating spirit of a particular thing, but, rather, an impersonal "power" whose efficacy is no longer locatable anywhere in the natural world. The characteristic tendency of the metaphysical mind is not so much to animate nature as to "reify" ideas, not so much to impute feelings to the wind or purposes to the sea as to invest concepts with a subsistent "reality" on a par with the world of rocks, chairs, and bugs. "Essences," "tendencies," "potentialities," and "natures" now begin to populate the universe as entities in their own right, and are accorded a causal efficacy which had hitherto been granted only to spirits. In place of the invisible divinities of the theologians, the metaphysicians conceive of a "logos" or "reason" as determining the order of the natural world. Most characteristically of all, the metaphysician identifies "reason" with "cause," and supposes thereby that by reasoning alone he may explain the causes of things. He offers "proofs," arrived at by deduction from rationally self-evident truths, of the existence of a necessary being which he usually calls "God," and imputes the "necessity" which he claims for his inference, to the things which he supposes himself to have inferred.

The beginning of the end of the metaphysical stage is reached when the great controversies break out between the so-called "realists" and "nominalists" over the status of universal concepts. These controversies are still "metaphysical" since both sides still suppose that by purely logical analysis alone it is possible to settle questions of existence. But the fact that the "reality" of universals, independently of the particulars which are characterized by them, is now regarded as a problem is itself indicative of the gradual loosening of the bonds of metaphysics itself.

The third or "positive" stage is finally reached when all such "problems" are permanently bypassed as futile, and positive science alone is accepted as the repository of human knowledge. At this stage "explanation" is conceived solely in terms of empirical hypotheses or laws which describe the constant relations which hold among classes of observable phenomena. Now the only admissible "causal connections" are verifiable correlations among classes of phenomena, and the role of reason is limited exclusively to tracing the logical relations that hold between scientific hypotheses themselves.

In characterizing the third stage, Comte gives us, in effect, his own theory of knowledge, which is "empirical," however, only in the most general sense of that term. All scientific thinking, according to him, is bound to accept observational tests as decisive in determining the validity of any hypothesis. But science is more than observational reports, and such a science as physics is distinguished, not by a vast accumulation of particular facts, but by the formulation of general hypotheses and theories which connect those facts with other facts in a systematic way. Genuine science emerges only when the facts are brought into correlation with one another and, above all, when individual phenomena are conceived as members of whole classes of similar phenomena that stand in law-like relations of coexistence or of succession to the members of other such classes. When the relations described by a given scientific theory are those of coexistence Comte calls the theory a "static" law; when they are relations of succession or continuity, the law is a "dynamic" law. Both types of law, according to Comte, are essential to science; neither is finally to be preferred to the other. It may be added in this connection that a great deal of futile debate over the possibility or nature of so-called laws of historical development might have been avoided had this simple distinction always been kept clearly in mind. In this, as in many other respects, Comte shows a clear-headedness which is well in advance of his time.

Comte accepts, in one sense, the ideal of the unity of science. But this does not appear to have meant for him what it has meant to certain other scientifically-minded philosophers. Comte's position comes out clearly in his interesting views concerning the classification of the sciences, a problem, incidentally, which provided nineteenth-century philosophers of science with one of their favorite indoor sports. In the first place, Comte is an anti-reductionist. He opposes any classification which seeks to reduce sociology to biology or the latter to physics. According to him, the difference between the sciences arise only in part from differences in the scope or generality of their laws. They are due also to the fact that experience discloses a great variety of distinct types of phenomena whose explanation, therefore, requires an ineradicable diversity of concepts and an irreducible plurality of theories. The only unity of science which Comte's philosophy advocates, then, is a methodological unity, that is, a common commitment on the part of all scientific inquirers to logic and to the tests of empirical observation. In the second place, Comte does not think of philosophy itself as a great master science, more general than physics, of which the hypotheses of less general sciences are logical consequences or special applications. It is a highly significant feature of Comte's positivism that he rejects any form of materialism, not only because it is "metaphysical," but also because it blurs vital observable differences between the kinds of phenomena that are dealt with in the physical, biological, and social sciences.

This does not, however, mean that Comte was willing to countenance what the German philosophers called *"Geisteswissenschaft,"* particularly if that connotes a discipline which covertly reintroduces spiritualistic categories into science, or which appeals to supposedly "private" data of experience that are accessible, on principle, only to introspection, or, finally, which employs a peculiar dialectical "logic" unlike that employed in the physical sciences. On the contrary, Comte refuses to regard the human mind as a unique sphere of inquiry which is unaccessible to public, intersubjective modes of analysis and observation. For him there are, at bottom, only two basic sciences of human behavior, physiology and sociology. Any third discipline which purports to deal with some special "psychical" phenomena Comte regards as pure mythology. It should be added here that Comte himself coined the bastard word "sociology" in order to designate an as yet non-existent science of human society, in terms of whose laws alone, as he believed, the economic, political, and moral behavior of men can be understood. Comte is strongly opposed to any purely historical approach to the study of social processes, and he is united, on this point, with his younger English contemporary, John Stuart Mill, against those exponents of the so-called historical method who think that the study of history alone provides adequate knowledge for the conduct of life. History, according to Comte, provides an agglomeration of particular observations that can at best provide data for generalization and the testing of social theories; it does not provide the theories themselves. For him, there can be no knowledge of the dynamics of history that is not based upon a science of society.

One further twist to Comte's philosophy remains to be pointed out. In his later writings, Comte came more and more to regard his philosophy as providing the basis for a new "religion of humanity," which alone, he thought, was suitable to the mentality of human beings in an age of science. Traditional religion requires the acceptance of unscientific theological beliefs and directs our energies away from the problems of individual and collective well-being "in this world." Comte was so far opposed to it. In its place he sought to substitute the new religious ideal of a progressively enlightened humanity unselfishly dedicated to principles of service and love. Unfortunately, however, Comte was not content to advocate his new religion; he was also impelled to furnish it with an elaborate ritual, which became an object of ridicule on the part of his critics. Moreover, in his last years, Comte came increasingly to regard himself as the veritable prophet and his young mistress as the patron saint and symbol of his new religion. This has not enhanced his reputation as a thinker.

In his last years Comte became somewhat paranoid, and his last writings exhibit a degree of emotional unbalance that unfortunately has obscured the sobriety of his earlier work. For all his grandiosity Comte had one of the seminal minds of his age, and his positive philosophy unquestionably represents one of the high points of nineteenth-century thought. He was much more than a narrow propagandist for science. He believed that within the domain of knowledge the scientific method should be sovereign, but without for a moment supposing that the acquisition of scientific information is the sole end of human life. He believed in the unity of science, but only in the methodological sense, and it was no part of his program, as a positivist, to reduce man to the status of a merely physical object. In the case of Comte, moreover, it is unnecessary, as it is with Fichte or Hegel, to squint a bit in order to make sense of what he is saying. He speaks, for the most part, directly and clearly, with a minimum of mystification. His errors are serious, but they can at least be located. In short, any impartial reader will discover in Auguste Comte a thinker of considerable depth and originality, who, for all his faults, is the forerunner of much that is most alive in the empiricist and naturalistic philosophies of our own age. Most historians of nineteenth-century philosophy have done him scant justice; it has been a pleasure for me, in these brief pages, to try to even the score.

The following selection is from Chapter I, Volume I, of

*The Positive Philosophy of Auguste Comte.** In it Comte gives an account of the aim of his work and a statement of the nature and importance of the positive philosophy.

〔 A general statement of any system of philosophy may be either a sketch of a doctrine to be established, or a summary of a doctrine already established. If greater value belongs to the last, the first is still important, as characterizing from its origin the subject to be treated. In a case like the present, where the proposed study is vast and hitherto indeterminate, it is especially important that the field of research should be marked out with all possible accuracy. For this purpose, I will glance at the considerations which have originated this work, and which will be fully elaborated in the course of it.

In order to understand the true value and character of the Positive Philosophy, we must take a brief general view of the progressive course of the human mind, regarded as a whole; for no conception can be understood otherwise than through its history.

Law of human progress.——From the study of the development of human intelligence, in all directions, and through all times, the discovery arises of a great fundamental law, to which it is necessarily subject, and which has a solid foundation of proof, both in the facts of our organization and in our historical experience. The law is this:——that each of our leading conceptions,——each branch of our knowledge,——passes successively through three different theoretical conditions: the Theological, or fictitious; the Metaphysical, or abstract; and the Scientific, or positive. In other words, the human mind, by its nature, employs in its progress three methods of philosophizing, the character of which is essentially different, and even radically opposed: viz., the theological method, the metaphysical, and the positive. Hence arise three philosophies, or general systems of conceptions on the aggregate of phenomena, each of

* *The Positive Philosophy of Auguste Comte,* translated by Harriet Martineau. London: Trubner and Co., 1853. This free translation is a condensation of Comte's *Cours de Philosophie Positive,* 1840–42.

which excludes the others. The first is the necessary point of departure of the human understanding; and the third is its fixed and definitive state. The second is merely a state of transition.

First stage.—In the theological state, the human mind, seeking the essential nature of beings, the first and final causes (the origin and purpose) of all effects,—in short, Absolute knowledge,—supposes all phenomena to be produced by the immediate action of supernatural beings.

Second stage.—In the metaphysical state, which is only a modification of the first, the mind supposes, instead of supernatural beings, abstract forces, veritable entities (that is, personified abstractions) inherent in all beings, and capable of producing all phenomena. What is called the explanation of phenomena is, in this stage, a mere reference of each to its proper entity.

Third stage.—In the final, the positive state, the mind has given over the vain search after Absolute notions, the origin and destination of the universe, and the causes of phenomena, and applies itself to the study of their laws,— that is, their invariable relations of succession and resemblance. Reasoning and observation, duly combined, are the means of this knowledge. What is now understood when we speak of an explanation of facts is simply the establishment of a connection between single phenomena and some general facts, the number of which continually diminishes with the progress of science.

Ultimate point of each.—The Theological system arrived at the highest perfection of which it is capable when it substituted the providential action of a single Being for the varied operations of the numerous divinities which had been before imagined. In the same way, in the last stage of the Metaphysical system, men substitute one great entity (Nature) as the cause of all phenomena, instead of the multitude of entities at first supposed. In the same way, again, the ultimate perfection of the Positive system would be (if such perfection could be hoped for) to represent all phenomena as particular aspects of a single general fact;— such as Gravitation, for instance.

The importance of the working of this general law will be

established hereafter. At present, it must suffice to point out some of the grounds of it.

Evidences of the law. Actual.—There is no science which, having attained the positive stage, does not bear marks of having passed through the others. Some time since it was (whatever it might be) composed, as we can now perceive, of metaphysical abstractions; and, further back in the course of time, it took its form from theological conceptions. We shall have only too much occasion to see, as we proceed, that our most advanced sciences still bear very evident marks of the two earlier periods through which they have passed.

The progress of the individual mind is not only an illustration, but an indirect evidence of that of the general mind. The point of departure of the individual and of the race being the same, the phases of the mind of a man correspond to the epochs of the mind of the race. Now, each of us is aware, if he looks back upon his own history, that he was a theologian in his childhood, a metaphysician in his youth, and a natural philosopher in his manhood. All men who are up to their age can verify this for themselves.

Theoretical.—Besides the observation of facts, we have theoretical reasons in support of this law.

The most important of these reasons arises from the necessity that always exists for some theory to which to refer our facts, combined with the clear impossibility that, at the outset of human knowledge, men could have formed theories out of the observation of facts. All good intellects have repeated, since Bacon's time, that there can be no real knowledge but that which is based on observed facts. This is incontestable, in our present advanced stage; but, if we look back to the primitive stage of human knowledge, we shall see that it must have been otherwise then. If it is true that every theory must be based upon observed facts, it is equally true that facts cannot be observed without the guidance of some theory. Without such guidance, our facts would be desultory and fruitless; we could not retain them: for the most part we could not even perceive them.

Thus, between the necessity of observing facts in order to form a theory, and having a theory in order to observe facts, the human mind would have been entangled in a vicious circle, but for the natural opening afforded by Theological conceptions. This is the fundamental reason for the theological character of the primitive philosophy. This necessity is confirmed by the perfect suitability of the theological philosophy to the earliest researches of the human mind. It is remarkable that the most inaccessible questions, —those of the nature of beings, and the origin and purpose of phenomena,—should be the first to occur in a primitive state, while those which are really within our reach are regarded as almost unworthy of serious study. The reason is evident enough:—that experience alone can teach us the measure of our powers; and if men had not begun by an exaggerated estimate of what they can do, they would never have done all that they are capable of. Our organization requires this. At such a period there could have been no reception of a positive philosophy, whose function is to discover the laws of phenomena, and whose leading characteristic it is to regard as interdicted to human reason those sublime mysteries which theology explains, even to their minutest details, with the most attractive facility. It is just so under a practical view of the nature of the researches with which men first occupied themselves. Such inquiries offered the powerful charm of unlimited empire over the external world,—a world destined wholly for our use, and involved in every way with our existence. The theological philosophy, presenting this view, administered exactly the stimulus necessary to incite the human mind to the irksome labour without which it could make no progress. We can scarcely conceive of such a state of things, our reason having become sufficiently mature to enter upon laborious scientific researches, without needing any such stimulus as wrought upon the imaginations of astrologers and alchemists. We have motive enough in the hope of discovering the laws of phenomena, with a view to the confirmation or rejection of a theory. But it could not be so in the earliest days; and it is to the chimeras of astrology and alchemy that we owe the long series of observations and experiments on which our positive science is based. Kepler felt this on behalf of astronomy, and Berthollet on behalf of chemistry.

Thus was a spontaneous philosophy, the theological, the only possible beginning, method, and provisional system, out of which the Positive philosophy could grow. It is easy, after this, to perceive how Metaphysical methods and doctrines must have afforded the means of transition from the one to the other.

The human understanding, slow in its advance, could not step at once from the theological into the positive philosophy. The two are so radically opposed, that an intermediate system of conceptions has been necessary to render the transition possible. It is only in doing this, that Metaphysical conceptions have any utility whatever. In contemplating phenomena, men substitute for supernatural direction a corresponding entity. This entity may have been supposed to be derived from the supernatural action: but it is more easily lost sight of, leaving attention free for the facts themselves, till, at length, metaphysical agents have ceased to be anything more than the abstract names of phenomena. It is not easy to say by what other process than this our minds could have passed from supernatural considerations to natural; from the theological system to the positive.

The Law of human development being thus established, let us consider what is the proper nature of the Positive Philosophy.

Character of the Positive Philosophy.—As we have seen, the first characteristic of the Positive Philosophy is that it regards all phenomena as subjected to invariable natural *Laws.* Our business is,—seeing how vain is any research into what are called *Causes,* whether first or final,—to pursue an accurate discovery of these Laws, with a view to reducing them to the smallest possible number. By speculating upon causes, we could solve no difficulty about origin and purpose. Our real business is to analyse accurately the circumstances of phenomena, and to connect them by the natural relations of succession and resemblance. The best illustration of this is in the case of the doctrine of Gravitation. We say that the general phenomena of the universe are *explained* by it, because it connects under one head the whole immense variety of astronomical facts; exhibiting the constant tendency of atoms towards each other in direct proportion to their masses, and in inverse proportion to the squares of their distances; whilst the general fact itself is a mere extension of one which is perfectly familiar to us, and which we therefore say that we know;—the weight of bodies on the surface of the earth. As to what weight and attraction are, we have nothing to do with that, for it is not a matter of knowledge at all. Theologians and metaphysicians may imagine and refine about such questions; but positive philosophy rejects them. When any attempt has been made to explain them, it has ended only in saying that attraction is universal weight, and that weight is terrestrial attraction: that is, that the two orders of phenomena are identical; which is the point from which the question set out. . . .

History of the Positive Philosophy.—Before ascertaining the stage which the Positive Philosophy has reached, we must bear in mind that the different kinds of our knowledge have passed through the three stages of progress at different rates, and have not therefore arrived at the same time. The rate of advance depends on the nature of the knowledge in question, so distinctly that, as we shall see hereafter, this consideration constitutes an accessary to the fundamental law of progress. Any kind of knowledge reaches the positive stage early in proportion to its generality, simplicity, and independence of other departments. Astronomical science, which is above all made up of facts that are general, simple, and independent of other sciences, arrived first; then terrestrial Physics; then Chemistry; and, at length, Physiology.

It is difficult to assign any precise date to this revolution in science. It may be said, like everything else, to have been always going on; and especially since the labours of Aristotle and the school of Alexandria; and then from the introduction of natural science into the West of Europe by the Arabs. But, if we must fix upon some marked period, to serve as a rallying point, it must be that,—about two centuries ago,—when the human mind was astir under the precepts of Bacon, the conceptions of Descartes, and the discoveries of Galileo. Then it was that the spirit of the

Positive philosophy rose up in opposition to that of the superstitious and scholastic systems which had hitherto obscured the true character of all science. Since that date, the progress of the Positive philosophy, and the decline of the other two, have been so marked that no rational mind now doubts that the revolution is destined to go on to its completion,—every branch of knowledge being, sooner or later, brought within the operation of Positive philosophy. This is not yet the case. Some are still lying outside: and not till they are brought in will the Positive philosophy possess that character of universality which is necessary to its definitive constitution.

New department of Positive philosophy.—In mentioning just now the four principal categories of phenomena,—astronomical, physical, chemical, and physiological,—there was an omission which will have been noticed. Nothing was said of social phenomena. Though involved with the physiological, social phenomena demand a distinct classification, both on account of their importance and of their difficulty. They are the most individual, the most complicated, the most dependent on all others; and therefore they must be the latest,—even if they had no special obstacle to encounter. This branch of science has not hitherto entered into the domain of Positive philosophy. Theological and metaphysical methods, exploded in other departments, are as yet exclusively applied, both in the way of inquiry and discussion, in all treatment of Social subjects, though the best minds are heartily weary of eternal disputes about divine right and the sovereignty of the people. This is the great, while it is evidently the only gap which has to be filled, to constitute, solid and entire, the Positive Philosophy. Now that the human mind has grasped celestial and terrestrial physics,—mechanical and chemical; organic physics, both vegetable and animal,—there remains one science, to fill up the series of sciences of observation,—Social physics. This is what men have now most need of: and this it is the principal aim of the present work to establish.

Social Physics.—It would be absurd to pretend to offer this new science at once in a complete state. Others, less new, are in very unequal conditions of forwardness. But the same character of positivity which is impressed on all the others will be shown to belong to this. This once done, the philosophical system of the moderns will be in fact complete, as there will then be no phenomenon which does not naturally enter into some one of the five great categories. All our fundamental conceptions having become homogeneous, the Positive state will be fully established. It can never again change its character, though it will be for ever in course of development by additions of new knowledge. Having acquired the character of universality which has hitherto been the only advantage resting with the two preceding systems, it will supersede them by its natural superiority, and leave to them only an historical existence.

Secondary aim of this work.—We have stated the special aim of this work. Its secondary and general aim is this:— to review what has been effected in the Sciences, in order to show that they are not radically separate, but all branches from the same trunk. If we had confined ourselves to the first and special object of the work, we should have produced merely a study of Social physics: whereas, in introducing the second and general, we offer a study of Positive philosophy, passing in review all the positive sciences already formed.

To review the philosophy of the Sciences.—The purpose of this work is not to give an account of the Natural Sciences. Besides that it would be endless, and that it would require a scientific preparation such as no one man possesses, it would be apart from our object, which is to go through a course of not Positive Science, but Positive Philosophy. We have only to consider each fundamental science in its relation to the whole positive system, and to the spirit which characterizes it; that is, with regard to its methods and its chief results.

The two aims, though distinct, are inseparable; for, on the one hand, there can be no positive philosophy without a basis of social science, without which it could not be all-comprehensive; and, on the other hand, we could not pursue Social science without having been prepared by the study of phenomena less complicated than those of society, and furnished with a knowledge of laws and anterior facts which have a bearing upon social science. Though the fundamental sciences are not all equally interesting to ordinary minds, there is no one of them that can be neglected in an inquiry like the present; and, in the eye of philosophy, all are of equal value to human welfare. Even those which appear the least interesting have their own value, either on account of the perfection of their methods, or as being the necessary basis of all the others.

*   *   *   *   *   *   *   *   *

Advantages of the Positive Philosophy.—The general spirit of a course of Positive Philosophy having been thus set forth, we must now glance at the chief advantages which may be derived, on behalf of human progression, from the study of it. Of these advantages, four may be especially pointed out.

Illustrates the intellectual function.—I. The study of the Positive Philosophy affords the only rational means of exhibiting the logical laws of the human mind, which have hitherto been sought by unfit methods. To explain what is meant by this, we may refer to a saying of M. de Blainville, in his work on Comparative Anatomy, that every active, and especially every living being, may be regarded under two relations—the Statical and the Dynamical; that is, under conditions or in action. It is clear that all considerations range themselves under the one or the other of these heads. Let us apply this classification to the intellectual functions.

If we regard these functions under their Statical aspect—that is, if we consider the conditions under which they exist—we must determine the organic circumstances of the case, which inquiry involves it with anatomy and physiology. If we look at the Dynamic aspect, we have to study simply the exercise and results of the intellectual powers of the human race, which is neither more nor less than the general object of the Positive Philosophy. In short, looking at all scientific theories as so many great logical facts, it is only by the thorough observation of these facts that we can arrive at the knowledge of logical laws. These being the only means of knowledge of intellectual phenomena, the illusory psychology, which is the last phase of theology, is excluded. It pretends to accomplish the discovery of the laws of the human mind by contemplating it in itself; that is, by separating it from causes and effects. Such an attempt, made in defiance of the physiological study of our intellectual organs, and of the observation of rational methods of procedure, cannot succeed at this time of day.

The Positive Philosophy, which has been rising since the time of Bacon, has now secured such a preponderance, that the metaphysicians themselves profess to ground their pretended science on an observation of facts. They talk of external and internal facts, and say that their business is with the latter. This is much like saying that vision is explained by luminous objects painting their images upon the retina. To this the physiologists reply that another eye would be needed to see the image. In the same manner, the mind may observe all phenomena but its own. It may be said that a man's intellect may observe his passions, the seat of the reason being somewhat apart from that of the emotions in the brain; but there can be nothing like scientific observation of the passions, except from without, as the stir of the emotions disturbs the observing faculties more or less. It is yet more out of the question to make an intellectual observation of intellectual processes. The observing and observed organ are here the same, and its action cannot be pure and natural. In order to observe, your intellect must pause from activity; yet it is this very activity that you want to observe. If you cannot effect the pause, you cannot observe: if you do effect it, there is nothing to observe. The results of such a method are in proportion to its absurdity. After two thousand years of psychological pursuit, no one proposition is established to the satisfaction of its followers. They are divided, to this day, into a multitude of schools, still disputing about the very elements of their doctrine. This interior observation gives birth to almost as many theories as there are observers. We ask in vain for any one discovery, great or small, which has been made under this method. The psychologists have done some good in keeping up the activity of our understandings, when there was no better work for our faculties to do; and they may have added something to our stock of knowledge. If they have done so, it is by practising the Positive method—by observing the progress of the human mind in the light of science; that is, by ceasing, for the moment, to be psychologists.

The view just given in relation to logical Science becomes yet more striking when we consider the logical Art.

The Positive Method can be judged of only in action. It cannot be looked at by itself, apart from the work on which it is employed. At all events, such a contemplation would be only a dead study, which could produce nothing in the mind which loses time upon it. We may talk for ever about the method, and state it in terms very wisely, without knowing half so much about it as the man who has once put it in practice upon a single particular of actual research, even without any philosophical intention. Thus it is that psychologists, by dint of reading the precepts of Bacon and the discourses of Descartes, have mistaken their own dreams for science.

Without saying whether it will ever be possible to establish *à priori* a true method of investigation, independent of a philosophical study of the sciences, it is clear that the thing has never been done yet, and that we are not capable of doing it now. We cannot as yet explain the great logical procedures, apart from their applications. If we ever do, it will remain as necessary then as now to form good intellectual habits by studying the regular application of the scientific methods which we shall have attained.

This, then, is the first great result of the Positive Philosophy—the manifestation by experiment of the laws which rule the Intellect in the investigation of truth; and, as a consequence, the knowledge of the general rules suitable for that object.

Must regenerate Education.—II. The second effect of the Positive Philosophy, an effect not less important and far more urgently wanted, will be to regenerate Education.

The best minds are agreed that our European education,

still essentially theological, metaphysical, and literary, must be superseded by a Positive training, conformable to our time and needs. Even the governments of our day have shared, where they have not originated, the attempts to establish positive instruction; and this is a striking indication of the prevalent sense of what is wanted. While encouraging such endeavours to the utmost, we must not however conceal from ourselves that everything yet done is inadequate to the object. The present exclusive speciality of our pursuits, and the consequent isolation of the sciences, spoil our teaching. . . . The specialities of science can be pursued by those whose vocation lies in that direction. They are indispensable; and they are not likely to be neglected; but they can never of themselves renovate our system of Education; and, to be of their full use, they must rest upon the basis of that general instruction which is a direct result of the Positive Philosophy.

*   *   *   *   *   *   *   *   *

Must reorganize society.—IV. The Positive Philosophy offers the only solid basis for that Social Reorganization which must succeed the critical condition in which the most civilized nations are now living.

It cannot be necessary to prove to anybody who reads this work that Ideas govern the world, or throw it into chaos; in other words, that all social mechanism rests upon Opinions. The great political and moral crisis that societies are now undergoing is shown by a rigid analysis to arise out of intellectual anarchy. While stability in fundamental maxims is the first condition of genuine social order, we are suffering under an utter disagreement which may be called universal. Till a certain number of general ideas can be acknowledged as a rallying-point of social doctrine, the nations will remain in a revolutionary state, whatever palliatives may be devised; and their institutions can be only provisional. But whenever the necessary agreement on first principles can be obtained, appropriate institutions will issue from them, without shock or resistance; for the causes of disorder will have been arrested by the mere fact of the agreement. It is in this direction that those

must look who desire a natural and regular, a normal
state of society.

Now, the existing disorder is abundantly accounted for
by the existence, all at once, of three incompatible philosophies,—the theological, the metaphysical, and the positive.
Any one of these might alone secure some sort of social
order; but while the three co-exist, it is impossible for us
to understand one another upon any essential point whatever. If this is true, we have only to ascertain which of the
philosophies must, in the nature of things, prevail; and,
this ascertained, every man, whatever may have been his
former views, cannot but concur in its triumph. The problem once recognized cannot remain long unsolved; for all
considerations whatever point to the Positive Philosophy as
the one destined to prevail. It alone has been advancing
during a course of centuries, throughout which the others
have been declining. The fact is incontestable. Some may
deplore it, but none can destroy it, nor therefore neglect
it but under penalty of being betrayed by illusory speculations. This general revolution of the human mind is nearly
accomplished. We have only to complete the Positive
Philosophy by bringing Social phenomena within its comprehension, and afterwards consolidating the whole into
one body of homogeneous doctrine. The marked preference
which almost all minds, from the highest to the commonest,
accord to positive knowledge over vague and mystical conceptions, is a pledge of what the reception of this philosophy will be when it has acquired the only quality that it
now wants—a character of due generality. When it has
become complete, its supremacy will take place spontaneously, and will re-establish order throughout society. There
is, at present, no conflict but between the theological and
the metaphysical philosophies. They are contending for the
task of reorganizing society; but it is a work too mighty
for either of them. The positive philosophy has hitherto
intervened only to examine both, and both are abundantly
discredited by the process. It is time now to be doing something more effective, without wasting our forces in needless controversy. It is time to complete the vast intellectual
operation begun by Bacon, Descartes, and Galileo, by

constructing the system of general ideas which must henceforth prevail among the human race. This is the way to put an end to the revolutionary crisis which is tormenting the civilized nations of the world.

Leaving these four points of advantage, we must attend to one precautionary reflection.

No hope of reduction to a single law.—Because it is proposed to consolidate the whole of our acquired knowledge into one body of homogeneous doctrine, it must not be supposed that we are going to study this vast variety as proceeding from a single principle, and as subjected to a single law. There is something so chimerical in attempts at universal explanation by a single law, that it may be as well to secure this Work at once from any imputation of the kind, though its development will show how undeserved such an imputation would be. Our intellectual resources are too narrow, and the universe is too complex, to leave any hope that it will ever be within our power to carry scientific perfection to its last degree of simplicity. Moreover, it appears as if the value of such an attainment, supposing it possible, were greatly overrated. . . .

The consideration of all phenomena as referable to a single origin is by no means necessary to the systematic formation of science, any more than to the realization of the great and happy consequences that we anticipate from the positive philosophy. The only necessary unity is that of Method, which is already in great part established. As for the doctrine, it need not be *one;* it is enough that it should be *homogeneous.* It is, then, under the double aspect of unity of method and homogeneousness of doctrine that we shall consider the different classes of positive theories in this work. While pursuing the philosophical aim of all science, the lessening of the number of general laws requisite for the explanation of natural phenomena, we shall regard as presumptuous every attempt, in all future time, to reduce them rigorously to one.]

CHAPTER VII

The Saint of Liberalism:
John Stuart Mill (1806-1873)

ONE OF THE FIRST ENGLISHMEN TO APPRECIATE THE importance of Comte's philosophy was his younger contemporary, John Stuart Mill. Despite the fact that he was subsequently disillusioned and repelled by the megalomania and religiosity of Comte's later writings, Mill well understood how many philosophical commitments they shared in common. Comte construed Mill's favorable notices of his ideas as coming from an English disciple who would help to carry the good news of the positive philosophy to the gentiles. This was wholly Comte's idea. Both by temperament and by conviction, Mill was not cut out to be the disciple of any man or the mere propagandist for any dispensation. He had not worked himself free, at great personal cost, from the rigid dogmas of the Benthamite utilitarianism into which he had been indoctrinated as a youth by his father, James Mill, in order to become a convert to Comte's religion of humanity. Comte's mystical adoration of Humanity came perilously close to the sort of animistic reification of a concept which he himself had exposed in the thinking of the theological and metaphysical stages. And Comte's increasingly organistic conception of the relation of the individual member to society had overtones that were not far removed from the statism of Fichte and Hegel. Such tendencies in Comte's later thought could not possibly appeal to Mill, for whom the major problem of nineteenth-century social life was the spiritual, intellectual, and social freedom of individual men. Mill was profoundly imbued, as Comte was not, with the ingrained atomistic and psychologistic habits of mind that are characteristic of the tradition of classical British empiricism, of which he himself was the last great representative. For him it was virtually instinctive to conceive the human mind, as Locke and Hume had done before him, in terms of "bundles" of particular impressions and ideas. It was also instinctive for him to think of society as a collection of individual persons united together only by common interests and mutual responsibilities. Until late in life, he was never able to conceive the problem of human freedom in institutional terms. It was always a cardinal thesis of Mill's own classification of the social sciences that psychological laws of association and motivation are the foundation of any science of society which seeks to understand man's communal behavior. Unlike Comte, he believed that any theory which seeks to explain human activities *en bloc* presupposes a psychological theory of human nature.

Throughout his life, and in all of his books, Mill was first of all a polemicist who conducted an unremitting campaign against the myriadic forms of obscurantism, dogmatism and irrationalism which afflicted nineteenth-century thought. His whole ramified "philosophy of experience," as he called it, was directed against absolutes of any sort, whether they be disguised as self-evident truths, traditional verities, categorical imperatives, natural rights, or logical axioms. Many of Mill's critics have not fully appreciated the fact that his logical theories and his theory of knowledge, as well as his moral and political philosophy, are all finally directed to the same fundamental end. For example, his attempt to provide a purely inductive basis for deductive logic was itself part of his grand campaign against the intuitionists and transcendentalists who invariably cited the non-empirical character of logical and mathematical truths in support of their own apriorism and dogmatism in the spheres of religion, morality, and politics. So long, Mill thought, as logic and mathematics are exempted from the tests of observation, a case remains in principle for those who appeal to intuition, self-evidence, and authority, in other domains which more directly affect the happiness of men. Mill took the heroic step of denying the distinction between logical and factual truths which had been the cornerstone of Hume's own radical empiricism. He did so, however, primarily in order to make good the claim that *all* knowledge whatever must be grounded in and tested by experience, a thesis which he believed to be essential if the spirit of philosophical liberalism is to prevail against its enemies.

Mill's philosophy is radically empirical. But still more basic to his point of view is what may be called his "reasonablism," his conviction that no proposition of whatever sort should be exempted from criticism and that for any dictum that may properly claim our assent reasons may properly be asked which should be capable of "determining the intellect." The root of all authoritarianism and absolutism, which Mill regards as the greatest remediable source of human misery, is the exemption of certain propositions from such review. If these evils are to be removed, then no belief, however deeply felt, can be regarded as infallible. The growth of human knowledge and wisdom, upon which the progress of mankind chiefly depends, is the pooled result of innumerable individual observations and speculations, criticisms and countercriticisms. So long as any proposition is exempted from the demand for reasons, that growth is fatally impaired, and the whole case for freedom of thought, which for Mill is the essential liberty, is placed in jeopardy.

The motives animating Mill's *Logic* are thus all of a piece with those which govern his great essay on *Liberty*. And if he is still remembered with gratitude by free men everywhere, it is because his whole philosophy, whatever its faults, is perhaps the greatest nineteenth-century symbol of spiritual liberality and intellectual reasonableness. There is scarcely a wind of doctrine blowing in his age which failed to touch Mill, and if, as he tells us in his *Autobiography,* he could never read Hegel himself without feeling slightly nauseated, he was by no means unresponsive to the poetic and religious impulses which animated most of what was significant in the romantic and transcendental philosophies of his English contemporaries, Coleridge and Carlyle. He departed from them only at the point where their genuine spirituality passed over into an obscurantist spiritualism which is incompatible with the philosophy of experience.

Mill called his philosophy "the philosophy of experience," precisely in order to distinguish it from the vulgar, know-nothing empiricism which, by refusing to acknowledge any proposition which is not immediately and conclusively confirmed by sense-perception, rejects not only transcendental metaphysics and revealed religion, but also science itself. All propositions, according to Mill, must meet the tests of experience. But not all valid propositions are reports of immediate experience. Like Comte, Mill was fully aware that science cannot exist without hypotheses and theories as well as observations, and that although reliable hypotheses must be tested by observation they are not merely accumulated observation reports. It was also a salient point of his theory of knowledge that raw observations, made at random and uncritically reported, have little evidential value. It is for this reason, as he never tired of reminding Macaulay and other conservative representatives of the historical school, that the "lessons of history" provide no adequate basis for the conduct of political affairs. A principal aim of Mill's famous "canons of induction" was to provide a method for sifting the evidence for the correlations upon which scientific laws are based. Mill understood the fallacy of *post hoc ergo propter hoc,** and he was quite aware of the crucial importance of experimentation for the scientific testing of theories. Real continuities in nature, said Mill, do not always lie upon the surface of experience. Valid causal connections can be established only through meticulous sorting and independent variation of the complex antecedent conditions and consequences that are concealed from casual observation. Unwashed appearances, including appearances of correlation, are notoriously deceptive. It should be the function of inductive logic, among other things, to provide reliable technique for cleaning them.

* "After this, therefore because of this."

With the details of Mill's elaborate theory of inductive logic it is impossible to deal in a brief space. Our concern here must be with its main philosophical interest, and with the philosophical problems which it raises.

Mill understood as I have said, that all scientific hypotheses and predictions go beyond the "facts." Science is never a mere record of what has happened in numerous particular cases. The concern of science is with causal uniformities which hold regularly for all members of a given class. Its business is to extrapolate in a responsible way from past experience to a future which has not yet been experienced. How, then, can the belief in such general uniformities and predictions be justified in spite of the fact that what they comprehend always outruns the available data? Kant's answer, as we have seen, is that the principle of causality is an a priori synthetic principle of the human understanding which is presupposed by all rational beings in thinking about objects in space and time. Such a solution, however, was not available to Mill. He was obliged, therefore, to suppose that the principle of the uniformity of nature, as he called it, is itself wholly grounded in experience. He himself puts the point with uncommon clarity and succinctness: "We must first observe that there is a principle implied in the very statement of what Induction is; an assumption with regard to the course of nature and the order of the universe; namely that there are such things in nature as parallel cases; that what happens once will, under a sufficient degree of similarity of circumstances, happen again, and not only again, but as often as the same circumstances recur. . . . And if we consult the actual course of nature we find that the assumption is warranted. The universe, so far as known to us, is so constituted that whatever is true in any one case is true in all cases of a certain description; the only difficulty is, to find what description."

But the principle that the course of nature is uniform, although apparently the fundamental principle of induction, does not, in Mill's view, explain the inductive process or independently justify it. For it also is in need of justification, being itself, as he believes, no more than the most general hypothesis that can be formulated about the order of things in nature. Moreover, it is not our first induction from experience, but one of the last. We arrive at it only after making innumerable special inductions and generalizations upon which its own plausibility largely depends. In effect, then, Mill appears to think that the law of the uniformity of nature is a second-order, synoptic generalization whose own validity is attested by the whole battery of limited hypotheses of science and common sense. This implies that the law is at best an inductive hypothesis which is in need of and in fact receives an overwhelming convergence of evidence from the more restricted generalizations of the special sciences and of ordinary experience. But, then, how can it provide the "warrant" for the latter? Is there not here an obvious circularity, a futile attempt to lift oneself by one's inductive bootstraps?

So, at any rate, most of Mill's critics have argued. If the only warrant for the thesis that the course of nature is uniform lies in the lower-order generalizations that have already been induced from experience, how can it, in turn, reasonably provide the warrant for them? The underlying problem of induction thus still remains: what authorizes *any* induction from experience, restricted or unrestricted? To this question, Mill's critics contend, he does not provide the ghost of an answer. Nor has he stopped to ask the more fundamental question whether such a principle as that of universal causality is really an hypothesis at all, whether, that is to say, what it asserts is a law of nature which describes correlations that hold classes of phenomena. This pressing question, which might have given Mill pause, had he more deeply pondered Hume's *Treatise* or Kant's *Critique,* is the serious upshot of their analyses of causation. If the answer lies in the negative, then perhaps the whole "problem of induction" may be found to resolve itself into one of formulating the validating conditions which we ourselves, as inquirers, are prepared to accept in seeking to justify our ideas concerning the world of phenomena. So construed, these conditions would then specify what we take to be the conditions of rationality within the sphere of factual inquiry. From this standpoint, questions concerning their own validity would be pointless since there is no higher court of reason to which an appeal can intelligibly be made. To question them would be like questioning, in the moral sphere, whether we ought to do what is right.

If, in spite of this, someone should still question them, the only way to deal with him would be along the lines Mill himself adopted in trying to answer those who professed skeptical doubts about the principle of utility. What is required, at such a point, is not proof, but self-study and clarification of one's underlying commitments as a human being. First principles, as Mill himself tells us, are not amenable to proof, even though, in some sense, they may be supported. But before they are so supported, it would appear desirable to ask what sort of support they might be thought to require. Had Mill pondered this question from the standpoint of the problem of knowledge as thoroughly as he did in relation to the problem of conduct, he might perhaps have seen that what is involved in both cases is essentially a question of motivation, and that in both cases the only cure is a practical cure. At this point, the empiricist might discover that he could learn something about the defense of reason from his archenemy, Fichte.

Mill's philosophy of experience has another important aspect which remains to be mentioned. Here he follows more closely in the footsteps of his predecessors, Berkeley and Hume. The grand design of all these philosophers is to provide an account of the faculties and furniture of the human mind which accepts nothing beyond the data of sense-perception, feeling, and the "natural" principles of association whereby the "material" of sensation and feeling are organized into the ideas and beliefs which form our picture of the world in which we live. Nothing, on this view, is represented in the imagination which, directly or indirectly, is not first found in sense-experience, and the imagination itself is nothing but the propensity of our ideas to form associations with other ideas. What we think of as the world of nature, therefore, consists at bottom in nothing but certain constant uniformities among classes of sensations, and what we conceive as a material object is nothing, finally, but a complex "possibility of sensation." According to this view, which is sometimes called "phenomenalism," every statement of fact is, in principle, reducible to a conjunction of statements about actual or possible sense-impressions. And, on this view, there is no term of reference which does not designate some potentially experienceable item of sensation or feeling. What we call "matter" is merely one system of uniformities among sensations, and what we call "mind" is another. In referring, therefore, to the human mind, we are not talking about some immaterial substance that lies behind the world of sense, but only, as Hume had put it, about a "bundle of impressions." But by "impressions" it is essential to understand that we are not referring to something which exists only "in the mind," since by hypothesis "mind" is itself a portmanteau word which refers merely to a particular organization of the impressions themselves. The distinction between "appearance" and "reality" is, so to say, an intramural distinction that has an application solely within the domain of possible experience itself.

The underlying intention of Mill's philosophy is always broadly ethical. Its concern is to formulate a general view of human knowledge and of the world of nature which will be of the greatest utility in the conduct of life. The philosophy of experience, with its inductive logic and its phenomenalism, is thus adumbrated primarily as the orientation course for the utilitarian philosophy of life which Mill had inherited from Jeremy Bentham and which, with his own characteristic revisions, he restated in his famous essays, *Utilitarianism* and *Liberty*.

Mill's so-called "proof" of utilitarianism has been badly misunderstood by his critics. He was quite aware of the distinction between what is and what ought to be, between statements of fact and judgments which prescribe what ought to be done. In his *Logic*, a book which too many of the critics of his moral philosophy have neglected, Mill

explains very clearly wherein the essential difference between science and morality, which he speaks of significantly
as an "art," might be thought to lie. In his own mind he was
not seriously confused about the distinction between the
desired and the desirable, and he was under no illusion as
to the possibility of deducing a science of morals from
psychological or sociological laws of human behavior. Mill,
like Bentham, holds that actions are to be judged by their
consequences; but science cannot dictate what consequences are to be preferred. Moreover, the principle of
utility, which prescribes that actions are right only in so
far as they promote the general happiness, or greatest happiness of the greatest number, is a principle of conduct, and
not a definition in which the logical function of the word
"right" is explicated. In short, utilitarianism is, for Mill
as it was for Bentham, a way of life, not a theory of moral
discourse. And it was so construed in the nineteenth century by most of its enemies as well as by its friends.

Morality, then, is or should be the art of individual and
social happiness. And happiness or well-being is understood by Mill in terms of the harmonious satisfaction of
the desires of the individual. Actually there is much in
common between Mill's generic conception of happiness
and that of Aristotle. The difference lies chiefly in the
fact that Mill is a greater environmentalist than Aristotle
and views human nature itself in more variable terms. The
humanism of the ancient Greeks has been much applauded
as a capacious ethics whose conception of human well-
being does full justice to the range of man's interests and
capacities. Mill's conception of well-being is equally large,
although somewhat different in emphasis. It is his conviction that man is a social as well as an intellectual animal,
and that a large part of his happiness depends upon the
satisfaction of his social impulses and other-regarding sentiments. Some of the older forms of hedonism have been
charged with being egoistic. This may perhaps be true of
Epicureanism, but it cannot be fairly ascribed to Mill's
version of utilitarianism. For him, a life of personal pleas-
ure-seeking is as self-frustrating as any other pattern of

conduct which does not encompass the whole range of human sentiments.

There is, according to Mill, no serious problem of supplying a motive for the principle of utility; in principle that motive is already present in the simpler forms of human sympathy or fellow feeling. The chief moral problem, on the contrary, is the problem of enlightenment. If men adequately understood themselves, and were not distracted by misconceptions of the human situation which are inculcated through bad religion, bad philosophy, and bad government, the moral progress of mankind would be less faltering. What is most needed for enlightenment at the present time is, in Mill's opinion, liberty. The primary social factor in modern life which blocks the way of individual and collective well-being is the widespread interference of institutions, formal and informal, with individual self-development. Mill realizes, as most of his critics again fail to acknowledge, that any form of organized society is bound, in some degree, to frustrate the individual's desire to do exactly as he pleases. That, indeed, is a truism. The trouble is that such frustrations have long since ceased to serve the general happiness. It is unquestionably reasonable and necessary to restrict the liberty of the individual, but only to the extent that such restrictions are essential to the self-development of others.

Mill's passionate and complex defense of liberty is perhaps the most powerful and imaginative defense that has ever been made of the open society and the ideal of individual self-development. For him, liberty is both a means and an end, a condition of the general welfare and an intrinsic component of personal happiness. Moreover, it is not simply liberty in general which he defends but the specific liberties that are essential to the conduct of life. Freedom of thought, freedom to choose one's vocation, freedom of association and speech, which together comprise Mill's ideal of Liberty, are, in his view, the paramount goods which politically organized society can bestow. The extent to which they are realized in any society is, for Mill, the only test of its degree of civilization and its capacity for progress.

Mill understood, perhaps better than any other nineteenth-century liberal, that democracy and technological science are not automatic cure-alls. Within every human institution there is always a drift toward orthodoxy and conformity. Neither democracy nor institutionalized science are immune to such tendencies. The only way to offset them is through the constant extension of individual freedom, and through the criticism which freedom makes possible. No philosopher of his age held science or its methods in higher esteem than Mill. But he was never remotely tempted by the ideal of large-scale scientific social planning by an intellectual elite. On the contrary, in Mill's view the advancement of knowledge which is the condition of social progress is possible only in a society in which no person, however humble, is precluded from making an effective contribution to our all too skimpy fund of human knowledge. Authority invariably breeds orthodoxy, and orthodoxy, however "sound," is always the sign of a closed society which has reached the limit of its capacity for self-correction and self-development. If authority is also necessary for law and order, as Mill knows, it must also be continually checked and held to account by the free criticism of men who are unafraid.

Whatever its faults of detail, Mill's philosophy remains to this day the starting point for most liberal reflection concerning the good society and the good life. His name is cherished by many who have found inadequate his solutions to the logical and epistemological problems which concerned him. He has been called "the saint of rationalism," but his rationalism, if such it be, is a far cry indeed from that of his seventeenth- and eighteenth-century predecessors. I prefer to think of him as "the saint of liberalism," who kept alive in the Age of Ideology the ideal of reasonableness with a small "r." It is not an ideal which is easily dramatized or which appeals to most questers after certainty. But it is the mark of a civilized mind, and general acceptance of it is the mark of a civilized society.

The following selections are taken from Mill's essay "Nature" which was published posthumously by his wife's daughter as the first of three essays on religion, the other two of which are entitled "The Utility of Religion" and "Theism."* Whatever may be said of the latter two essays, "Nature" surely represents Mill's mature and considered opinion on its subject.

ʃ Nature, then, in this its simplest acceptation, is a collective name for all facts, actual and possible: or (to speak more accurately) a name for the mode, partly known to us and partly unknown, in which all things take place. For the word suggests, not so much the multitudinous detail of the phenomena, as the conception which might be formed of their manner of existence as a mental whole, by a mind possessing a complete knowledge of them: to which conception it is the aim of science to raise itself, by successive steps of generalization from experience.

Such, then, is a correct definition of the word Nature. But this definition corresponds only to one of the senses of that ambiguous term. It is evidently inapplicable to some of the modes in which the word is familiarly employed. For example, it entirely conflicts with the common form of speech by which Nature is opposed to Art, and natural to artificial. For in the sense of the word Nature which has just been defined, and which is the true scientific sense, Art is as much Nature as anything else; and everything which is artificial is natural—Art has no independent powers of its own: Art is but the employment of the powers of Nature for an end. Phenomena produced by human agency, no less than those which as far as we are concerned are spontaneous, depend on the properties of the elementary forces, or of the elementary substances and their compounds. The united powers of the whole human race could not create a new property of matter in general, or of any one of its species. We can only take advantage for our purposes of the properties which we find. . . .

It thus appears that we must recognize at least two principal meanings in the word Nature. In one sense, it means all the powers existing in either the outer or the inner world and everything which takes place by means of

* *Nature, The Utility of Religion*, and *Theism*, 3rd edition. London: Longmans, Green and Co., 1885, pp. 6–28, 54–65.

those powers. In another sense, it means, not everything which happens, but only what takes place without the agency, or without the voluntary and intentional agency, of man. This distinction is far from exhausting the ambiguities of the word; but it is the key to most of those on which important consequences depend.

Such, then, being the two principal senses of the word Nature; in which of these is it taken, or is it taken in either, when the word and its derivatives are used to convey ideas of commendation, approval, and even moral obligation?

*   *   *   *   *   *   *   *   *

Is it necessary to recognize in these forms of speech, another distinct meaning of the word Nature? Or can they be connected, by any rational bond of union, with either of the two meanings already treated of? At first it may seem that we have no option but to admit another ambiguity in the term. All inquiries are either into what is, or into what ought to be: science and history belonging to the first division, art, morals and politics to the second. But the two senses of the word Nature first pointed out, agree in referring only to what is. In the first meaning, Nature is a collective name for everything which is. In the second, it is a name for everything which is of itself, without voluntary human intervention. But the employment of the word Nature as a term of ethics seems to disclose a third meaning, in which Nature does not stand for what is, but for what ought to be; or for the rule or standard of what ought to be. A little consideration, however, will show that this is not a case of ambiguity; there is not here a third sense of the word. Those who set up Nature as a standard of action do not intend a merely verbal proposition; they do not mean that the standard, whatever it be, should be *called* Nature; they think they are giving some information as to what the standard of action really is. Those who say that we ought to act according to Nature do not mean the mere identical proposition that we ought to do what we ought to do. They think that the word Nature affords some external criterion of what we should do; and if they lay down as a rule for what ought to be, a word which in its proper signification denotes what is, they do so because they have a notion, either clearly or confusedly, that what is, constitutes the rule and standard of what ought to be.

The examination of this notion, is the object of the present Essay. It is proposed to inquire into the truth of the doctrines which make Nature a test of right and wrong, good and evil, or which in any mode or degree attach merit or approval to following, imitating, or obeying Nature. To this inquiry the foregoing discussion respecting the meaning of terms, was an indispensable introduction. Language is as it were the atmosphere of philosophical investigation, which must be made transparent before anything can be seen through it in the true figure and position. In the present case it is necessary to guard against a further ambiguity, which though abundantly obvious, has sometimes misled even sagacious minds, and of which it is well to take distinct note before proceeding further. No word is more commonly associated with the word Nature, than Law; and this last word has distinctly two meanings, in one of which it denotes some definite portion of what is, in the other, of what ought to be. We speak of the law of gravitation, the three laws of motion, the law of definite proportions in chemical combination, the vital laws of organized beings. All these are portions of what is. We also speak of the criminal law, the civil law, the law of honour, the law of veracity, the law of justice; all of which are portions of what ought to be, or of somebody's suppositions, feelings, or commands respecting what ought to be. The first kind of laws, such as the laws of motion, and of gravitation, are neither more nor less than the observed uniformities in the occurrence of phenomena: partly uniformities of antecedence and sequence, partly of concomitance. These are what, in science, and even in ordinary parlance, are meant by laws of nature. Laws in the other sense are the laws of the land, the law of nations, or moral laws; among which, as already noticed, is dragged in, by jurists and publicists, something which they think proper to call the Law of Nature. . . .

When it is asserted, or implied, that Nature, or the laws

of Nature, should be conformed to, is the Nature which is meant, Nature in the first sense of the term, meaning all which is—the powers and properties of all things? But in this signification, there is no need of a recommendation to act according to nature, since it is what nobody can possibly help doing, and equally whether he acts well or ill. There is no mode of acting which is not conformable to Nature in this sense of the term, and all modes of acting are so in exactly the same degree. Every action is the exertion of some natural power, and its effects of all sorts are so many phenomena of nature, produced by the powers and properties of some of the objects of nature, in exact obedience to some law or laws of nature. . . . To bid people conform to the laws of nature when they have no power but what the laws of nature give them—when it is a physical impossibility for them to do the smallest thing otherwise than through some law of nature, is an absurdity. The thing they need to be told is, what particular law of nature they should make use of in a particular case. . . .

Yet, idle as it is to exhort people to do what they cannot avoid doing, and absurd as it is to prescribe as a rule of right conduct what agrees exactly as well with wrong; nevertheless a rational rule of conduct *may* be constructed out of the relation which it ought to bear to the laws of nature in this widest acceptation of the term. Man necessarily obeys the laws of nature, or in other words the properties of things, but he does not necessarily *guide* himself by them. Though all conduct is in conformity to laws of nature, all conduct is not grounded on knowledge of them, and intelligently directed to the attainment of purposes by means of them. Though we cannot emancipate ourselves from the laws of nature as a whole, we can escape from any particular law of nature, if we are able to withdraw ourselves from the circumstances in which it acts. Though we can do nothing except through laws of nature, we can use one law to counteract another. According to Bacon's maxim, we can obey nature in such a manner as to command it. Every alteration of circumstances alters more or less the laws of nature under which we act; and by every choice which we make either of ends or of means, we place ourselves to a greater or less extent under one set of laws of nature instead of another. If, therefore, the useless precept to follow nature were changed into a precept to study nature; to know and take heed of the properties of the things we have to deal with, so far as these properties are capable of forwarding or obstructing any given purpose; we should have arrived at the first principle of all intelligent action, or rather at the definition of intelligent action itself. And a confused notion of this true principle, is, I doubt not, in the minds of many of those who set up the unmeaning doctrine which superficially resembles it. They perceive that the essential difference between wise and foolish conduct consists in attending, or not attending, to the particular laws of nature on which some important result depends. And they think, that a person who attends to a law of nature in order to shape his conduct by it, may be said to obey it, while a person who practically disregards it, and acts as if no such law existed, may be said to disobey it: the circumstance being overlooked, that what is thus called disobedience to a law of nature is obedience to some other or perhaps to the very law itself. . . .

But however much of its authority the "Naturam sequi" doctrine may owe to its being confounded with the rational precept "Naturam observare," its favourers and promoters unquestionably intend much more by it than that precept. To acquire knowledge of the properties of things, and make use of the knowledge for guidance, is a rule of prudence, for the adaptation of means to ends; for giving effect to our wishes and intentions whatever they may be. But the maxim of obedience to Nature, or conformity to Nature, is held up not as a simply prudential but as an ethical maxim; and by those who talk of *jus naturae,* even as a law, fit to be administered by tribunals and enforced by sanctions. Right action, must mean something more and other than merely intelligent action: yet no precept beyond this last, can be connected with the word Nature in the wider and more philosophical of its acceptations. We must try it therefore in the other sense, that in which Nature stands distinguished from Art, and denotes, not the whole course of the phenomena which come under our observation, but only their spontaneous course.

Let us then consider whether we can attach any meaning to the supposed practical maxim of following Nature, in this second sense of the word, in which Nature stands for that which takes place without human intervention. In Nature as thus understood, is the spontaneous course of things when left to themselves, the rule to be followed in endeavouring to adapt things to our use? But it is evident at once that the maxim, taken in this sense, is not merely, as it is in the other sense, superfluous and unmeaning, but palpably absurd and self-contradictory. For while human action cannot help conforming to Nature in the one meaning of the term, the very aim and object of action is to alter and improve Nature in the other meaning. If the natural course of things were perfectly right and satisfactory, to act at all would be a gratuitous meddling, which, as it could not make things better, must make them worse. Or if action at all could be justified, it would only be when in direct obedience to instincts, since these might perhaps be accounted part of the spontaneous order of Nature; but to do anything with forethought and purpose, would be a violation of that perfect order. If the artificial is not better than the natural, to what end are all the arts of life? To dig, to plough, to build, to wear clothes, are direct infringements of the injunction to follow nature.

*   *   *   *   *   *   *   *   *

All praise of Civilization, or Art, or Contrivance, is so much dispraise of Nature; an admission of imperfection, which it is man's business, and merit, to be always endeavouring to correct or mitigate.

The consciousness that whatever man does to improve his condition is in so much a censure and a thwarting of the spontaneous order of Nature, has in all ages caused new and unprecedented attempts at improvement to be generally at first under a shade of religious suspicion; as being in any case uncomplimentary, and very probably offensive to the powerful beings (or, when polytheism gave place to monotheism, to the all-powerful Being) supposed to govern the various phenomena of the universe, and of whose will the course of nature was conceived to be the expression. Any attempt to mould natural phenomena to the convenience of mankind might easily appear in interference with the government of those superior beings: and though life could not have been maintained, much less made pleasant, without perpetual interferences of the kind, each new one was doubtless made with fear and trembling, until experience had shown that it could be ventured on without drawing down the vengeance of the Gods. . . . But there still exists a vague notion that though it is very proper to control this or the other natural phenomenon, the general scheme of nature is a model for us to imitate: that with more or less liberty in details, we should on the whole be guided by the spirit and general conception of nature's own ways: that they are God's work, and as such perfect; that man cannot rival their unapproachable excellence, and can best show his skill and piety by attempting, in however imperfect a way, to reproduce their likeness; and that if not the whole, yet some particular parts of the spontaneous order of nature, selected according to the speaker's predilections, are, in a peculiar sense, manifestations of the Creator's will; a sort of finger posts pointing out the direction which things in general, and therefore our voluntary actions, are intended to take. Feelings of this sort, though repressed on ordinary occasions by the contrary current of life, are ready to break out whenever custom is silent, and the native promptings of the mind have nothing opposed to them but reason: and appeals are continually made to them by rhetoricians, with the effect, if not of convincing opponents, at least of making those who already hold the opinion which the rhetorician desires to recommend, better satisfied with it. . . .

If this notion of imitating the ways of Providence as manifested in Nature, is seldom expressed plainly and downrightly as a maxim of general application, it also is seldom directly contradicted. Those who find it on their path, prefer to turn the obstacle rather than to attack it, being often themselves not free from the feeling, and in any case afraid of incurring the charge of impiety by saying anything which might be held to disparage the works of the

Creator's power. They therefore, for the most part, rather endeavour to show, that they have as much right to the religious argument as their opponents, and that if the course they recommend seems to conflict with some part of the ways of Providence, there is some other part with which it agrees better than what is contended for on the other side. In this mode of dealing with the great *à priori* fallacies, the progress of improvement clears away particular errors while the causes of errors are still left standing, and very little weakened by each conflict: yet by a long series of such partial victories precedents are accumulated, to which an appeal may be made against these powerful prepossessions, and which afford a growing hope that the misplaced feeling, after having so often learnt to recede, may some day be compelled to an unconditional surrender. For however offensive the proposition may appear to many religious persons, they should be willing to look in the face the undeniable fact, that the order of nature, in so far as unmodified by man, is such as no being, whose attributes are justice and benevolence, would have made, with the intention that his rational creatures should follow it as an example. If made wholly by such a Being, and not partly by beings of very different qualities, it could only be as a designedly imperfect work, which man, in his limited sphere, is to exercise justice and benevolence in amending. The best persons have always held it to be the essence of religion, that the paramount duty of man upon earth is to amend himself: but all except monkish quietists have annexed to this in their inmost minds (though seldom willing to enunciate the obligation with the same clearness) the additional religious duty of amending the world, and not solely the human part of it but the material; the order of physical nature.

*   *   *   *   *   *   *   *   *

This brief survey is amply sufficient to prove that the duty of man is the same in respect to his own nature as in respect to the nature of all other things, namely not to follow but to amend it. Some people, however, who do not attempt to deny that instinct ought to be subordinate to reason, pay deference to nature so far as to maintain that every natural inclination must have some sphere of action granted to it, some opening left for its gratification. All natural wishes, they say, must have been implanted for a purpose: and this argument is carried so far, that we often hear it maintained that every wish, which it is supposed to be natural to entertain, must have a corresponding provision in the order of the universe for its gratification: insomuch (for instance) that the desire of an indefinite prolongation of existence, is believed by many to be in itself a sufficient proof of the reality of a future life.

I conceive that there is a radical absurdity in all these attempts to discover, in detail, what are the designs of Providence, in order when they are discovered to help Providence in bringing them about. Those who argue, from particular indications, that Providence intends this or that, either believe that the Creator can do all that he will or that he cannot. If the first supposition is adopted—if Providence is omnipotent, Providence intends whatever happens, and the fact of its happening proves that Providence intended it. If so, everything which a human being can do, is predestined by Providence and is a fulfilment of its designs. But if, as is the more religious theory, Providence intends not all which happens, but only what is good, then indeed man has it in his power, by his voluntary actions, to aid the intentions of Providence; but he can only learn those intentions by considering what tends to promote the general good, and not what man has a natural inclination to; for, limited as, on this showing, the divine power must be, by inscrutable but insurmountable obstacles, who knows that man *could* have been created without desires which never are to be, and even which never ought to be, fulfilled? The inclinations with which man has been endowed, as well as any of the other contrivances which we observe in Nature, may be the expression not of the divine will, but of the fetters which impede its free action; and to take hints from these for the guidance of our own conduct may be falling into a trap laid by the enemy. The assumption that everything which infinite goodness can desire, actually comes to pass in this universe, or at least that we must never say or suppose that it does not, is worthy only of those whose slavish fears make them offer the homage of lies to a Being who, they profess to think, is incapable of being deceived and holds all falsehood in abomination.

With regard to this particular hypothesis, that all natural impulses, all propensities sufficiently universal and sufficiently spontaneous to be capable of passing for instincts, must exist for good ends, and ought to be only regulated, not repressed; this is of course true of the majority of them, for the species could not have continued to exist unless most of its inclinations had been directed to things needful or useful for its preservation. But unless the instincts can be reduced to a very small number indeed, it must be allowed that we have also bad instincts which it should be the aim of education not simply to regulate but to extirpate, or rather (what can be done even to an instinct) to starve them by disuse. . . .

But even if it were true that every one of the elementary impulses of human nature has its good side, and may by a sufficient amount of artificial training be made more useful than hurtful; how little would this amount to, when it must in any case be admitted that without such training all of them, even those which are necessary to our preservation, would fill the world with misery, making human life an exaggerated likeness of the odious scene of violence and tyranny which is exhibited by the rest of the animal kingdom, except in so far as tamed and disciplined by man. There, indeed, those who flatter themselves with the notion of reading the purposes of the Creator in his works, ought in consistency to have seen grounds for inferences from which they have shrunk. If there are any marks at all of special design in creation, one of the things most evidently designed is that a large proportion of all animals should pass their existence in tormenting and devouring other animals. . . . If we are not obliged to believe the animal creation to be the work of a demon, it is because we need not suppose it to have been made by a Being of infinite power. But if imitation of the Creator's will, as revealed in nature, were applied as a rule of action in this case, the most atrocious enormities of the worst men would be more than justified by the apparent intention of Providence that throughout all animated nature the strong should prey upon the weak.

*   *   *   *   *   *   *   *   *

Conformity to nature, has no connection whatever with right and wrong. The idea can never be fitly introduced into ethical discussions at all, except, occasionally and partially, into the question of degrees of culpability. . . . That a thing is unnatural, in any precise meaning which can be attached to the word, is no argument for its being blamable; since the most criminal actions are, to a being like man, not more unnatural than most of the virtues.

*   *   *   *   *   *   *   *   *

It will be useful to sum up in a few words the leading conclusions of this Essay.

The word Nature has two principal meanings: it either denotes the entire system of things, with the aggregate of all their properties, or it denotes things as they would be, apart from human intervention.

In the first of these senses, the doctrine that man ought to follow nature is unmeaning; since man has no power to do anything else than follow nature; all his actions are done through, and in obedience to, some one or many of nature's physical or mental laws.

In the other sense of the term, the doctrine that man ought to follow nature, or in other words, ought to make the spontaneous course of things the model of his voluntary actions, is equally irrational and immoral.

Irrational, because all human action whatever, consists in altering, and all useful action in improving, the spontaneous course of nature:

Immoral, because the course of natural phenomena being replete with everything which when committed by human beings is most worthy of abhorrence, any one who endeavoured in his actions to imitate the natural course of things would be universally seen and acknowledged to be the wickedest of men.

The scheme of Nature regarded in its whole extent, cannot have had, for its sole or even principal object, the good of human or other sentient beings. What good it brings to them, is mostly the result of their own exertions. Whatsoever, in nature, gives indication of beneficent design, proves this beneficence to be armed only with limited power; and the duty of man is to co-operate with the beneficent powers, not by imitating but by perpetually striving to amend the course of nature—and bringing that part of it over which we can exercise control, more nearly into conformity with a high standard of justice and goodness.]

CHAPTER VIII

The Apostle of Evolution:
Herbert Spencer (1820-1903)

THE EVOLUTIONARY APPROACH TO THE STUDY OF ORGANIC
phenomena, until fairly recently, dominated not only all
the sciences of life but also the sciences of man. It is a
point of view which also profoundly affected the course of
philosophical reflection in the nineteenth century. It is
therefore essential that something should be said in these
pages about the theories of Charles Darwin. For they stand
to nineteenth-century scientific philosophies in much the
same relation as the astronomical and physical theories of
Copernicus, Kepler, Galileo, and Newton stood to the
philosophical speculations of the previous age.

The concept of evolution did not originate with Darwin.
But it was he who first gave the theory of organic evolution
its scientific basis, and it was his great works, *Origin of
Species* and *Descent of Man,* that ultimately carried the
day for the evolutionary method. Darwin himself was not a
philosopher, and he was content to let others draw out
the philosophical implications of his own scientific hypotheses. The main ideas of his theory had long been in the
air: the struggle for existence, the mutability of species
and natural selection, the inheritance of traits favorable to
biological survival, and the descent of man from a "lower"
order of primates. It was Darwin's role to bring all these
ideas together within a unified theory which sought to
explain in terms of natural causes the development of all
living things.

By "struggle for existence," Darwin did not intend a

teleological theory which imputes to all organic beings a purpose or will to live. For him, it was a figurative expression which refers exclusively to the observable facts of the continual dependence of all life upon the natural environment and the tendency of living things in such an environment to compete for survival. The struggle for existence, moreover, is only one aspect of the general phenomenon of organic adaptation to an environment which involves both changing physical conditions and the competitive adaptation of species. By "natural selection" Darwin meant merely the manner in which the total environment favors certain traits and discourages others, so that specific variations which conduce to survival are preserved while those which jeopardize survival simply disappear.

The famous slogan "survival of the fittest" is not Darwin's but Herbert Spencer's. Darwin himself was careful to disavow any supposed ethical implications of his theories, and the widespread view of the so-called "Social Darwinists" that those who are best adapted to survive ought to survive is no part of what Darwin himself sought to prove. Darwin was also very careful to observe the limits of his hypothesis. He did not profess to explain the origins of life itself; nor did he claim to know the precise causes of those variations which determine different organic species in the first place. And he rejected the implication which some sought to draw from his theory, namely, that the "higher" species are more perfectly adapted to their environment than the "lower" ones. It remained for his contemporary, Herbert Spencer, to draw out the major philosophical implications of the evolutionary theory. In his hands, it is transformed into a grand synthesis of human knowledge, complete with a cosmology, an ethics, and a politics.

To place Spencer's philosophy it is necessary not only to trace his relations to Darwin but also to contrast him with his philosophical predecessors, in particular Hegel and Comte. Both Hegel and Comte had elaborate theories of historical development, but their interest was primarily in the development of human ideas and institutions. Neither of them was seriously concerned with cosmological questions, and neither of them made any serious attempt to formulate universal laws of historical development which would apply not only to the progress of human thought and institutions but also to life as a whole and even to the physical universe. In fact, most nineteenth-century philosophers before Spencer were uninterested in the cosmological questions which had so much concerned philosophers during the seventeenth century. It took the evolutionary theory to once again stimulate the philosophical imagination to speculate freely about the cosmos as a whole, and to formulate a total world-view in terms of the concept of evolutionary development.

The contrast between Spencer and Comte sharply defines two different ways in which modern science has made its impact upon philosophy. For Comte, as for most positivists, the philosophically important thing about science is its method. As we have seen, the only unity of science which Comte defended was a methodological unity.

Spencer, who also professed to be a scientific philosopher, reacted to science rather differently. In a broad sense he, like Comte, regarded the scientific method as the only method of human knowledge. And his philosophy has many affinities with positivism and empiricism. But it was not merely the method of science which impressed him but the picture of the world and of man's place in it which was suggested by the substantive hypotheses of physical and, especially, biological science. His "synthetic philosophy," taken as a whole, is perhaps the greatest effort on the part of a nineteenth-century philosopher to organize and extend the scientific knowledge of his day into a grand speculative synthesis which seeks to provide a general description of the entire natural world.

Spencer's philosophy, then, is primarily naturalistic and materialistic rather than positivistic. In this respect it belongs more to the great materialist tradition of Lucretius and Hobbes than to the merely epistemological tradition of empiricism and positivism represented by Comte and Mill. The primary difference between Spencer and his predecessors in the materialist tradition is that the latter, on the whole, generalized from the model of the physical object whereas Spencer uses evolutionary biology as the clue to his metaphysical generalizations.

Spencer's *System of Synthetic Philosophy* opens, significantly, with a critical discussion of the limits of human knowledge and of the relations between science and religion. This discussion is characteristically conciliatory. It also shows evidences of the eclecticism that makes Spencer's philosophy rather difficult to place in relation to the main currents of nineteenth-century thought. Like Kant, he regards all positive knowledge as limited to phenomena appearing in space and time. But also like Kant, he does not limit "reality" to what appears or could appear to our senses. He also speaks of an external, independent reality which he calls "The Unknowable." The reconciliation of science and religion will finally be reached, on his view, when scientists and scientific philosophers acknowledge that the ultimate mystery of existence cannot be penetrated by the methods of positive science and when proponents of religion give up the attempt to explain the existence of things by reference to a Being whose nature we cannot know. Spencer thinks that his view is already implicit in the historical development of religion from fetishism and polytheism to the more advanced monotheistic theologies, according to which any attempt on the part of man to know God or to apply to Him such human attributes as volition, intelligence, and personality is the greatest of blasphemies. For Spencer, the inward essence of religion has nothing to do with explanations of God's nature, His relations to the world, or the history of mankind. It lies simply in the acknowledgment of the ultimate mystery of being, and in the sense of awe which men feel toward it.

In saying that religion is concerned with the mysterious Unknowable, it might be argued that Spencer is not, or at any rate should not, be saying that religion is concerned with some "entity" which, as it happens, we cannot know, but rather that it is not properly concerned with "knowables" at all, and that its interest in "what there is" has a completely different focus. From this point of view, religion is not at all a thwarted proto-science, which, by definition, cannot achieve its aim; it is something else altogether which, unfortunately, has gotten mixed up, historically, with problems of explanation which are not its proper concern and which it must henceforth leave alone if it is to do its own proper work.

Spencer's own clues to his evolutionary metaphysics came, in the first instance, not from Darwin but from the German idealist philosopher Schelling. According to the latter, there is exhibited within the domain of organic life a development toward increasing differentiation, organization, and individualization. Schelling's speculations appeared to be confirmed by the work of the embryologist K. E. von Baer, who proposed the hypothesis that the structural changes occurring in the growth of all embryos exhibit a progressive development from indeterminate and homogeneous to more determinate and heterogeneous forms. It seemed evident to Spencer that such a development need not be restricted to life forms only, but may in fact be ascribed to inorganic processes as well, and he sought to support his more general claim by numerous analogies taken from the physical sciences.

But Spencer believed that there was also another aspect of this universal process of evolutionary development. Counterbalancing the process of differentiation, there is a tendency toward integration, the re-formation of the gradually differentiated processes into new, more inclusive wholes. According to Spencer, the increasing complexity and individuality of organic species which culminates in man is offset by another tendency within human life toward more and more powerful integrations of behavior through intelligence. The evolutionary differentiation which is exhibited at the social level in the increasing division of human labor is also offset, as societies advance, by the progressive integration of individuals within more comprehensive and more organically related associations of men.

If all this is metaphysics, it is, at any rate, an empirically oriented metaphysics, which, by intention, is based upon evidence gathered from the empirical sciences. It sounds, from one standpoint, like a great cosmological success

story, and it provides the basis for the widespread view of
Spencer as merely an apostle of that great nineteenth-century
delusion, Progress. One can easily imagine an unfriendly
critic entitling his interpretation of Spencer's philosophy
"From Chaos to Cosmos, or the Gospel of Universal
Progress." Such an interpretation would be unfair. Like
most of his fellow Victorians, Spencer was not unaware
that the evolutionary march of history has its seamier side.
He well understood that change is a process of dissolution
as well as evolution, of disintegration as well as integration. In this respect Spencer was not alone. Nearly
all of the philosophers of development, evolution, and
progress, who view human life and institutions under
the form of history rather than of eternity, at some point
sound the same note of the transitoriness, mutability, and
conflict inherent in all things human. Underneath the superficial buoyancy and hopefulness and the complacent assurance which we tend to identify with the Victorian mentality
there is nearly always something very like fear. This is
hardly to be wondered at, for the majestic portrait of evolutionary development is also a portrait of the predatory
struggle for existence.

Spencer and Darwin were both influenced by Malthus,
whose theory of population, read in one way, contains such
a terrifying prophecy for the future of the human race. The
pressure of population, which has always tended to outrun
the means of subsistence, is, according to Spencer, "the
proximate cause of progress," compelling men to settle new
territories, to abandon the predatory habits of the hunter
and to cultivate the arts of husbandry and agriculture, to
improve modes of production, and to adopt the "moral"
attitudes that foster collective security and order. The pressing question, however, is whether such progressive advances can permanently offset the increasing intensity of
the individual struggle for survival engendered by the continual increase in population. Spencer's own semicyclical
theory of development, at any rate, does not suggest an
unequivocally optimistic answer.

Spencer's philosophy may at least lay claim to the qualities of its defects. If it too often seems "synthetic" in the

pejorative sense, it also exhibits the major philosopher's serious impulse toward system. One of its most impressive features is Spencer's systematic attempt to apply and indirectly to confirm the fruitfulness of his general theory of evolutionary development within the domains of social theory and ethics. Here also one finds Spencer in his characteristic role as a mediator between opposing points of view. Accordingly he stands in these spheres somewhere between the radical individualism and psychologism of Mill and the collectivism and sociologism of Comte and Hegel.

Like Comte, but with interesting modifications of his own, Spencer proposes a law of three stages of social development. In the first stage, there are no well-defined social types or classes; societies are still small, and the mode of social organization is relatively homogeneous and undifferentiated, with each individual or family doing everything for itself. The second is a "militaristic" phase in which government is more highly centralized and usually monarchical, in which customs are rigid, class distinctions strictly maintained, and religion authoritarian. Finally, a third stage is reached which is characteristic of modern industrial societies. At this stage, there is an increased differentiation of labor, an emphasis upon commerce and production, a lessening of centralized governmental controls, and a gradual weakening of the old authoritarian social forms. This system, with its rapid scientific and technological advance, its free and world trade, its increasingly liberal political and social institutions, within which human relations are determined by agreement or contract rather than pre-established status or function has been in Spencer's view, more and more closely approximated by the culture of nineteenth-century England.

Unlike Mill, who, in his later years, looked upon socialism with increasing favor, Spencer regarded socialism, not as the next development of society which will supersede liberal democracy and private enterprise, but rather as a by-product of the militaristic, feudal type of society. Nor was he at all surprised to find that in Germany the autocrat, Bismarck, should favor a form of state socialism. Socialism, he thought, would produce a form of society like that of the ants or bees, in which the regimentation of individual activities would finally be complete. And he predicted, prophetically, that in a socialized society, the bureaucracy would give rise to a new form of aristocracy, more powerful than any that had gone before, for whose support the masses would be obliged to labor unceasingly and without effective recourse.

In an age of practicing as well as theoretical Marxism, Spencer's highly un-Marxian theory of the origins and nature of socialism has been derided as "unhistorical" or "merely bourgeois." But perspectives change, and it is possible to suppose that the anti-Marxists will soon rediscover in Spencer a major prophet as well as a brilliant diagnostician of the later developments of Western culture.

Spencer was not unaware of the imperfections of nineteenth-century society. But it was characteristic of Spencer, as it is characteristic of most fundamentally civilized minds, to think in terms of degree. He was neither a traditionalist nor a revolutionist, but a gradualist for whom the transition from any stage of society to another involves a period of evolutionary development. Moreover, Spencer leaves open the door to an ethical development which transcends the very modest paradise of nineteenth-century industrial democracy. In order to envisage what this development may be, he contends, we must turn from sociology and history to ethics. Every ethical code is geared to a particular social system, and inevitably envisages the preservation as well as the perfecting of the form of life which exists within that particular system. His own code, accordingly, is aimed at the greatest completeness of life as this would be understood by an enlightened representative of the society in which he himself lived. In that society, ethical activity is bound to be inclusive and integrative, directed toward the general happiness. But in the good society, which is an ideal projection of tendencies and aspirations already afoot, enforced duties will gradually be replaced by a free, sympathetic altruism which will be animated, not by a Kantian "conscience" or the sense of obligation, but by spontaneous and immediately satisfying other-regarding impulses.

Unfortunately, as Spencer realizes, the good society does

not as yet exist. In the present order, altruism, being animated primarily by the sense of duty, remains half-hearted and sporadic. Ethical improvement will come, he thinks, only with a further development of the social order as a whole. Spencer's realism, as an ethicist, is a function of his evolutionism and environmentalism. Like any other form of activity moral behavior is a form of adaptation, conditioned by the specific circumstances in which the individual finds himself. All individuals are implicated willy-nilly in the incessant struggle for existence. How they will respond to the struggle depends not so much upon certain abstract "motives" of selfishness or love, as upon the social situation in which they, as socially conditioned organisms, are obliged to act. Altruism, as an effective form of social behavior, is possible only in a society which demands altruism for survival. Spencer is saying, in effect, that the good society cannot be approximated until there is a more perfect compatibility between the individual's private interests and his social obligations, or until the pursuit of personal happiness also includes the fulfillment of his other-regarding or "moral" attitudes.

In concluding these remarks on Spencer's philosophy I find that I cannot forbear a final word of measured praise and perhaps also of prophecy. On the whole, when his system is compared with other pretentious philosophical systems of the nineteenth-century, it will be found to be more firm and substantial than most. He often went wrong, but this was not due to any want of industry or any deliberate ignoring of the facts on his part. No philosopher of his age was more addicted to facts than Spencer, or so assiduous in their pursuit. This is a great virtue. If Spencer generalized too readily, he at any rate generalized from observable facts, and his errors can be corrected by the same process of observation and inductive generalization. The same cannot be said of many of his contemporaries. Spencer's writing is insufferably discursive and prosy. Yet if his words are heavy and unpoetic, his essentially cosmological and historical imagination has its own poetic aspect, and in his own lumbering way he is the philosophical poet of the evolutionary tragicomedy. And the common reader may

at any rate read his philosophy for what it is, and not as
a concealed allegory whose essential meaning lies elsewhere. One may take him or leave him, but at least one
knows, for the most part, what one takes or leaves. The
trouble is that, although he is much criticized, he is little
read. If he were read, my guess is that his philosophical
stock would rise a bit. Unlike Hegel, Spencer has no secrets.
But if his philosophy is not at all mysterious, he is more
aware than some of his critics of the brooding mystery that
lies at the heart of existence. On the whole, and with many
reservations, I am, like Santayana, "in Spencer's camp."

My prophecy is that Spencer is due for a revival. If his
own age overrated him, ours has underestimated his merits. His ideals are not essentially different from those of
that half of the world which, somewhat fatuously, calls itself "free." In times like these Spencer's dull, discursive
sanity has a good deal to commend it.

The following selection is from the concluding chapter
(Chapter XXIV) of Spencer's *First Principles*.* In it Spencer states the main theses of his evolutionary philosophy
and draws out what he takes to be their most important implications.

[. . . A coherent knowledge implies something more than
the establishment of connexions: we must not rest after
seeing how each minor group of truths falls into its place
within some major group, and how all the major groups fit
together. It is requisite that we should retire a space, and,
looking at the entire structure from a distance at which
details are lost to view, observe its general character.

Something more than recapitulation—something more
even than an organized re-statement, will come within the
scope of the chapter. We shall find that in their *ensemble*
the general truths reached exhibit, under certain aspects, a
oneness not hitherto observed.

There is, too, a special reason for noting how the various
divisions and sub-divisions of the argument consolidate;
namely, that the theory at large thereby obtains a final illus-

* *First Principles*. New York and London: D. Appleton and Co.,
1900, pp. 494–509. This work first appeared in 1862.

tration. The reduction of the generalizations which have been set forth separately to a completely integrated state, exemplifies once more the process of Evolution, and strengthens still further the general fabric of conclusions.

§ 185. Here, indeed, we find ourselves brought round unexpectedly to the truth with which we set out, and with which our re-survey must commence. For this integrated form of knowledge is the form which, apart from the doctrine of Evolution, we decided to be the highest form.

When we inquired what constitutes Philosophy—when we compared men's various conceptions of Philosophy, so that, eliminating the elements in which they differed, we might see in what they agreed; we found in them all the tacit implication that Philosophy is completely unified knowledge. Apart from each scheme of unified knowledge, and apart from proposed methods by which unification is to be effected, we traced in every case a belief that unification is possible, and that the end of Philosophy is achievement of it.

After reaching this conclusion we considered the data with which Philosophy must set out. Fundamental propositions, or propositions not deducible from deeper ones, can be established only by showing the complete congruity of all the results reached through the assumption of them; and, premising that they were simply assumed till thus established, we took as our data those components of our intelligence without which there cannot go on the mental processes implied by philosophizing.

From the specification of these we passed to certain primary truths—"The Indestructibility of Matter," "The Continuity of Motion," and "The Persistence of Force"; of which the last is ultimate and the others derivative. Having previously seen that our experiences of Matter and Motion are resolvable into experiences of Force, we further saw the truths that Matter and Motion are unchangeable in quantity, to be implications of the truth that Force is unchangeable in quantity. This we concluded is the truth by derivation from which all other truths are to be proved.

The first of the truths which presented itself to be so proved, is "The Persistence of the Relations among

Forces." This, which is ordinarily called Uniformity of Law, we found to be a necessary implication of the truth that Force can neither arise out of nothing nor lapse into nothing.

The next deduction was that forces which seem to be lost are transformed into their equivalents of other forces; or, conversely, that forces which become manifest, do so by disappearance of pre-existing equivalent forces. These truths are found illustrated by the motions of the heavenly bodies, by the changes going on over the Earth's surface, and by all organic and super-organic actions.

It was shown to be the same with the law that everything moves along the line of least resistance, or the line of greatest traction, or their resultant. Among movements of all orders, from those of stars down to those of nervous discharges and commercial currents, it was shown both that this is so, and that, given the Persistence of Force, it must be so.

*   *   *   *   *   *   *   *   *

§ 186. These truths holding of existences at large, were recognized as of the kind required to constitute what we distinguish as Philosophy. But, on considering them, we perceived that as they stand they do not form a Philosophy; and that a Philosophy cannot be formed by any number of such truths separately known. Each expresses the law of some one factor by which phenomena, as we experience them, are produced; or, at most, expresses the law of co-operation of some two factors. But knowing what are the elements of a process, is not knowing how these elements combine to effect it. That which alone can unify knowledge must be the law of co-operation of the factors—a law expressing simultaneously the complex antecedents and the complex consequents which any phenomenon as a whole presents.

A further inference was that Philosophy, as we understand it, must not unify the changes displayed in separate concrete phenomena only; and must not stop short with unifying the changes displayed in separate classes of concrete phenomena; but must unify the changes displayed in all concrete phenomena. If the law of operation of each factor holds true throughout the Cosmos, so, too, must the law of their co-operation. And hence in comprehending the Cosmos as conforming to this law of co-operation, must consist that highest unification which Philosophy seeks.

Descending to a more concrete view, we saw that the law sought must be the law of the continuous re-distribution of Matter and Motion. The changes everywhere going on, from those which are slowly altering the structure of our galaxy down to those which constitute a chemical decomposition, are changes in the relative positions of component parts; and everywhere necessarily imply that along with a new arrangement of Matter there has arisen a new arrangement of Motion. Hence it follows that there must be a law of the concomitant re-distribution of Matter and Motion which holds of every change, and which, by thus unifying all changes, must be the basis of a Philosophy.

In commencing our search for this universal law of re-distribution, we contemplated from another point of view the problem of Philosophy, and saw that its solution could not but be of the nature indicated. It was shown that an ideally complete Philosophy must formulate the whole series of changes passed through by existences separately and as a whole in passing from the imperceptible to the perceptible and again from the perceptible to the imperceptible. If it begins its explanations with existences that already have concrete forms, or leaves off while they still retain concrete forms, then, manifestly, they had preceding histories, or will have succeeding histories, or both, of which no account is given. Whence we saw it to follow that the formula sought, equally applicable to existences taken singly and in their totality, must be applicable to the whole history of each and to the whole history of all. This must be the ideal form of a Philosophy, however far short of it the reality may fall.

By these considerations we were brought within view of the formula. For if it had to express the entire progress from the imperceptible to the perceptible and from the perceptible to the imperceptible; and if it was also to express the continuous re-distribution of Matter and Motion, then, obviously, it could be no other than one defining the opposite processes of concentration and diffusion in terms of Matter and Motion. And if so, it must be a statement of the truth that the concentration of Matter implies the dissipation of Motion, and that, conversely, the absorption of Motion implies the diffusion of Matter.

Such, in fact, we found to be the law of the entire cycle of changes passed through by every existence. Moreover we saw that besides applying to the whole history of each existence, it applies to each detail of the history. Both processes are going on at every instant; but always there is a differential result in favour of the first or the second. And every change, even though it be only a transposition of parts, inevitably advances the one process or the other.

Evolution and Dissolution, as we name these opposite transformations, though thus truly defined in their most general characters, are but incompletely defined; or rather, while the definition of Dissolution is sufficient, the definition of Evolution is extremely insufficient. Evolution is always an integration of Matter and dissipation of Motion; but it is in nearly all cases much more than this. The primary re-distribution of Matter and Motion is accompanied by secondary re-distributions.

Distinguishing the different kinds of Evolution thus produced as simple and compound, we went on to consider under what conditions the secondary re-distributions which make Evolution compound, take place. We found that a concentrating aggregate which loses its contained motion rapidly, or integrates quickly, exhibits only simple Evolution; but in proportion as its largeness, or the peculiar constitution of its components, hinders the dissipation of its motion, its parts, while undergoing that primary re-distribution which results in integration, undergo secondary re-distributions producing more or less complexity.

§ 187. From this conception of Evolution and Dissolution as together making up the entire process through which things pass; and from this conception of Evolution as divided into simple and compound; we went on to consider the law of Evolution, as exhibited among all orders of existences, in general and in detail.

The integration of Matter and concomitant dissipation of

Motion, was traced not in each whole only, but in the parts
into which each whole divides. By the aggregate Solar System, as well as by each planet and satellite, progressive
concentration has been, and is still being, exemplified. In
each organism that general incorporation of dispersed materials which causes growth, is accompanied by local in-
corporations, forming what we call organs. Every society,
while it displays the aggregative process by its increasing
mass of population, displays it also by the rise of dense
masses in special parts of its area. And in all cases, along
with these direct integrations there go the indirect integrations by which parts are made mutually dependent.

From this primary re-distribution we were led on to consider the secondary re-distributions, by inquiring how there
came to be a formation of parts during the formation of a
whole. It turned out that there is habitually a passage from
homogeneity to heterogeneity, along with the passage from
diffusion to concentration. While the matter composing the
Solar System has been assuming a denser form, it has
changed from unity to variety of distribution. Solidification
of the Earth has been accompanied by a progress from
comparative uniformity to extreme multiformity. In the
course of its advance from a germ to a mass of relatively
great bulk, every plant and animal also advances from simplicity to complexity. The increase of a society in numbers
and consolidation has for its concomitant an increased
heterogeneity both of its political and its industrial organization. And the like holds of all super-organic products
—Language, Science, Art, and Literature.

But we saw that these secondary re-distributions are not
thus completely expressed. While the parts into which each
whole is resolved become more unlike one another, they
also become more sharply marked off. The result of the
secondary re-distributions is therefore to change an indefinite homogeneity into a definite heterogeneity. This additional trait also we found in evolving aggregates of all
orders. Further consideration, however, made it apparent
that the increasing definiteness which goes along with increasing heterogeneity is not an independent trait, but that
it results from the integration which progresses in each of

the differentiating parts, while it progresses in the whole they form.

Further, it was pointed out that in all evolutions, inorganic, organic, and super-organic, this change in the arrangement of Matter is accompanied by a parallel change in the arrangement of contained Motion: every increase in structural complexity involving a corresponding increase in functional complexity. It was shown that along with the integration of molecules into masses, there arises an integration of molecular motion into the motion of masses; and that as fast as there results variety in the sizes and forms of aggregates and their relations to incident forces, there also results variety in their movements.

The transformation thus contemplated under separate aspects, being in itself but one transformation, it became needful to unite these separate aspects into a single conception—to regard the primary and secondary re-distributions as simultaneously working their various effects. Everywhere the change from a confused simplicity to a distinct complexity, in the distribution of both matter and motion, is incidental to the consolidation of the matter and the loss of its internal motion. Hence the re-distribution of the matter and of its retained motion, is from a relatively diffused, uniform, and indeterminate arrangement, to a relatively concentrated, multiform, and determinate arrangement.

§ 188. We come now to one of the additions that may be made to the general argument while summing it up. Here is the fit occasion for observing a higher degree of unity in the foregoing inductions, than we observed while making them.

The law of Evolution has been thus far contemplated as holding true of each order of existences, considered as a separate order. But the induction as so presented, falls short of that completeness which it gains when we contemplate these several orders of existences as forming together one natural whole. While we think of Evolution as divided into astronomic, geologic, biologic, psychologic, sociologic, &c., it may seem to some extent a coincidence that the same law of metamorphosis holds throughout all its divisions.

But when we recognize these divisions as mere conventional groupings, made to facilitate the arrangement and acquisition of knowledge—when we remember that the different existences with which they severally deal are component parts of one Cosmos; we see at once that there are not several kinds of Evolution having certain traits in common, but one Evolution going on everywhere after the same manner. We have repeatedly observed that while any whole is evolving, there is always going on an evolution of the parts into which it divides itself; but we have not observed that this equally holds of the totality of things, which is made up of parts within parts from the greatest down to the smallest. We know that while a physically-cohering aggregate like the human body is getting larger and taking on its general shape, each of its organs is doing the same; that while each organ is growing and becoming unlike others, there is going on a differentiation and integration of its component tissues and vessels; and that even the components of these components are severally increasing and passing into more definitely heterogeneous structures. But we have not duly remarked that while each individual is developing, the society of which he is an insignificant unit is developing too; that while the aggregate mass forming a society is integrating and becoming more definitely heterogeneous, so, too, that total aggregate, the Earth, is continuing to integrate and differentiate; that while the Earth, which in bulk is not a millionth of the Solar System, progresses towards its more concentrated structure, the Solar System similarly progresses.

So understood, Evolution becomes not one in principle only, but one in fact. There are not many metamorphoses similarly carried on, but there is a single metamorphosis universally progressing, wherever the reverse metamorphosis has not set in. In any locality, great or small, where the occupying matter acquires an appreciable individuality or distinguishableness from other matter, there Evolution goes on; or rather, the acquirement of this appreciable individuality is the commencement of Evolution. And this holds regardless of the size of the aggregate, and regardless of its inclusion in other aggregates.

§ 189. After making them, we saw that the inductions which, taken together, establish the law of Evolution, do not, so long as they remain inductions, form that whole rightly named Philosophy; nor does even the foregoing passage of these inductions from agreement into identity, suffice to produce the unity sought. For, as was pointed out at the time, to unify the truths thus reached with other truths, they must be deduced from the Persistence of Force. Our next step, therefore, was to show why, Force being persistent, the transformation which Evolution shows us necessarily results.

The first conclusion was, that any finite homogeneous aggregate must lose its homogeneity, through the unequal exposures of its parts to incident forces, and that the imperfectly homogeneous must lapse into the decidedly non-homogeneous. It was pointed out that the production of diversities of structure by diverse forces, and forces acting under diverse conditions, has been illustrated in astronomic evolution; and that a like connexion of cause and effect is seen in the large and small modifications undergone by our globe. The early changes of organic germs supplied further evidence that unlikenesses of structure follow unlikenesses of relations to surrounding agencies—evidence enforced by the tendency of the differently-placed members of each species to diverge into varieties. And we found that the contrasts, political and industrial, which arise between the parts of societies, serve to illustrate the same principle. The instability of the relatively homogeneous thus everywhere exemplified, we saw also holds in each of the distinguishable parts into which any whole lapses; and that so the less heterogeneous tends continually to become more heterogeneous.

A further step in the inquiry disclosed a secondary cause of increasing multiformity. Every differentiated part is not simply a seat of further differentiations, but also a parent of further differentiations; since in growing unlike other parts, it becomes a centre of unlike reactions on incident forces, and by so adding to the diversity of forces at work, adds to the diversity of effects produced. This multiplication of effects proved to be similarly traceable throughout all Nature—in the actions and reactions that go on throughout the Solar System, in the never-ceasing geologic complications, in the involved changes produced in organisms by new influences, in the many thoughts and feelings generated by single impressions, and in the ever-ramifying results of each additional agency brought to bear on a society. To which was joined the corollary that the multiplication of effects advances in a geometrical progression along with advancing heterogeneity.

Completely to interpret the structural changes constituting Evolution, there remained to assign a reason for that increasingly-distinct demarcation of parts, which accompanies the production of differences among parts. This reason we discovered to be the segregation of mixed units under the action of forces capable of moving them. We saw that when unlike incident forces have made the parts of an aggregate unlike in the natures of their component units, there necessarily arises a tendency to separation of the dissimilar units from one another, and to a clustering of those units which are similar. This cause of the definiteness of the local integrations which accompany local differentiations, turned out to be likewise exemplified by all kinds of Evolution—by the formation of celestial bodies, by the moulding of the Earth's crust, by organic modifications, by the establishment of mental distinctions, by the genesis of social divisions.

At length, to the query whether these processes have any limit, there came the answer that they must end in equilibrium. That continual division and sub-division of forces which changes the uniform into the multiform and the multiform into the more multiform, is a process by which forces are perpetually dissipated; and dissipation of them, continuing as long as there remain any forces unbalanced by opposing forces, must end in rest. It was shown that when, as happens in aggregates of various orders, many movements go on together, the earlier dispersion of the smaller and more resisted movements, establishes moving equilibria of different kinds: forming transitional stages on the way to complete equilibrium. And further inquiry made it apparent that for the same reason, these moving equilibria have certain self-conserving powers; shown in the neutralization of perturbations, and in the adjustment to new conditions. This general principle of equilibration, like the preceding general principles, was traced throughout all forms of Evolution—astronomic, geologic, biologic, mental, and social. And our concluding inference was, that the penultimate stage of equilibration in the organic world, in which the extremest multiformity and most complex moving equilibrium are established, must be one implying the highest state of humanity.

*   *   *   *   *   *   *   *   *

§ 190. Finally we turned to contemplate, as exhibited throughout Nature, that process of Dissolution which forms the complement of Evolution, and which, at some time or other, undoes what Evolution has done.

Quickly following the arrest of Evolution in aggregates that are unstable, and following it at periods often long delayed but reached at last in the stable aggregates around us, we saw that even to the vast aggregate of which all these are parts—even to the Earth as a whole—Dissolution must eventually come. Nay we even saw grounds for the belief that local assemblages of those far vaster masses we know as stars will eventually be dissipated: the question remaining unanswered whether our Sidereal System as a whole may not at a time beyond the reach of finite imagination share the same fate. While inferring that in many parts of the visible universe dissolution is following evolution, and that throughout these regions evolution will presently recommence, the question whether there is an alternation of evolution and dissolution in the totality of things is one which must be left unanswered as beyond the reach of human intelligence.

If, however, we lean to the belief that what happens to the parts will eventually happen to the whole, we are led to entertain the conception of Evolutions that have filled an immeasurable past and Evolutions that will fill an immeasurable future. We can no longer contemplate the visible creation as having a definite beginning or end, or as being isolated. It becomes unified with all existence before and after; and the Force which the Universe presents, falls into the same category with its Space and Time, as admitting of no limitation in thought.

§ 191. This conception is congruous with the conclusion reached in Part I., where we dealt with the relation between the Knowable and the Unknowable.

It was there shown by analysis of both religious and scientific ideas, that while knowledge of the Cause which produces effects on consciousness is impossible, the existence of a Cause for these effects is a datum of consciousness. Belief in a Power which transcends knowledge is that fundamental element in Religion which survives all its changes of form. This inexpugnable belief proved to be likewise that on which all exact Science is based. And this is also the implication to which we are now led back by our completed synthesis. The recognition of a persistent Force, ever changing its manifestations but unchanged in quantity throughout all past time and all future time, is that which we find alone makes possible each concrete interpretation, and at last unifies all concrete interpretations.

Towards some conclusion of this order, inquiry, scientific, metaphysical, and theological, has been, and still is, manifestly advancing. The coalescence of polytheistic conceptions into the monotheistic conception, and the reduction of the monotheistic conception to a more and more general form, in which personal superintendence becomes merged in universal immanence, clearly shows this advance. It is equally shown in the fading away of old theories about "essences," "potentialities," "occult virtues," &c.; in the abandonment of such doctrines as those of "Platonic Ideas," "Pre-established Harmonies," and the like; and in the tendency towards the identification of Being as present in consciousness, with Being as otherwise conditioned beyond consciousness. Still more conspicuous is it in the progress of Science, which, from the beginning, has been grouping isolated facts under laws, uniting special laws under more general laws, and so reaching on to laws of higher and higher generality; until the conception of universal laws has become familiar to it.

Unification being thus the characteristic of developing

thought of all kinds, and eventual arrival at unity being fairly inferable, there arises yet a further support to our conclusion. Since, unless there is some other and higher unity, the unity we have reached must be that towards which developing thought tends.

*   *   *   *   *   *   *   *   *

§ 193. If these conclusions be accepted—if it be agreed that the phenomena going on everywhere are parts of the general process of Evolution, save where they are parts of the reverse process of Dissolution; then we may infer that all phenomena receive their complete interpretation, only when recognized as parts of these processes. Whence it follows that the limit towards which Knowledge advances can be reached only when the formulae of these processes are so applied as to yield interpretations of phenomena in general. But this is an ideal which the real must ever fall short of.

For true though it may be that all phenomenal changes are direct or indirect results of the persistence of force, the proof that they are such can never be more than partially given. Scientific progress is progress in that adjustment of thought to things which we saw is going on, and must continue to go on, but which can never arrive at anything like perfection. Still, though Science can never be reduced to this form, and though only at a far distant time can it be brought anywhere near it, a good deal may even now be done in the way of approximation.

Of course, what may now be done cannot be done by any single individual. No one can possess that encyclopaedic information required for rightly organizing even the truths already established. Nevertheless, as all organization, beginning in faint and blurred outlines, is completed by successive modifications and additions, advantage may accrue from an attempt, however rude, to reduce the facts now accumulated—or rather certain classes of them—to something like co-ordination.]

CHAPTER IX

Dialectics and Materialism:
Karl Marx (1818-1883) and
Friedrich Engels (1820-1895)*

HISTORICALLY, THE PHILOSOPHY OF MARX AND ENGELS
may be regarded as a joint product of Hegelian dialectics,
materialism, and empiricism. But in philosophy, as elsewhere, historical classifications can be misleading. What is
original or arresting in the thought of Marx and Engels
is inadequately conveyed by such a description. It misses
altogether that feature of Marxism which has made it the
symbol of revolutionary ideology for our age: its radical

* In this chapter I have treated Marx and his alter-ego Engels as
virtually one philosopher. There are several reasons for this.
In the first place, it is next to impossible to gain a coherent picture of Marx's more philosophical doctrines from his writings
alone. Although Marx's mind was unquestionably more profound and original than Engels', it was the latter who did most
of their writing on the foundations of dialectical materialism.
In treating Engels' writings as a kind of annex to those of Marx,
I do not wish to do Engels himself an injustice. He was no mere
mouthpiece, and Marx learned almost as much from him as
Engels did from Marx. My willingness to allow him to speak,
in the selections, for the philosophy of Marxism plainly shows
that I consider him quite able to do so. I believe that most later
Marxists have been right, in short, in regarding the writings of
Marx and Engels as merely different books of the same testa-
ment. And I am convinced that an impartial comparison of the
works on which they worked together as collaborators with
those written by Engels alone will vindicate this view. I should
perhaps add that Engels' letters provide an indispensable auxiliary source book for an understanding of orthodox Marxism; in
them the unattractive dogmatism of the more formal works is
considerably softened.

and deliberate break with all the major social traditions of Western culture. Nor does it make clear the main difference in perspective between Marx and the philosophers previously considered in this book. For all his borrowings from them, Marx disagreed with all of them more radically than any of them disagreed with the rest.

As I have interpreted them, the major disagreements between the idealists and the positivists have to do, not with questions of fact, but with questions of method and of value. These disagreements always remained within certain limits. Neither the idealists, Fichte and Hegel, the positivist, Comte, the liberal, Mill, nor the evolutionary naturalist, Spencer, regarded themselves as social revolutionaries or as renegades from the underlying cultural tradition in which their own philosophies had been conceived and nurtured. They were critics and reformers who sought only to clarify, purify, and amend the tradition; they had no intention of breaking with it altogether. They were, to be sure, involved in the progressively intense crisis of reason in which all philosophies since Kant have been implicated. But the philosophical disagreements between the idealists and the positivists, serious as they were, may still be viewed as phases of a continuing parliamentary debate between tolerably well-bred liberals and conservatives, all of whom were committed, in greater or less degree, to the developing institutional life of bourgeois Christendom. It was a debate, moreover, in which party lines continued to be well-defined and party discipline, at least on major issues, was fairly well preserved. When we come to Marx and, in the following chapters, to Nietzsche and Kierkegaard, we find that these lines have become obscured, and that philosophical oppositions of a different and more radical kind begin to emerge. None of these men was content merely to amend the tradition; each, in his own way, tried to destroy it. What they sought to accomplish as philosophers was not just a new way of ideas or a new critique of reason, but virtually the creation of a new kind of man. So different both in form and substance are their writings from those of their predecessors that many academic historians have scarcely recognized that they are philosophers at all. Yet it

has been their doctrines rather than the "respectable" theories of their more conventional contemporaries that have had the greater impact, for better or worse, upon the effective thought of our own age.

It seemed clear to Marx, Nietzsche, and Kierkegaard, if to few others, that any cultural synthesis or compromise between Christianity, positive science, and political liberalism is impossible. They were not interested in being reasonable but in salvation or success. The philosophical problem, said Marx, is not to understand the world, but to change it. For Nietzsche, "truth" itself becomes virtually a term of derision; where truth is of no avail Nietzsche resorts openly to the noble lie. His point, however, is usually misunderstood. What he objects to is not truth, but easy philosophical assumptions concerning the objectivity and universality of traditional standards of rationality. Standards of any sort are either freely accepted for the sake of some end or else passively acquiesced in through fear or habit. The philosophically important questions, for Nietzsche, are not so much "What is true?", "What is rational?", or "What is right?", but "What do I want to do?" and "What do I want to become?". Kierkegaard is equally intransigent. He simply turns his back upon the "rational" theologies of our tradition. In his view, they are merely so many unchristian attempts to rationalize the idea of Christ and hence so many ways of accommodating its inner, subjective meaning to the irrelevant demands of the secular order. For him, there is no more possibility of reconciling the idea of a Christian life with the demands of the historical institutions with which Hegel identifies "objective spirit" or "reason" than there is of equating spiritual freedom with historical necessity. His break with theological rationalism is at the same time a radical break with the bourgeois institutional life of the nineteenth century, and it is as radical and final a break as that of either Marx or Nietzsche.

All three made a series of bold attempts to state the predicament of spiritually and socially alienated men in the modern world. The philosophical tasks of Marx, Nietzsche, and Kierkegaard are therefore only incidentally theoretical. Their aim is nothing less than the construction of a new

way of life which will answer to the demands of men who refuse to accept what Matthew Arnold calls "this strange disease of modern life" either as an act of God or as a fatality of reason. Were they prophets or madmen? The answer remains unclear.

Marx himself is the most rationalistic of the three. This shows itself, first of all, in his preoccupation with the problem of method. But Marx's method is also the source of some of the greatest perplexities which Marxism presents to the intellectual historian. As his admirers are never tired of reiterating, Marx himself was, among other things, a serious social scientist whose theory of historical development has had an incalculable effect upon subsequent social theory. He was not, they insist, a mere dialectician, like Hegel, spinning out theses and antitheses a priori which prescribe how the course of human history must proceed. In part this is true. His historical materialism was intended, in part, to provide the framework for a verifiable theory of the executive causes of social change. Marx and Engels bitterly criticized not only the idealist Hegel, but also the materialist Feuerbach, precisely on the ground that their philosophies of history were too grandiose and vague and too little concerned with observable social causes and effects.

Yet Marx was much more than a scientist spinning out theories of historical development. He was also a moralist and a prophet. He employed his theory of history not merely to explain what has happened or even to predict what might happen under certain historical conditions, but also to prophesy the ultimate destiny of mankind as a whole. The proletarian revolution and the eventual classless society are, for him, necessary consequences of the contradictions inherent in a capitalistic economy; they not only are likely to occur if certain empirical conditions are fulfilled, they must—and, more covertly, should—occur. For Marx as for Hegel the history of mankind is to be read as a necessary development in which every social system passes fatally into its opposite. His dialectical conception of change, again like Hegel's, is less an inductive generalization than a rigid rule of analysis which seeks to impose

Marx. The fact that Hegel tended to confuse logical contradiction with material contrariety or conflict did not faze Marx, who was even less interested in the proprieties of formal logic than Hegel himself. The dialectical law of thesis, antithesis, and synthesis might be worthless as a theory of logical inference, but it provided Marx with a first-rate clue for unraveling the threads of historical development. By interpreting it "materialistically," rather than as a mere law of thought, he was only showing, for the first time, how the dialectic really operates. Hegel's own use of the dialectic always seemed arbitrary precisely because he had no concrete material basis for ascribing a causal connection between thesis and antithesis or between the latter and the ensuing synthesis. By reinterpreting it, it was Marx's intention to give it, for the first time, a determinate meaning which might serve the purpose of serious causal explanation and prediction.

Thus, by uniting Hegel's dialectic of history with materialism, Marx sought at once to transform materialism itself from speculative mechanics into a philosophy of historical development and to turn the dialectic from an apparently arbitrary law of thought into a veritable law of historical causation. Perhaps, in Marx's sense, the term "dialectic" has now lost even a vestigial connection with its original meaning. That, in truth, is merely a matter of words. And although, in its most important sense, "matter" is no longer used by Marx to refer to an underlying substratum or substance, but rather to the observable "materials" with which men work and upon which they expend their energy, that, again, merely reflects the shift in Marx's interest as an ideologist. The important thing is that the ideology called "dialectical materialism," regardless of the propriety of its title, has taken hold of the imaginations of men as perhaps no doctrine has been able to do since the time of Christ.

Marx again and again protested that his only use of the dialectic was merely scientific. At the same time, it must be pointed out that there were other features of it, as characterized by Hegel, which also strongly appealed to Marx. One of these is the inherent "rationality" which Hegel ascribed to it. Playing perhaps on the dual meaning of "rational," Hegel could insist that any rational process must be both intelligible and right. And because both intelligibility and propriety are built into the very meaning of "rationality," he could use it as a term of impersonal commendation in the very act of asserting the rationality or lawlike character of any dialectical development. Ideologically, this had the great advantage of relieving Hegel of the necessity of expressing his own approval of it in the form of an explicit value judgment. Perhaps without quite realizing what he had done, Marx himself adopted this essentially normative side of the Hegelian dialectic for his own very different ideological purposes. But it was precisely this ambiguity in the word "rational" which enabled him to preserve his own magisterial air of scientific impartiality without denying himself the benefits of the language of impersonal edification. In virtue of it he could leave the dialectic to point its own moral without intruding upon it any supposedly irrelevant and subjective judgment of right or wrong.

Thus was the idea of progress cunningly written into the very constitution of the dialectic, and thus did Marx's own materialistic interpretation of history carry with it, without any special emphasis on his part, the unexpressed but essential implication that the revolutionary development of society is always a lawlike movement toward better things. But there is still another feature of the dialectic which appealed to Marx. This was its "necessity." For Marx the scientist, it might suffice merely to describe the conditions of social change. But it was highly essential to his purpose as an ideologist that he should be able to speak of the great waltz of history as "necessary" or "inevitable." Doubtless any rational development should be acquiesced in with good grace by all men of good will; but if such a development is also inevitable, as Marx claimed the ultimate victory of the proletariat to be, then resistance to it becomes pointless. The only practical question, as Marx's apologists contend, has to do with the timetable: Nothing can forever postpone a necessary historical change; yet the dialectic prescribes only a direction of change, not a calendar of events to come. Something may be done, therefore, by revolutionary organizations, such as the communist party, to hasten the inevitable and much to be desired end—the classless society.

Critics of Marx have frequently argued that the logic of Marx's theory is not impeccable. As a necessitarian, so it is said, he leaves no room for freedom, and thus deprives ideological exhortation itself of any point. In this matter, as it seems to me, his critics have failed to see that the term "inevitable," as used by Marx, is primarily a term of encouragement for some and of doom for others. It belongs not to the language of scientific description, but to that of ideological conflict. Its function is the prophetic one of awakening the workingmen of the world to a sense of their own historic mission as deliverers of mankind. Or, so, at any rate, Marx might have argued when his more pragmatic mood was upon him.

One further implication of Marx's interpretation of history remains to be observed. For Marx, developments in religious, philosophical, or political thought are essentially by-products of modifications in the modes of material production and organization. What he proposed, in effect, was to invert Hegel's idealistic interpretation of history so that the ideational "superstructure" could be correctly understood for the first time as an effect rather than as a determining cause of basic changes in the social system. The consequence of this inversion is that Marx construed progress, not in terms of spiritual self-development or "freedom," but, rather, in terms of the improvement of the underlying economic conditions of social life. The amelioration of man's lot, for Marx, thus begins, even if it does not end, with a solution to the problem of poverty. And the salvation of man, the cure for his loneliness as well as for his misery, lies, at bottom, in a collective attack upon this problem. "The anatomy of civil society," said Marx, "is to be sought in political economy." So also, he might have added, with the anatomy of human progress.

Marx's collectivism is largely a product of his early training as a Hegelian. From the beginning, Marx conceived the problem of human salvation, as he also conceived human action itself, in social terms. Man is a social animal, however, not because he has an instinct for brotherhood, but rather because he is conditioned to think and act as the member of a social class. Such self-regarding or other-regarding impulses as the individual may possess always work themselves out through channels determined by the social environment to which he is subject. In his interesting book, *The Open Society and Its Enemies,* Professor Karl Popper credits Marx with being the first to state what he calls "the autonomy of sociology." This, I think, is mistaken. Hegel's philosophy of history, although spiritualistic, was also formulated in essentially sociological rather than in psychological terms. And it was from him that Marx learned to think of human action in terms of certain institutionalized roles. Popper's thesis is also mistaken on another count since, as we have seen, Auguste Comte had already insisted, in the clearest terms, that sociological laws are not reducible to psychological laws of human nature. Nevertheless we may agree with Popper to this extent: Marx did more than any other nineteenth-century philosopher to popularize the autonomy of sociology, and it has been his influence, rather than Comte's or Hegel's, which has been most effective in combating the psychologism inherent in most earlier social theories. Such a theory as Marx's, it should be added, is not incompatible with a certain ethical individualism. And it is only fair to Marx to point out that unlike Hegel or Comte, his vision of the good society is virtually anarchistic. The good or classless society, for him, cannot be instituted without collective action. But the ultimate end of such action and of all institutions is not the preservation of a great social organism, but the happiness of individual men. In this respect, Marx, unlike Hegel, can never properly be regarded as a forerunner of Fascism.

It must also be pointed out that Marx's materialistic philosophy cannot properly be thought to involve an egoistic theory of human nature. Marx is an environmentalist. From his point of view, if most men have hitherto lived by the sword, this is not because they are instinctively aggressive, but because the circumstances of the social environment determine them to act aggressively. It is capitalism, according to Marx, and not the love of power, which breeds imperialism and war. By the same token, it is not the inborn depravity of man that is responsible for the venality of the capitalists, but the predatory effects of the profit system. Voltaire had said that men have not always been wolves, but have become wolves. Marx conceived it to be his business to explain why. But he also considered it his business to tell men on what terms they might cease to act like wolves.*

The first of the following selections is Marx's *Theses on Feuerbach*. The Theses were written in 1845 and first published as an appendix in the 1888 edition of Engels' *Ludwig Feuerbach*. The second selection is from Part I of Engels' *Anti-Dühring*.** The latter work, which was the last that Engels wrote in collaboration with Marx, contains perhaps the best general statement of the materialist interpretation of history. In it Engels attacks the current undialectical materialism of Dühring, a now forgotten lecturer on economics at the University of Berlin.

I. The chief defect of all hitherto existing materialism that Feuerbach included—is that the object, reality, sensuousness, is conceived only in the form of the *object* of *contemplation* but not as *human sensuous activity, practice,* not subjectively. Thus it happened that the *active* side, in opposition to materialism, was developed by idealism—but only abstractly, since, of course, idealism does not know real sensuous activity as such. Feuerbach wants sensuous objects, really differentiated from the thought-objects, but he does not conceive human activity itself as activity

* For further discussion of Marx's philosophy, particularly with respect to his views concerning the relations of philosophy and ideology to science, the reader is referred to Chapter I.

** These selections are reprinted from *A Handbook of Marxism,* edited by E. Burns. New York: Random House, 1935. London: Victor Gollancz, Ltd. The original title of Engels' *Ludwig Feuerbach* was *Ludwig Feuerbach und der Ausgang der klassischen deutschen Philosophie;* it was published in 1888. The original title of the *Anti-Dühring* was *Herr Eugen Dührings Umwälzung der Wissenschaft;* it was published in 1878.

through objects. Consequently, in the *Essence of Christianity,* he regards the theoretical attitude as the only genuinely human attitude, while practice is conceived and fixed only in its dirty-Jewish form of appearance. Hence he does not grasp the significance of "revolutionary," of practical-critical, activity.

II. The question whether objective truth can be attributed to human thinking is not a question of theory but is a practical question. In practice man must prove the truth, i.e., the reality and power, the "this-sidedness," of his thinking. The dispute over the reality or non-reality of thinking which is isolated from practice is a purely scholastic question.

III. The materialistic doctrine that men are products of circumstances and upbringing and that, therefore, changed men are products of other circumstances and changed upbringing, forgets that circumstances are changed precisely by men and that the educator must himself be educated. Hence this doctrine necessarily arrives at dividing society into two parts, of which one towers above society (in Robert Owen, for example).

The coincidence of the changing of circumstances and of human activity can only be conceived and rationally understood as revolutionising practice.

IV. Feuerbach starts out from the fact of religious self-alienation, the duplication of the world into a religious, imaginary world and a real one. His work consists in the dissolution of the religious world into its secular basis. He overlooks the fact that after completing this work, the chief thing still remains to be done. For the fact that the secular foundation lifts itself above itself and establishes itself in the clouds as an independent realm is only to be explained by the self-cleavage and self-contradictoriness of this secular basis. The latter must itself, therefore, first be understood in its contradiction and then, by the removal of the contradiction, revolutionised in practice. Thus, for instance, once the earthly family is discovered to be the secret of the holy family, the former must then itself be theoretically criticised and radically changed in practice.

V. Feuerbach, not satisfied with *abstract thinking,* appeals to *sensuous contemplation,* but he does not conceive sensuousness as a practical, human-sensuous activity.

VI. Feuerbach resolves the religious essence into the human. But the human essence is no abstraction inherent in each single individual. In its reality it is the *ensemble* of the social relations.

Feuerbach, who does not attempt the criticism of this real essence, is consequently compelled:

1. To abstract from the historical process and to fix the religious sentiment as something for itself and to presuppose an abstract—*isolated*—human individual.

2. The human essence, therefore, can with him be comprehended only as "genus," as a dumb internal generality which merely *naturally* unites the many individuals.

VII. Feuerbach, consequently, does not see that the "religious sentiment" is itself a *social product,* and that the abstract individual whom he analyses belongs in reality to a particular form of society.

VIII. Social life is essentially *practical.* All mysteries which mislead theory to mysticism find their rational solution in human practice and in the comprehension of this practice.

IX. The highest point attained by comtemplative materialism, i.e., materialism which does not understand sensuousness as practical activity, is the outlook of single individuals in "civil society."

X. The standpoint of the old materialism is "civil society"; the standpoint of the new is *human* society or socialised humanity.

XI. The philosophers have only *interpreted* the world in various ways; the point however is to *change* it.]

[ANTI-DÜHRING

Classification. A Priorism

. . . Logical schemata can only relate to *forms of thought;* but what we are dealing with here are only forms of *being,* of the external world, and these forms can never be created and derived by thought out of itself, but only from the external world. But with this the whole relationship is inverted: the principles are not the starting point of the investigation, but its final result; they are not applied to Nature and human history, but abstracted from them; it is not Nature and the realm of humanity which conform to these principles, but the principles are only valid in so far as they are in conformity with Nature and history. That is the only materialistic conception of the matter, and Herr Dühring's contrary conception is idealistic, makes things stand completely on their heads, and fashions the real world out of ideas, out of schemata, schemes or categories existing somewhere before the world, from eternity—just like a *Hegel*.

Such a result comes of accepting in quite a naturalistic way "consciousness," "reasoning," as something given, something from the outset, in contrast to being, to Nature. If this were so, it must seem extremely remarkable that consciousness and Nature, thinking and being, the laws of thought and the laws of Nature, should be so closely in correspondence. But if the further question is raised: what then are thought and consciousness, and whence they come, it becomes apparent that they are products of the human brain and that man himself is a product of Nature, which has been developed in and along with its environment; whence it is self-evident that the products of the human brain, being in the last analysis also products of Nature, do not contradict the rest of Nature but are in correspondence with it. . . .

If we deduce the world schematism not from our minds, but only *through* our minds from the real world, deducing the basic principles of being from what is, we need no philosophy for this purpose, but positive knowledge of the world and of what happens in it; and what this yields is also not philosophy, but positive science.

Further: if no philosophy as such is any longer required, then also there is no more need of any system, not even of any natural system of philosophy. The perception that all the phenomena of Nature are systematically interconnected drives science on to prove this systematic interconnection throughout, both in general and in detail. But an adequate, exhaustive scientific statement of this interconnection, the formulation on thought of an exact picture of the world system in which we live, is impossible for us, and will always remain impossible. If at any time in the evolution of mankind such a final, conclusive system of the interconnections within the world—physical as well as mental and historical—were brought to completion, this would mean that human knowledge had reached its limit, and, from the moment when society had been brought into accord with that system, further historical evolution would be cut short—which would be an absurd idea, pure nonsense. . . . Each mental image of the world system is and remains in actual fact limited, objectively through the historical stage and subjectively through the physical and mental constitution of its maker. . . .

Natural Philosophy; Cosmogony, Physics, Chemistry

. . . The materialists before Herr Dühring spoke of matter and motion. He reduces motion to mechanical force as its supposed basic form, and thereby makes it impossible for himself to understand the real connection between matter and motion, which in fact was also unclear to all former materialists. And yet it is simple enough. *Motion is the mode of existence of matter.* Never anywhere has there been matter without motion, nor can there be. Motion in cosmic space, mechanical motion of smaller masses on the various celestial bodies, the motion of molecules as heat or as electrical or magnetic currents, chemical combination or disintegration, organic life—at each given moment each individual atom of matter in the world is in one or other of these forms of motion, or in several forms of them at once. All rest, all equilibrium, is only relative, and only has meaning in relation to one or other definite form of motion. . . . Matter without motion is just as unthinkable as motion without matter. Motion is therefore as uncreatable and indestructible as matter itself; as the older philosophy (Descartes) expressed it, the quantity of motion existing in the world is always the same. Motion therefore cannot be created; it can only be transferred. When motion is transferred from one body to another, in so far as it transfers itself, is active, it may be regarded as the cause of motion, in so far as the latter is transferred, is passive. We call this active motion *force*, and the passive, the *manifestation of force*. In this it is as clear as daylight that the force is equal to its manifestation, because in fact it is the *same* motion which takes place in both.

A motionless state of matter is therefore one of the most empty and nonsensical of ideas—a "delirious phantasy" of the purest water. In order to arrive at such an idea it is necessary to conceive the relative mechanical equilibrium, in which state a body on the earth may in fact be, as absolute rest, and then to extend this over the whole universe. This is certainly made easier if universal motion is reduced to purely mechanical force. And the restriction of motion to purely mechanical force has the further advantage that a force can be conceived as at rest, as tied up, and as therefore for the moment inactive. When in fact, as is very often the case, the transfer of a motion is a somewhat complex process containing a number of intermediate points, it is possible to postpone the actual transmission to any moment desired by omitting the last link in the chain. . . .

It is therefore possible to imagine that during its motionless, identical state, matter was loaded with force, and this, if anything at all, seems to be what Herr Dühring understands by the unity of matter and mechanical force. This concept is nonsensical, because it tranfers to the universe, as if it were absolute, a state which by its nature is relative and therefore can only apply to *one part* of matter at one time. . . . We may turn and twist as much as we like, but under Herr Dühring's guidance we always come back again to—the finger of God.

*   *   *   *   *   *   *   *   *

. . . It is a hard nut and a bitter pill for our metaphysician that motion should find its measure in its opposite, in rest. That is indeed a crying contradiction, and every contradiction, according to Herr Dühring, is nonsensical. It is none the less a fact that the suspended stone, just like the loaded gun, represents a definite quantity of mechanical motion, that this definite quantity is measurable exactly by its weight and its distance from the ground, and that the mechanical motion may be used in various ways at will, for example, by its direct fall, by sliding down an inclined plane, or by turning a shaft. From the dialectical standpoint, the possibility of expressing motion in its opposite, in rest, presents absolutely no difficulty. To dialectical philosophy the whole contradiction, as we have seen, is only relative; there is no such thing as absolute rest, unconditional equilibrium. Each separate movement strives towards equilibrium, and the motion as whole puts an end to the equilibrium. When therefore rest and equilibrium occur they are the result of arrested motion, and it is self-evident that this motion is measurable in its result, can be expressed in it, and can be restored out of it again in one form or another. But Herr Dühring cannot allow himself to be satisfied with such a simple presentation of the matter. As a good metaphysician he first tears open a yawning gulf, which does not exist in reality, between motion and equilibrium, and is then surprised that he cannot find any bridge across this self-fabricated gulf. He might just as well mount his metaphysical Rosinante and chase the Kantian "thing-in-itself"; for it is that and nothing else which in the last analysis is hiding behind this undiscoverable bridge.

*   *   *   *   *   *   *   *   *

Dialectics; Quantity and Quality

. . . So long as we consider things as static and lifeless, each one by itself, alongside of and after each other, it is true that we do not run up against any contradictions in them. We find certain qualities which are partly common to, partly diverse from, and even contradictory to each other, but which in this case are distributed among different objects and therefore contain no contradiction. Within the limits of this sphere of thought we can get along on the basis of the usual metaphysical mode of thought. But the position is quite different as soon as we consider things in their motion, their change, their life, their reciprocal influence on each other. Then we immediately become involved in contradictions. Motion itself is a contradiction: even simple mechanical change of place can only come about through a body at one and the same moment of time being both in one place and in another place, being in one and the same place and also not in it. And the continuous assertion and simultaneous solution of this contradiction is precisely what motion is.

And if simple mechanical change of place contains a contradiction, this is even more true of the higher forms of motion of matter, and especially of organic life and its development. We saw above that life consists just precisely in this—that a living thing is at each moment itself and yet something else. Life is therefore also a contradiction which is present in things and processes themselves, and which constantly asserts and solves itself; and as soon as the contradiction ceases, life too comes to an end, and death steps in. We likewise saw that also in the sphere of thought we could not avoid contradictions, and that for example the contradiction between man's inherently unlimited faculty of knowledge and its actual realisation in men who are limited by their external conditions and limited also in their intellectual faculties finds its solution in what is, for us at least, and from a practical standpoint, an endless succession of generations, in infinite progress. . . .

On Page 336* Marx, on the basis of the previous examination of constant and variable capital and surplus value, draws the conclusion that "not every sum of money, or of value, is at pleasure tranformable into capital. To effect this transformation, in fact, a certain minimum of money or of exchange-value must be presupposed in the hands of the individual possessor of money or commodities."

He then takes as an example the case of a labourer in any branch of industry, who works eight hours for himself —that is, in producing the value of his wages—and the following four hours for the capitalist, in producing surplus value, which immediately flows into the pocket of the

* *Capital*, Vol. 1 (Kerr Edition).

capitalist. In this case a capitalist would have to dispose
of a sum of value sufficient to enable him to provide two
labourers with raw materials, instruments of labour, and
wages, in order to appropriate enough surplus value every
day to enable him to live on it even as well as one of his
labourers. And as the aim of capitalist production is not
mere subsistence but the increase of wealth, our man
with his two labourers would still not be a capitalist. Now
in order that he may live twice as well as an ordinary
labourer, and besides turn half of the surplus value produced again into capital, he would have to be able to em-
ploy eight labourers, that is he would have to dispose of
four times the sum of value assumed above. And it is only
after this, and in the course of still further explanations
elucidating and establishing the fact that not every petty
sum of value is enough to be transformable into capital,
but that the minimum sum required varies with each period
of development and each branch of industry, it is only then
that Marx observes: "Here, as in natural science, is *verified*
the correctness of the law discovered by Hegel (in his
Logic) that merely quantitative changes beyond a certain
point pass into qualitative differences." . . .]

CHAPTER X

Salvation Without A Savior:
Friedrich Nietzsche (1844-1900)

HAD A POLL OF PROFESSIONAL PHILOSOPHERS BEEN TAKEN before the Second World War concerning the achievement of Friedrich Nietzsche, the general consensus, at least in English-speaking countries, would probably have been that he is a brilliant but irresponsible "literary philosopher" whose rather shocking ideas are not to be taken too seriously. Santayana expressed the prevailing opinion when he spoke, in his *Egotism in German Philosophy*, of Nietzsche's "genial imbecility" and "boyish blasphemies." Writing somewhat later, Bertrand Russell sums it up by saying that Nietzsche "invented no new technical theories in ontology; his importance is primarily in ethics, and secondarily as an acute historical critic." Concerning Nietzsche's influence, he adds that Nietzsche's followers "have had their innings, but we may hope that it is coming rapidly to an end."

Russell's powers as a prophet have, in this case, proved very imperfect. Nevertheless, he has, by implication, posed a question which goes to the root of the problem concerning the meaning of Nietzsche's philosophy: Who *are* his true followers? For a time it was fashionable to treat him as a forerunner of the irrationalist ideologies of power which achieved their apotheosis in Fascism and Nazism. Mussolini openly avowed his admiration for Nietzsche, and the at least superficial similarities between Nietzsche's luridly antiliberal and antidemocratic transvaluation of values and the Nazi cult of power and destiny have frequently been noted. These unsavory associations, damaging as they have been to Nietzsche's reputation, cannot be lightly brushed aside. Nietzsche's talk, if not his thought, is full of cruelty, and his blazing hatred of "the herd" is more virulent than that of Swift. There is another, half-hidden Nietzsche who distinguishes the anti-Christ from the anti-Christian, and who, no doubt, would have been horrified by the brutality, or at least the vulgarity, of Nazism. But his praise of the military "virtues" was sincere, and his intemperate attack upon "the party of humanity" is reiterated again and again throughout his works.

There are many aspects of Nietzsche's philosophy, however, which are plainly incompatible with Nazism, and he cannot be held responsible for all the sins that have been committed in his name. He was, certainly, no admirer of the German "soul" or of German nationalism. Although he was an authoritarian, he opposed the cult of statism. He always thought of himself as a "good European," in contrast to most of his German contemporaries. He hated the "slave morality" of which he thought the Jewish people were the originators. But that was the real basis of his alleged anti-Semitism. He much admired "great men" like Napoleon, but primarily as romantic symbols of inward self-assurance and external freedom of action in an age in which both assurance and freedom were increasingly impossible. I am convinced, moreover, that his ideal *Übermensch,* or "superman" as it is usually translated, more closely resembles the creative artist or the religious prophet than the empire builder.

Since the last War, another wave of interest in Nietzsche's philosophy has emerged from a more sympathetic quarter, and with the advent of existentialism, he is now widely hailed, along with Kierkegard, as one of the most important precursors of that highly individualistic philosophy. Accordingly, a somewhat more favorable view of Nietzsche's thought is now developing. From this standpoint, the picture of a rather sophomoric and unbalanced fire-eater who used his pen as a substitute for the sword he could not carry is being replaced by another which represents him as a lonely, estranged man, obsessed by the absurdity of human existence and more deeply conscious than any of this contemporaries that he was living "at the end of the world." From this standpoint, also, we are invited to consider the first philosopher since Hume who knew "in his bones" that there are no necessary connections between matters of fact, and who faced the fact, emotionally as well as intellectually, that existence itself is a surd.

Much is now made of Nietzsche's powers as a "depth psychologist." Like Schopenhauer, whose influence upon him was very great, Nietzsche recognized how small a part conscious choice and realistic thinking play in determining human action. He also understood the extent to which ideological affiliations, religious as well as political, are determined by deep-lying frustrations and anxieties of which the individual is usually unaware. And, far more profoundly than anyone else before him, Nietzsche knew the myriadic ways in which emotive symbols may be employed in controlling and manipulating human attitudes. In fact no nineteenth-century philosopher so well understood the essential precariousness of the life of reason, and the innumerable symbolic masks that unreason can wear. If, at times, he also seems to fall in love with his own discoveries, and takes an inordinate pleasure in showing his contempt for a creature who can be gulled in so many ways by his emotions, he is merely exhibiting in his own behavior some of the characteristics which his own philosophy may help us to understand. In fact, Nietzsche himself was a pitiful victim of some of the very psychological and social maladies which he did so much to clarify. The wonder is that, sick as he was, he could penetrate so deeply behind the masks which men use to conceal their loneliness and frustration.

Nietzsche never succeeded in formulating a system of philosophy. It seems to me a mistake, therefore, to try to describe his complex and ambiguous philosophy in the usual way. For this reason, I shall adopt a somewhat different procedure in characterizing it. I will begin by making a number of comparisons between Nietzsche and other philosophers whom we have considered, in order to bring out some of the more salient and interesting features of his thought. I will then conclude with some general remarks about his historical philosophical position.

Let us first compare him with Hegel. In both cases the style is deeply characteristic of the philosopher. Superficially, no two writers could be more unlike. If there is one word for Hegel's style, it is "opaque." Rejecting the Cartesian doctrine of "clear and distinct ideas," and distrusting the capacity of ordinary language to express his thought, Hegel wrote in a heavy, lumbering manner which is loaded with jargon and with qualifying phrases that frequently complicate, without thereby clarifying his ideas. Nietzsche, on the contrary, writes completely unlike a "school philosopher." He uses ordinary language like a master to express everything he has to say. He is informal, racy, aphoristic, and his works are full of arresting metaphors and figures that seem to grow enigmatically in significance, the more one ponders them. Like Hegel, he is a great master of irony and antithesis. But if his own underlying meaning is also hard to come by, the surface of his prose, unlike Hegel's is remarkably clear. Where Hegel is sometimes almost comically impersonal and "objective," hiding himself behind a pose of historical omniscience, Nietzsche always speaks for himself and glories in his own subjectivity. His "historical consciousness" is at least as well-developed as Hegel's, but he also has the saving grace, as Hegel did not, of turning it upon himself. Nietzsche never forgets, or allows his reader to forget, his own exceedingly ambiguous historical position. He is also well aware of the weaknesses of the historical consciousness, for example, its tendency to substitute a kind of imaginative re-enactment of past actions for moral choice and responsibility, its evasion of the existential predicament of human life, and its decadence. Unlike Hegel, finally, Nietzsche is not merely a philosopher, and his *Thus Spake Zarathustra* is one of the great philosophical poems of Western literature.

Nietzsche's complex attitudes toward Christianity and Christ are, like Hegel's, full of ambiguities. Hegel, as we have seen, was able to make some sort of spiritual identification with his own historical and symbolic interpretation of Christianity. Nietzsche, however, had no use for Hegel's semi-Christian spirituality. Hegel said, but Nietzsche believed, that "God is dead." His atheism is both intellectual and emotional: God not only does not exist; He is dead. "If," his Zarathustra asks, "there were Gods, how could I bear to be no God? *Consequently* there are no Gods." But it is not just the matter of God's existence which is at stake in Nietzsche's rejection of Christianity. He is bitterly opposed to historical Christianity, which he thought universalized the slave morality of the Hebrews and, at every stage, blocked the path toward intellectual enlightenment and spiritual freedom.

It has been said that Nietzsche did not so much regard himself as an anti-Christ as an anti-Christian, and that his real devil is Paul, who made a pundit of his Master, and an institutionalized theology of His pretty myths. What Nietzsche really opposed, so it is argued, is the do-good ethics of service and the false humility and charity which are enshrined as the Christian virtues. But Nietzsche himself covertly preaches a not un-Christlike gospel, full of paradoxes, which announces that human salvation is possible only through renunciation, sacrifice, and suffering. In this guise, he is sometimes pictured as one who is harsh only in order to be kind, whose only desire is to drive the money-changers and time-servers from the temple, and, like Christ himself, to slay the dragons of spiritual sloth, complacency, and humdrum pleasure seeking. And indeed one can even go a step beyond this and point out that Nietzsche's own mystical doctrine of eternal recurrence is nothing but a thinly disguised version of the Christian doctrines of incarnation and resurrection.

Very well; but this must not allow us to deny Nietzsche's detestation of Christianity and all its spiritual fruits. Contrary to the opinion of Bertrand Russell, I cannot believe that Nietzsche's opposition to Christianity is merely ethical. It is ethical, certainly, but it is also much more. For behind his repudiation of the ethics of brotherly love, and behind his inability to believe *in* Christ as a Saviour, is his inability, as a philosopher, to believe that there is an Incarnate God who enters, paradoxically, into the historical order, who intervenes in and controls the destinies of men, and who guarantees to men a supernatural resurrection of their bodies. Thus, again, speaks Zarathustra: "I conjure you, my brethren, remain faithful to earth, and do not believe those who speak unto you of superterrestrial hopes! Poisoners they are, whether they know it or not."

Some comparisons between Nietzsche and Marx may also be helpful in placing his philosophy. Both are naturalists, and both are committed, up to a point, to the scientific description of the natural world and of man's place in nature. Like Marx, Nietzsche is a Romantic almost in spite of himself, and he resembles Marx in his distrust of the obscurantism, the anti-intellectualism, the medievalism, and the contempt for the Enlightenment which are characteristic of certain sides of nineteenth-century Romanticism. But he realizes, as fully as Marx, how profoundly the predicament of men in the nineteenth century had changed since "the good old time" of Mozart, Voltaire, and Hume. And, although he is nostalgic for the Enlightenment, he knows that its ideals can no longer be his. The knowledge of this is bitter for Nietzsche. In his case, the historical consciousness has imbued him with a profounder tragic sense than Marx, or even Hegel, possessed. Despite the buoyancy of Zarathustra, Nietzsche does not share Marx's grim assurance that the historical development of mankind, for all its bloody conflicts and waste, is a forced march toward the good society.

As a prophet, Nietzsche comes off much better than Marx. He foretells the rise of a new generation of tyrants who will play, half-cynically, upon the fears and insecurities of the masses and who will manipulate them at their pleasure by elaborate social myths. He also predicts, with extraordinary insight, the degeneration of Hegel's ideal of the state into a vulgar plutocratic ideal whose only aim will be war "and once again war." But he regards socialism (it is interesting on this point to compare him with Herbert Spencer) as merely another development of the democratic, utilitarian morality of the herd which he takes to be the primary secular aftereffect of Christianity. Socialism, in Nietzsche's view, is not at all radical; what it offers is merely more of the same. What is required, he thinks, is not a mere reorganization of modes of production or an overhaul of the political forms of liberal democracy, but a thoroughgoing transvaluation of values which explicitly renounces the whole underlying ethics of service upon which socialism and liberalism alike rest.

Nietzsche shares many of Marx's convictions concerning the radical evils of modern social and political life. Both his diagnosis and his cure, however, are radically different. In the first place, it is largely foreign to Nietzsche's mind to think "materialistically" in terms of economic modes of production and institutionalized class conflict. Nietzsche has no faith whatever in the saving grace of collective action and social identification. Nor can he take seriously a primarily economic or political solution to the problem of man's lost freedom and creativity. Nietzsche is perhaps the most extreme anticollectivist in the history of modern philosophy. It is no accident that his habitual symbol for the masses is "the herd." It is, indeed, his own obsessive anxiety lest he be trampled on by the herd, and his claustrophobic fear of being smothered by the anonymous, collective life of modern society that are inversely symbolized by his gospel of the will to power. Power, for Nietzsche as for Spinoza, symbolizes self-determination. It means, for him, doing and being able to do what you will, not what some class, institution, or general will considers to be "right" for you. In Nietzsche's view, so long as the individual remains caught in a web of collective rituals and impersonal social routines, however much they may conduce to something called the general "welfare," all tampering with the political or economic order leaves the fundamental predicament of modern life completely untouched.

One of Nietzsche's favorite antipathies was Mill. He despised what he called the "pig philosophy" of utilitarianism; to him it was a timidly prudential gospel of collective material comforts fit only for a society of unimaginative shopkeepers, such as he imagined the English to be. He called Mill a "blockhead," and professed to abhor "the man's vulgarity." Actually Nietzsche differed from Mill less than he supposed. For one thing, they shared a common commitment to naturalism and, within certain limits, to science. Their attitudes toward the Church and its nay-saying, other-wordly ethics were not unlike. Mill was as deeply oppressed as Nietzsche himself by the mediocrity, the tastelessness, the uniformitarianism which seemed to be the inevitable by-products of democratic social and political institutions. For Mill also the problem of human freedom in the modern world did not stop with the question of civil liberties. It meant for him, as for Nietzsche, the ability of the individual to fulfill himself, to realize his highest capacities as a man. It is their language, as it seems to me, not its fundamental import, which is so different. Moreover, Nietzsche's aristocratic hatred of purely quantitative standards of excellence has its own counterpart in Mill's recognition of the preference of "qualified judges" as an independent standard of value.

But while they share a desire to protect what Matthew Arnold called "the saving remnant," this is balanced in Mill's case, but not in Nietzsche's, by a deep compassion for the herd. Mill is therefore never tempted to renounce his allegiance to democratic political ideals in order to save the aristocratic values of taste, personal merit, and individual distinction. The good society, for him, must include both. The advantage, however, does not lie exclusively with Mill. For if Mill's ethics is more humane, Nietzsche is more deeply aware of the difficulties of reconciling an ethics of welfare with one of self-fulfillment for "superior" men or "qualified judges." He believes that a choice has to be made, and he is quite clear what his own decision must be. In trying to have it both ways, Nietzsche might argue, Mill's ethics is a confused and futile hodgepodge of irreconcilable ideals. Bentham, at any rate, was a consistent philistine who was quite willing to face the consequences of his purely quantitative standards: if push-pin gives as much pleasure as poetry, said Bentham, then it is as *good* as poetry, and that is the end of it. To which, of course, Mill would reply that there is no self-fulfillment without love, and no general happiness which ignores or blurs the qualitative differences between kinds of human good.

Nietzsche's relations to Schopenhauer are more easily defined. The root metaphor of Nietzsche's philosophy, the will to power, is a modification, via Darwin, of Schopenhauer's will to live. Nietzsche construes "the struggle for existence" more literally than Darwin; for him it is a ceaseless, competitive, predatory effort, not simply to live, as Schopenhauer had thought, but for ascendancy. Nietzsche's conception of will, moreover, is less metaphysical than Schopenhauer's. For him it is entirely a matter of action. There is, according to Nietzsche, no question of "free" will, but only of stronger and weaker wills. Schopenhauer, perhaps inconsistently, sought to turn the will upon itself, and for him the good life is one of will-less contemplation. Perceiving the inconsistency, Nietzsche accepts it as a fact that will is inherent in all life, and remains as long as life itself lasts. For him, therefore, there can be no question of denying or transcending will. The only question is: whose will shall prevail? And this, he holds, is simply a question of power.

Yet is it, even for him? It has frequently been said that Nietzsche, like all naturalists, blurs the distinction between the willed and the desirable or good, and that he passes, with no show of justification, from the fact, if such it be, of the will to power to its glorification. Formally this is true. And it involves Nietzsche in the same dilemma in which the sophist Thrasymachus in Plato's *Republic* was caught. His objection to the slave morality of Christianity is that it puts the strong in irons. But who, after all, are the strong? As Nietzsche himself describes them, Christian morality and democratic institutions are devices by means of which the individually weak wills of the many are organized, in effect, into a great collective will which holds in check the otherwise stronger wills of their superiors. In this way Nietzsche seems inadvertently to acknowledge the bitter truth of the principle that "in union there is strength." Hence, it might be argued, he ought, as a consistent lover of power, to admire Christian morality and democratic politics more than his own superman and his own political ideal of an aristocratic elite. The fact is that Nietzsche admires power, but only when possessed by his superior men, not when it is used by the herd to keep them within bounds.

Nietzsche is sometimes classified as a Social Darwinist, who converts the struggle for existence into a moral parable. Actually, Nietzsche's doctrine of the superman is only superficially an evolutionary theory. What it really prophesies is not a new biological species but a new kind of *man* who recognizes his own capacity for self-transcendence, and who demands for himself and all other superior men the right to self-transcendence and self-fufillment. Essentially, his doctrine is an ethical or religious call to action, a demand that men of superior capacities, by disciplined effort and sacrifice, rise above their animal heritage of reflexive, instinctual response and their social heritage of routine, herdlike conformity. In short, Nietzsche is not seriously interested in the scientific question concerning the possibility of an evolution of a new species beyond *homo sapiens,* but rather with the spiritual possibilities of *homo sapiens* himself.

It would not be unfair, I think, to say that Nietzsche, whose own father was a minister, remained throughout his life a lay preacher in the best Protestant tradition of individual nonconformity. The gospel that he preaches, however, is essentially the possibility of individual salvation without a savior. Among the intellectually enlightened, whose worldview in an age of science is bound to be naturalistic, the main tenets of the Christian myth are no longer credible, and in consequence, as the proponents of "liberal" Christianity must in candor admit, that myth has finally lost its redemptive power. Those who, like Hegel, seek to preserve its saving grace in abstraction from its roots in passionate human belief and expectation deceive themselves; they merely procrastinate the advent of honest atheism.

This does not mean that in ceasing to be a Christian Nietzsche was able automatically to cast off the needs which had given efficacy to the myth of Resurrection for countless men. The question was, how can such a need be satisfied within the framework of a naturalistic worldview which can no longer credit the Christian myth either as prediction or as symbolic prophecy. Nietzsche thought he had found the answer in the ancient doctrine of eternal recurrence. There is some suggestion of this idea in Herbert Spencer's quasicyclical theory of evolutionary integration and disintegration. But Spencer made no religious use of it. In Nietzsche's case, the idea was essentially a religious conception of individual immortality. According to him, each individual is living through, at each moment, an eternally recurrent cycle of activity. In everything that the individual does or experiences, therefore, he himself is eternally present. What matters to the individual person, from Nietzsche's standpoint, is not the impersonal immortality of fame or influence upon the lives of men yet unborn, but his own personal immortality. He is not content that other lives like his own will be lived or that others will come to share, through his effort, the values which he most cherishes; what he demands is that his own consciousness itself shall somehow always *be*. This demand could only be satisfied, given a naturalistic world-view, by a doctrine of eternal recurrence according to which the same cycle of life is endlessly relived.

If you should ask what evidence Nietzsche might adduce for such a theory, the answer is none. But this way of putting the matter misses the point of the doctrine. For it wasn't, really, a theory at all, but a way of satisfying Nietzsche's own rage to be. Its merit consisted in the fact that it could make of every moment of human life, not merely a passing experience, but an absolutely and eternally momentous occasion.

The following selections are from the first chapter of Nietzsche's *Beyond Good and Evil*.* The chapter is entitled "Prejudices of Philosophers."

{ 1. The Will to Truth, which is to tempt us to many a hazardous enterprise, the famous Truthfulness of which all philosophers have hitherto spoken with respect, what questions has this Will to Truth not laid before us! What

---

* *Beyond Good and Evil*, authorized translation by Helen Zimmern. Edinburgh: The Good European Society, The Darien Press, 1907, pp. 5–12 and 20–34. The original title of this work was *Jenseits von Gut und Böse;* it was first published in 1886.

strange, perplexing, questionable questions! It is already a long story; yet it seems as if it were hardly commenced. Is it any wonder if we at last grow distrustful, lose patience, and turn impatiently away? That this Sphinx teaches us at last to ask questions ourselves? *Who* is it really that puts questions to us here? *What* really is this "Will to Truth" in us? In fact we made a long halt at the question as to the origin of this Will—until at last we came to an absolute standstill before a yet more fundamental question. We inquired about the *value* of this Will. Granted that we want the truth: *why not rather* untruth? And uncertainty? Even ignorance? The problem of the value of truth presented itself before us—or was it we who presented ourselves before the problem? Which of us is the Œdipus here? Which the Sphinx? It would seem to be a rendezvous of questions and notes of interrogation. And could it be believed that it at last seems to us as if the problem had never been propounded before, as if we were the first to discern it, get a sight of it, and *risk raising* it. For there is risk in raising it, perhaps there is no greater risk.

2. *"How could* anything originate out of its opposite? For example, truth out of error? or the Will to Truth out of the will to deception? or the generous deed out of selfishness? or the pure sun-bright vision of the wise man out of covetousness? Such genesis is impossible; whoever dreams of it is a fool, nay, worse than a fool; things of the highest value must have a different origin, an origin of *their own*— in this transitory, seductive, illusory, paltry world, in this turmoil of delusion and cupidity, they cannot have their source. But rather in the lap of Being, in the intransitory, in the concealed God, in the 'Thing-in-itself'—*there* must be their source, and nowhere else!"—This mode of reasoning discloses the typical prejudice by which metaphysicians of all times can be recognised, this mode of valuation is at the back of all their logical procedure; through this "belief" of theirs, they exert themselves for their "knowledge," for something that is in the end solemnly christened "the Truth." The fundamental belief of metaphysicians is *the belief in antitheses of values*. It never occurred even to the wariest of them to doubt here on the very threshold (where

doubt, however, was most necessary); though they had made a solemn vow, *"de omnibus dubitandum."* For it may be doubted, firstly, whether antitheses exist at all; and secondly, whether the popular valuations and antitheses of value upon which metaphysicians have set their seal, are not perhaps merely superficial estimates, merely provisional perspectives, besides being probably made from some corner, perhaps from below—"frog perspectives," as it were, to borrow an expression current among painters. In spite of all the value which may belong to the true, the positive, and the unselfish, it might be possible that a higher and more fundamental value for life generally should be assigned to pretence, to the will to delusion, to selfishness, and cupidity. It might even be possible that *what* constitutes the value of those good and respected things, consists precisely in their being insidiously related, knotted, and crocheted to these evil and apparently opposed things—perhaps even in being essentially identical with them. Perhaps! But who wishes to concern himself with such dangerous "Perhapses"! For that investigation one must await the advent of a new order of philosophers, such as will have other tastes and inclinations, the reverse of those hitherto prevalent—philosophers of the dangerous "Perhaps" in every sense of the term. And to speak in all seriousness, I see such new philosophers beginning to appear.

3. Having kept a sharp eye on philosophers, and having read between their lines long enough, I now say to myself that the greater part of conscious thinking must be counted amongst the instinctive functions, and it is so even in the case of philosophical thinking; one has here to learn anew, as one learned anew about heredity and "innateness." As little as the act of birth comes into consideration in the whole process and continuation of heredity, just as little is "being-conscious" *opposed* to the instinctive in any decisive sense; the greater part of the conscious thinking of a philosopher is secretly influenced by his instincts, and forced into definite channels. And behind all logic and its seeming sovereignty of movement, there are valuations, or to speak more plainly, physiological demands, for the maintenance of a definite mode of life. . . .

4. The falseness of an opinion is not for us any objection to it: it is here, perhaps, that our new language sounds most strangely. The question is, how far an opinion is life-furthering, life-preserving, species-preserving, perhaps species-rearing; and we are fundamentally inclined to maintain that the falsest opinions (to which the synthetic judgments *a priori* belong), are the most indispensable to us; that without a recognition of logical fictions, without a comparison of reality with the purely *imagined* world of the absolute and immutable, without a constant counterfeiting of the world by means of numbers, man could not live—that the renunciation of false opinions would be a renunciation of life, a negation of life. *To recognise untruth as a condition of life:* that is certainly to impugn the traditional ideas of value in a dangerous manner, and a philosophy which ventures to do so, has thereby alone placed itself beyond good and evil.

5. That which causes philosophers to be regarded half-distrustfully and half-mockingly, is not the oft-repeated discovery how innocent they are—how often and easily they make mistakes and lose their way, in short, how childish and childlike they are,—but that there is not enough honest dealing with them, whereas they all raise a loud and virtuous outcry when the problem of truthfulness is even hinted at in the remotest manner. They all pose as though their real opinions had been discovered and attained through the self-evolving of a cold, pure, divinely indifferent dialectic (in contrast to all sorts of mystics, who, fairer and foolisher, talk of "inspiration"); whereas, in fact, a prejudiced proposition, idea, or "suggestion," which is generally their heart's desire abstracted and refined, is defended by them with arguments sought out after the event. They are all advocates who do not wish to be regarded as such, generally astute defenders, also, of their prejudices, which they dub "truths,"—and *very* far from having the conscience which bravely admits this to itself; very far from having the good taste or the courage which goes so far as to let this be understood, perhaps to warn friend or foe, or in cheerful confidence and self-ridicule. The spectacle of the Tartuffery of old Kant, equally stiff and decent, with

which he entices us into the dialectic by-ways that lead
(more correctly mislead) to his "categorical imperative"—
makes us fastidious ones smile, we who find no small
amusement in spying out the subtle tricks of old moralists
and ethical preachers. Or, still more so, the hocus-pocus of
mathematical form, by means of which Spinoza has as it
were clad his philosophy in mail and mask—in fact, the
"love of *his* wisdom," to translate the term fairly and
squarely—in order thereby to strike terror at once into the
heart of the assailant who should dare to cast a glance on
that invincible maiden, that Pallas Athene:—how much
of personal timidity and vulnerability does this masquerade
of a sickly recluse betray!

6. It has gradually become clear to me what every great
philosophy up till now has consisted of—namely, the con-
fession of its originator, and a species of involuntary and
unconscious autobiography: and moreover that the moral
(or immoral) purpose in every philosophy has constituted
the true vital germ out of which the entire plant has always
grown. Indeed, to understand how the abstrusest metaphysical assertions of a philosopher have been arrived at,
it is always well (and wise) to first ask oneself: "What
morality do they (or does he) aim at?" Accordingly, I do
not believe that an "impulse to knowledge" is the father of
philosophy; but that another impulse, here as elsewhere,
has only made use of knowledge (and mistaken knowledge!) as an instrument. But whoever considers the fundamental impulses of man with a view to determining how far
they may have here acted as *inspiring* genii (or as demons
and cobolds), will find that they have all practised philosophy at one time or another, and that each one of them
would have been only too glad to look upon itself as the
ultimate end of existence and the legitimate *lord* over all
the other impulses. For every impulse is imperious, and as
such, attempts to philosophise. To be sure, in the case of
scholars, in the case of really scientific men, it may be
otherwise—"better," if you will; there there may really be
such a thing as an "impulse to knowledge," some kind of
small, independent clockwork, which, when well wound up,
works away industriously to that end, *without* the rest of the

scholarly impulses taking any material part therein. The actual "interests" of the scholar, therefore, are generally in quite another direction—in the family, perhaps, or in money-making, or in politics; it is, in fact, almost indifferent at what point of research his little machine is placed, and whether the hopeful young worker becomes a good philologist, a mushroom specialist, or a chemist; he is not *characterised* by becoming this or that. In the philosopher, on the contrary, there is absolutely nothing impersonal; and above all, his morality furnishes a decided and decisive testimony as to *who he is,*—that is to say, in what order the deepest impulses of his nature stand to each other.

* * * * * * * * *

13. Psychologists should bethink themselves before putting down the instinct of self-preservation as the cardinal instinct of an organic being. A living thing seeks above all to *discharge* its strength—life itself is *Will to Power;* self-preservation is only one of the indirect and most frequent *results* thereof. In short, here, as everywhere else, let us beware of *superfluous* teleological principles!—one of which is the instinct of self-preservation (we owe it to Spinoza's inconsistency). It is thus, in effect, that method ordains, which must be essentially economy of principles.

* * * * * * * * *

16. There are still harmless self-observers who believe that there are "immediate certainties"; for instance, "I think," or as the superstition of Schopenhauer puts it, "I will"; as though cognition here got hold of its object purely and simply as "the thing in itself," without any falsification taking place either on the part of the subject or the object. I would repeat it, however, a hundred times, that "immediate certainty," as well as "absolute knowledge" and the "thing in itself," involve a *contradictio in adjecto;* we really ought to free ourselves from the misleading significance of words! The people on their part may think that cognition is knowing all about things, but the philosopher must say to himself: "When I analyse the process that is expressed in the sentence, 'I think,' I find a whole series of daring assertions, the argumentative proof of which would be difficult, perhaps impossible: for in-

stance, that it is *I* who think, that there must necessarily be something that thinks, that thinking is an activity
and operation on the part of a being who is thought of as
a cause, that there is an 'ego,' and finally, that it is already
determined what is to be designated by thinking—that I
know what thinking is. For if I had not already decided
within myself what it is, by what standard could I determine whether that which is just happening is not perhaps
'willing' or 'feeling'? In short, the assertion 'I think,' assumes that I *compare* my state at the present moment with
other states of myself which I know, in order to determine
what it is; on account of this retrospective connection with
further 'knowledge,' it has at any rate no immediate certainty for me."—In place of the "immediate certainty" in
which the people may believe in the special case, the
philosopher thus finds a series of metaphysical questions
presented to him, veritable conscience questions of the intellect, to wit: "From whence did I get the notion of 'thinking'? Why do I believe in cause and effect? What gives
me the right to speak of an 'ego,' and even of an 'ego' as
cause, and finally of an 'ego' as cause of thought?" He who
ventures to answer these metaphysical questions at once
by an appeal to a sort of *intuitive* perception, like the
person who says, "I think, and know that this, at least, is
true, actual, and certain"—will encounter a smile and two
notes of interrogation in a philosopher nowadays. "Sir,"
the philosopher will perhaps give him to understand, "it
is improbable that you are not mistaken, but why should it
be the truth?"

17. With regard to the superstitions of logicians, I
shall never tire of emphasising, a small, terse fact, which
is unwillingly recognised by these credulous minds—
namely, that a thought comes when "it" wishes, and not
when "I" wish; so that it is a *perversion* of the facts of
the case to say that the subject "I" is the condition of the
predicate "think." *One* thinks; but that this "one" is precisely the famous old "ego," is, to put it mildly, only a supposition, an assertion, and assuredly not an "immediate
certainty." After all, one has even gone too far with this
"one thinks"—even the "one" contains an *interpretation*

of the process, and does not belong to the process itself. One infers here according to the usual grammatical formula —"To think is an activity; every activity requires an agency that is active; consequently" . . . It was pretty much on the same lines that the older atomism sought, besides the operating "power," the material particle wherein it resides and out of which it operates—the atom. More rigorous minds, however, learnt at last to get along without this "earth-residuum," and perhaps some day we shall accustom ourselves, even from the logician's point of view, to get along without the little "one" (to which the worthy old "ego" has refined itself).

18. It is certainly not the least charm of a theory that it is refutable; it is precisely thereby that it attracts the more subtle minds. It seems that the hundred-times-refuted theory of the "free will" owes its persistence to this charm alone; someone is always appearing who feels himself strong enough to refute it.

19. Philosophers are accustomed to speak of the will as though it were the best-known thing in the world; indeed, Schopenhauer has given us to understand that the will alone is really known to us, absolutely and completely known, without deduction or addition. But it again and again seems to me that in this case Schopenhauer also only did what philosophers are in the habit of doing— he seems to have adopted a *popular prejudice* and exaggerated it. Willing—seems to me to be above all something *complicated,* something that is a unity only in name— and it is precisely in a name that popular prejudice lurks, which has got the mastery over the inadequate precautions of philosophers in all ages. So let us for once be more cautious, let us be "unphilosophical": let us say that in all willing there is firstly a plurality of sensations, namely, the sensation of the condition *"away from which* we go," the sensation of the condition *"towards which* we go," the sensation of this *"from"* and *"towards"* itself, and then besides, an accompanying muscular sensation, which, even without our putting in motion "arms and legs," commences its action by force of habit, directly we "will" anything. Therefore, just as sensations (and indeed many

kinds of sensations) are to be recognised as ingredients of the will, so, in the second place, thinking is also to be recognised; in every act of the will there is a ruling thought; —and let us not imagine it possible to sever this thought from the "willing," as if the will would then remain over! In the third place, the will is not only a complex of sensation and thinking, but it is above all an *emotion,* and in fact the emotion of the command. That which is termed "freedom of the will" is essentially the emotion of supremacy in respect to him who must obey: "I am free, 'he' must obey"—this consciousness is inherent in every will; and equally so the straining of the attention, the straight look which fixes itself exclusively on one thing, the unconditional judgment that "this and nothing else is necessary now," the inward certainty that obedience will be rendered—and whatever else pertains to the position of the commander. A man who *wills* commands something within himself which renders obedience, or which he believes renders obedience. But now let us notice what is the strangest thing about the will,—this affair so extremely complex, for which the people have only one name. Inasmuch as in the given circumstances we are at the same time the commanding *and* the obeying parties, and as the obeying party we know the sensations of constraint, impulsion, pressure, resistance, and motion, which usually commence immediately after the act of will; inasmuch as, on the other hand. we are accustomed to disregard this duality, and to deceive ourselves about it by means of the synthetic term "I": a whole series of erroneous conclusions, and consequently of false judgments about the will itself, has become attached to the act of willing— to such a degree that he who wills believes firmly that willing *suffices* for action. Since in the majority of cases there has only been exercise of will when the effect of the command—consequently obedience, and therefore action— was to be *expected,* the *appearance* has translated itself into the sentiment, as if there were there a *necessity of effect;* in a word, he who wills believes with a fair amount of certainty that will and action are somehow one; he ascribes the success, the carrying out of the willing, to the will itself, and thereby enjoys an increase of the sensation of power which accompanies all success. "Freedom of Will"— that is the expression for the complex state of delight of the person exercising volition, who commands and at the same time identifies himself with the executor of the order —who, as such, enjoys also the triumph over obstacles, but thinks within himself that it was really his own will that overcame them.

*   *   *   *   *   *   *   *   *

21. The *causa sui* is the best self-contradiction that has yet been conceived, it is a sort of logical violation and unnaturalness; but the extravagant pride of man has managed to entangle itself profoundly and frightfully with this very folly. The desire for "freedom of will" in the superlative, metaphysical sense, such as still holds sway, unfortunately, in the minds of the half-educated, the desire to bear the entire and ultimate responsibility for one's actions oneself, and to absolve God, the world, ancestors, chance, and society therefrom, involves nothing less than to be precisely this *causa sui,* and, with more than Munchausen daring, to pull oneself up into existence by the hair, out of the slough of nothingness. If any one should find out in this manner the crass stupidity of the celebrated conception of "free will" and put it out of his head altogether, I beg of him to carry his "enlightenment" a step further, and also put out of his head the contrary of this monstrous conception of "free will": I mean "non-free will," which is tantamount to a misuse of cause and effect. One should not wrongly *materialise* "cause" and "effect," as the natural philosophers do (and whoever like them naturalise in thinking at present), according to the prevailing mechanical doltishness which makes the cause press and push until it "effects" its end; one should use "cause" and "effect" only as pure *conceptions,* that is to say, as conventional fictions for the purpose of designation and mutual understanding,—*not* for explanation. In "being-in-itself" there is nothing of "causal-connection," of "necessity," or of "psychological non-freedom"; there the effect does *not* follow the cause, there "law" does not obtain. It is *we* alone who have devised cause, sequence,

reciprocity, relativity, constraint, number, law, freedom, motive, and purpose; and when we interpret and intermix this symbol-world, as "being in itself," with things, we act once more as we have always acted—*mythologically*. The "non-free will" is mythology; in real life it is only a question of *strong* and *weak* wills.—It is almost always a symptom of what is lacking in himself, when a thinker, in every "causal-connection" and "psychological necessity," manifests something of compulsion, indigence, obsequiousness, oppression, and non-freedom; it is suspicious to have such feelings—the person betrays himself. And in general, if I have observed correctly, the "non-freedom of the will" is regarded as a problem from two entirely opposite standpoints, but always in a profoundly *personal* manner: some will not give up their "responsibility," their belief in *themselves,* the personal right to *their* merits, at any price (the vain races belong to this class); others on the contrary, do not wish to be answerable for anything, or blamed for anything, and owing to an inward self-contempt, seek *to get out of the business,* no matter how. The latter, when they write books, are in the habit at present of taking the side of criminals; a sort of socialistic sympathy is their favourite disguise. And as a matter of fact, the fatalism of the weak-willed embellishes itself surprisingly when it can pose as *"la religion de la souffrance humaine"; that is *its* "good taste."

22. Let me be pardoned, as an old philologist who cannot desist from the mischief of putting his finger on bad modes of interpretation, but "Nature's conformity to law," of which you physicists talk so proudly, as though—why, it exists only owing to your interpretation and bad "philology." It is no matter of fact, no "text," but rather just a naïvely humanitarian adjustment and perversion of meaning, with which you make abundant concessions to the democratic instincts of the modern soul! "Everywhere equality before the law—Nature is not different in that respect, nor better than we": a fine instance of secret motive, in which the vulgar antagonism to everything privileged and autocratic—likewise a second and more refined atheism—is once more disguised. *"Ni dieu, ni maître"*

—that, also, is what you want; and therefore "Cheers for natural law!"—is it not so? But, as has been said, that is interpretation, not text; and somebody might come along, who, with opposite intentions and modes of interpretation, could read out of the same "Nature," and with regard to the same phenomena, just the tyrannically inconsiderate and relentless enforcement of the claims of power—an interpreter who should so place the unexceptionalness and unconditionalness of all "Will to Power" before your eyes, that almost every word, and the word "tyranny" itself, would eventually seem unsuitable or like a weakening and softening metaphor—as being too human; and who should, nevertheless, end by asserting the same about this world as you do, namely, that it has a "necessary" and "calculable" course, *not,* however, because laws obtain in it, but because they are absolutely *lacking,* and every power effects its ultimate consequences every moment. Granted that this also is only interpretation—and you will be eager enough to make this objection?—well, so much the better.

23. All psychology hitherto has run aground on moral prejudices and timidities, it has not dared to launch out into the depths. In so far as it is allowable to recognise in that which has hitherto been written, evidence of that which has hitherto been kept silent, it seems as if nobody had yet harboured the notion of psychology as the Morphology and *Development-doctrine of the Will to Power,* as I conceive of it. The power of moral prejudices has penetrated deeply into the most intellectual world, the world apparently most indifferent and unprejudiced, and has obviously operated in an injurious, obstructive, blinding, and distorting manner. A proper physio-psychology has to contend with unconscious antagonism in the heart of the investigator, it has "the heart" against it: even a doctrine of the reciprocal conditionalness of the "good" and the "bad" impulses, causes (as refined immorality) distress and aversion in a still strong and manly conscience—still more so, a doctrine of the derivation of all good impulses from bad ones. If, however, a person should regard even the emotions of hatred, envy, covetousness, and imperious-

ness as life-conditioning emotions, as factors which must be present, fundamentally and essentially, in the general economy of life (which must, therefore, be further developed if life is to be further developed), he will suffer from such a view of things as from sea-sickness. And yet this hypothesis is far from being the strangest and most painful in this immense and almost new domain of dangerous knowledge; and there are in fact a hundred good reasons why everyone should keep away from it who *can* do so! On the other hand, if one has once drifted hither with one's bark, well! very good! now let us set our teeth firmly! let us open our eyes and keep our hand fast on the helm! We sail away right *over* morality, we crush out, we destroy perhaps the remains of our own morality by daring to make our voyage thither—but what do *we* matter! Never yet did a *profounder* world of insight reveal itself to daring travellers and adventurers, and the psychologist who thus "makes a sacrifice"—it is *not* the *sacrifizio dell'intelletto,* on the contrary!—will at least be entitled to demand in return that psychology shall once more be recognized as the queen of the sciences, for whose service and equipment the other sciences exist. For psychology is once more the path to the fundamental problems.]

CHAPTER XI

The Advent of Existentialism:
Sören Kierkegaard (1813-1855)

ONLY SINCE WORLD WAR II, WHEN EVEN THE WEEKLY
news magazines became excited about a strange new European philosophy known as "Existentialism," has there
been any substantial interest in Kierkegaard as a philosopher in England or the United States. Even now the
standard histories of philosophy rarely mention him, and
when they do there is no suggestion that he might be one
of the "greats" of nineteenth-century philosophy. The intrinsic merits of Kierkegaard's philosophical ideas are still
a subject for debate. But his historical importance can no
longer be denied, for his writings are the fountainhead of
one of the most influential philosophical movements of our
own age. Partly for this reason, but partly also because he
is symptomatic of another form which the crisis of reason
has taken since the time of Kant, I have considered it essential to include him in this book.

Kierkegaard is one of the most elusive writers in a period which might well have been called the age of obscurity.
His writings lend themselves even less than Nietzsche's
to the requirements of systematic exposition and analysis.
This does not mean that Kierkegaard lacks literary skill;
on the contrary, he has a great flair for style and he is
surely one of the greatest intellectual satirists in the history
of modern literature. When he chooses, as in his devastating counter-dialectic against Hegel, he can be an acute
philosophical critic, but he does not usually argue for his

own position at all; he merely presents it. As a distinguished Oxford philosopher recently said to me, Kierkegaard is not one of those philosophers upon whom you can sharpen your wits. In this respect, he is more like a poet who presents his reader with a strange new spiritual world within which, if you would understand him, you must, for the time being, live and breathe. Like Socrates, Kierkegaard is also a kind of gadfly who stings his audience until it performs the essential act of introspective self-knowledge. But it is you, the reader, who must do the essential work; all Kierkegaard does, or tries to do, is to shock you into facing the fact of your own existence as a conscious being. In short, Kierkegaard has not so much a doctrine to expound or a theory to defend, as a way of life, a sensibility, a perspective which he is prepared to share with his reader if the latter will make the necessary effort.

Perhaps the first thing to be said about Kierkegaard's point of view—and it is more a point of view than a "philosophy" in the traditional sense—is that he shares Nietzsche's extreme distaste for the comfortable, hypocritical, progressive, bourgeois world in which he lived. Nor does Nietzsche himself condemn historical, institutionalized Christianity with more savage bitterness than the Christian, Kierkegaard. A passionate follower of the Gospels, he denounces the existing Church as merely another respectable, timeserving institution which stands in the way of this spiritual progress of the individual Christian. And he utterly rejects the claim of the Church to be the true successor to apostolic Christianity.

But Kierkegaard reserves his bitterest invective for Hegel's idealistic rationalization of the Christian tradition. This, in his judgment, is the very symbol of the intellectualistic disease from which modern philosophy suffers. Hegel offers us, not a living God, but a dialectico-historical reconstruction of the Christian myth whose only function is to reconcile men to their stations on the cross of history. For Kierkegaard, Hegel's much vaunted historical consciousness is not a way of coming to more complete understanding of one's own condition as an existing being, but essentially an escape from it. As we saw earlier, Hegel himself objected to the supposedly false abstractness of the traditional formal logic of Aristotle, and proposed to replace it with a true logic of thought or being (for him, of course, they come to the same thing). By such a dialectical logic alone, he supposed, we may gain a proper idea of the reality of change. And he believed that only by viewing any process dialectically in terms of an ever-widening network of historical relations can we grasp its nature concretely. From Kierkegaard's point of view, however, all Hegel really accomplished was to absorb the individual's particular existence into that abstraction to end all abstractions, the Absolute, in which every remaining vestige of concrete existence is finally lost. What Hegel leaves us with, by a monstrous irony, is a great "pan-logism" in which the impersonal movement of the dialectic itself turns out to be the only reality. Kierkegaard speaks of his own thought, on the contrary, as a "qualitative dialectic." By this he meant a dialectic which renounces any show of explaining the transitions from thesis to antithesis as necessary moments of a continuous process of development. Actually, Kierkegaard's dialectic has nothing whatever to do with logic in any ordinary sense. It is, so to say, a purely "psycho-logic" which follows its own unpredictable course toward ends that are wholly remote from scientific truth. Such a psycho-logic is, you say, utterly fantastic. Precisely, replied Kierkegaard, that is its great merit, for existence itself is fantastic, and can only be reached subjectively by the paradoxes of inner reflection and self-consciousness.

But Kierkegaard's opposition to Hegel is not restricted to questions of dialectic. In his view, Hegel's philosophy of right is a gospel for institutionalized robots that have lost any sense of themselves as persons and are content to live passively as mere functionaries of the state, church, and family. For Kierkegaard, the whole side of Hegel's philosophy which has to do with "objective spirit" is nothing more than an elaborate piece of ontological mystification which distracts men from facing the only reality with which they have to do, their own conscious existence.

Hegel's objective spirit is purely a creature of his dialectic, a phantom of thought which has nothing to do with what exists. Reality can be reached, according to Kierkegaard, not by the manipulation of concepts, but only by immediate experience. Kant, in his way, was right: "existence" is not a predicate. What it means to exist can only be grasped ostensively by a direct intuition of one's self.

It is Kierkegaard's view that awareness of one's own existence becomes most acute in periods of extreme inner tension, when anxiety and dread, having passed beyond the stage of local concern for particular ends, now have become total or, so to say, "metaphysical." This total, objectless dread arises only when one is no longer preoccupied with the problem of getting particular results or keeping what one has, when, indeed, the whole point of getting results seems pointless and one's entire way of life is imperiled. Only then does one fully realize what it really means to *be*. It would be pointless to charge Kierkegaard with morbidity on this score. His only reply would be to shrug his shoulders and say "So what?" He is not trying to prove a point, but to express an attitude which he thinks is of the greatest importance for the only thing that matters, individual salvation.

It should be pointed out, in this connection, that Kierkegaard's obsession with abnormal states of consciousness, which was shared, incidentally, by that most "healthy-minded" American philosopher, William James, is also characteristic of several important nineteenth- and twentieth-century novelists and poets. In fact, anyone who has felt his way into the strange, febrile world of Dostoyevski's novels, or who has been at once fascinated and repelled by the metaphysical novels of Franz Kafka, has made perhaps the best possible literary preparation for understanding such works of Kierkegaard's as *The Sickness unto Death* and *The Concept of Dread*. Kierkegaard's interest in the "crisis mentality" is not, however, literary or psychological, but metaphysical and religious. For it is his contention that only by passing through such dark nights of the soul can one fully know what it means to be or not to be.

The word "means" in the preceding statement is, however, ambiguous. Read in one way, it may suggest that
Kierkegaard is primarily concerned to defend a certain
theory concerning the meaning and knowledge of "existence," not unlike that of Kant. But there is another way
of construing "means" which comes closer, I believe, to
Kierkegaard's fundamental interest as a philosopher. In
this sense, we may take him to be saying essentially that
only in states of extreme emotional crisis, when one faces
not just the possibility but the fact of one's own imminent
annihilation can one finally grasp the *significance* of one's
own existence. For it is only then that one at last decides
to live or die, to be or not to be. In short, it is the significance of life, rather than the meaning of "existence" which
is Kierkegaard's concern, and if his doctrine has "ontological" implications also, it is a form of ontology whose ulterior point is practical rather than theoretical. When this
point is reached, philosophy has passed to the farthest extreme from science, and its questions cease entirely to be
concerned, in any ordinary sense, with knowledge of what
there is.

So extreme, in fact, is Kierkegaard's aversion to rationalistic theology and metaphysics, that it might be argued that
he is in effect denying that reason and even philosophy itself, when conceived as it has been since the time of Socrates as rational reflection and criticism, are capable of
solving any of the basic spiritual problems of human experience. From such a standpoint, it may appear that
Kierkegaard is actually denying the very possibility of the
philosophical enterprise. Indeed, one might conclude from
this that he has reached, although by a very different route,
the same conclusion as the positivists themselves. Both
give us philosophies to end all philosophy.

Yet Kierkegaard, like the positivists, *is* a philosopher.
For, as Kant himself showed, the critique of reason, whatever its result, is a fundamental and indispensable philosophical task. Conceived in one way, Kierkegaard's anti-
intellectualism is nothing but an extreme form of the continuing Romantic reaction against rationalism. It may also

be regarded as a latter-day manifestation of a long tradition of anti-intellectualistic fideism within Christian theology, which includes such important names as Tertullian, St. Augustine, and Pascal. For all of these writers, the significance of the religious life does not consist in its ability to provide answers to questions that any persistent scientist might find himself asking in the course of his investigations into the causes of natural phenomena, but in certain suprarational commitments or acts of faith which are responses to doubts of an entirely different order. For Kierkegaard, as for all fideists, basic religious questions do not admit of rational answers. But this, no doubt, is because religious questions are not motivated by anything that could be called, in any normal sense, a desire for information. What they seek is not understanding, but something that passes understanding, namely, salvation. And for salvation there is no recourse save an act of faith.

Kierkegaard betrays his own historical position in another way in his employment of the concept of development. He is not interested, however, in formulating laws of historical development, as were Hegel and Marx; his concern is with what may be called the morphology of spiritual progress. This development he conceives as having three distinct stages, in a way that is partly reminiscent of Comte. But whereas Comte thought of his law of the three stages as applying to the intellectual development of the individual and the race, Kierkegaard's doctrine is concerned only with the ideal progress of the human soul from the aesthetic, through the ethical, to the religious consciousness. At first glance this may suggest that whereas Comte regards the man of science as the highest stage of human development, Kierkegaard, on the contrary, considers the religious man as representing the highest stage. But appearances, here, are somewhat deceptive, and the comparison itself is extremely misleading. Actually, Comte and Kierkegaard are not talking about the same dimension of progress in their respective theories of the three stages. This becomes clear when we remember that Comte does not identify theology with religion, and that he conceives the perfect man of science as also committed to the positive religion of humanity. For Comte, in short, science is not incompatible with religion, but with the theological way of representing and thinking about reality. Kierkegaard, on the other hand, does not mention scientific thought as one of his stages. The development he describes is not a progress from science to religion, but from art and morality to religion. Kierkegaard, in short, is not concerned with the sort of intellectual development which Comte characterizes in his theory of the three stages; his concern is with questions of value and with the problems of self-knowledge and self-transcendence.

I am not suggesting here that the positivism of Comte and the existentialism of Kierkegaard are easily reconciled. What I am saying is that the contrast between them cannot be properly represented as the opposition of science and religion. Kierkegaard has no great quarrel with science, so long as it keeps its place as a system of thought; and Comte has no quarrel with religion if it leaves the department of human knowledge to science. Moreover, in their common opposition to rationalistic theology and metaphysics, and in their common conviction that questions of existence cannot be settled by reason alone, they display a deep-lying historical affinity which more recent positivists and existentialists might do well to ponder. Recognition of this affinity, for all their differences in aim and method, might help to bridge the apparently complete gap between contemporary analytical philosophy in England and the United States and the new existential metaphysics of France and Germany.

Kierkegaard conceives of man's spiritual progress, not as Hegel did, as a necessary manifestation of the historical self-development of absolute spirit, but as an entirely free personal development which the individual may or may not pass through, as he chooses. From Kierkegaard's point of view, the Hegelian conception of freedom is completely specious. For him, every person must decide for himself whether he will ascend from the sphere of aesthetic contemplation to that of moral responsibility and action, and from thence to the level of religious faith. As I understand him, however, what Kierkegaard preaches is not mysticism. The phase of the religious life which he emphasizes is not mystical communion or contemplation of God, but active faith and worship. His God remains wholly transcendent, and is as inaccessible to intuition as He is to the discursive understanding or reason. In this way, Kierkegaard shows himself to be in the main line of Lutheran Protestantism. And in this way he also shows himself to be a true child of the Age of Ideology, which is not an age of contemplation, but of decision, affirmation, and faith.

One last word: like Nietzsche, Kierkegaard in effect denies any possibility of a collectivistic or social solution to the spiritual problems of human life. The "way" he preaches is a lonely, solitary way which each man must choose and follow for himself. Like Nietzsche also, although for a partly different goal, he rejects the humanistic-utilitarian ideal of a common good realizable in some measure by rational inquiry and joint social action. The difference between them lies in the fact that Kierkegaard is wholly disillusioned, as Nietzsche is not, with the ideal of an Earthly Kingdom of this-worldly self-development. From his own standpoint, he is calling men back to the lost faith in the God of their fathers. But it is a faith which, at least by intention, has nothing to do with historical Christianity or with its churches, either Protestant or Catholic. But what, really, does it *mean*?

The following selections are taken from perhaps the most important and certainly the most consecutive of Kierkegaard's philosophical writings, *Concluding Unscientific Postscript*.* The first selection is from Chapter II, which is called "The Subjective Truth; Inwardness; Truth Is Subjectivity"; the second selection is from Chapter III, which is called "Real or Ethical Subjectivity; The Subjective Thinker."

* *Concluding Unscientific Postscript,* translated by David F. Swenson and Walter Lowrie. Princeton: Princeton University Press, for the American-Scandinavian Foundation, 1944, pp. 176–82, and 312–18. The work originally appeared in 1846 under the title *Uvidenskabelig Eftersskrift.*

{ If an existing individual were really able to transcend himself, the truth would be for him something final and complete; but where is the point at which he is outside himself? The I-am-I is a mathematical point which does not exist, and in so far there is nothing to prevent everyone from occupying this standpoint; the one will not be in the way of the other. It is only momentarily that the particular individual is able to realize existentially a unity of the infinite and the finite which transcends existence. This unity is realized in the moment of passion. Modern philosophy has tried anything and everything in the effort to help the individual to transcend himself objectively, which is a wholly impossible feat; existence exercises its restraining influence, and if philosophers nowadays had not become mere scribblers in the service of a fantastic thinking and its preoccupation, they would long ago have perceived that suicide was the only tolerable practical interpretation of its striving. But the scribbling modern philosophy holds passion in contempt; and yet passion is the culmination of existence for an existing individual— and we are all of us existing individuals. In passion the existing subject is rendered infinite in the eternity of the imaginative representation, and yet he is at the same time most definitely himself. The fantastic I-am-I is not an identity of the infinite and the finite, since neither the one nor the other is real; it is a fantastic rendezvous in the clouds, an unfruitful embrace, and the relationship of the individual self to this mirage is never indicated.

All essential knowledge relates to existence, or only such knowledge as has an essential relationship to existence is essential knowledge. All knowledge which does not inwardly relate itself to existence, in the reflection of inwardness, is, essentially viewed, accidental knowledge; its degree and scope is essentially indifferent. That essential knowledge is essentially related to existence does not mean the above-mentioned identity which abstract thought postulates between thought and being; nor does it signify, objectively, that knowledge corresponds to something existent as its object. But it means that knowledge has a relationship to the knower, who is essentially an existing individual, and that for this reason all essential knowledge is essentially related to existence. Only ethical and ethico-religious knowledge has an essential relationship to the existence of the knower.

Mediation is a mirage, like the I-am-I. From the abstract point of view everything is and nothing comes into being. Mediation can therefore have no place in abstract thought because it presupposes *movement*. Objective knowledge may indeed have the existent for its object; but since the knowing subject is an existing individual, and through the fact of his existence in process of becoming, philosophy must first explain how a particular existing subject is related to a knowledge of mediation. It must explain what he is in such a moment, if not pretty nearly *distrait;* where he is, if not in the moon? There is constant talk of mediation and mediation; is mediation then a man, as Peter Deacon believes that *Imprimatur* is a man? How does a human being manage to become something of this kind? Is this dignity, this great *philosophicum,* the fruit of study, or does the magistrate give it away, like the office of deacon or gravedigger? Try merely to enter into these and other such plain questions of a plain man, who would gladly become mediation if it could be done in some lawful and honest manner, and not either by saying *ein zwei drei kokolorum,* or by forgetting that he is himself an existing human being, for whom existence is therefore something essential, and an ethico-religious existence a suitable *quantum satis.* A speculative philosopher may perhaps find it in bad taste to ask such questions. But it is important not to direct the polemic to the wrong point, and hence not to begin in a fantastic objective manner to discuss *pro* and *contra* whether there is a mediation or not, but to hold fast what it means to be a human being.

In an attempt to make clear the difference of way that exists between an objective and a subjective reflection, I shall now proceed to show how a subjective reflection makes its way inwardly in inwardness. Inwardness in an existing subject culminates in passion; corresponding to passion in the subject the truth becomes a paradox; and the fact that the truth becomes a paradox is rooted precisely in its having a relationship to an existing subject. Thus the one corresponds to the other. By forgetting that one is an existing subject, passion goes by the board and the truth is no longer a paradox; the knowing subject becomes a fantastic entity rather than a human being, and the truth becomes a fantastic object for the knowledge of this fantastic entity.

*When the question of truth is raised in an objective manner, reflection is directed objectively to the truth, as an object to which the knower is related. Reflection is not focussed upon the relationship, however, but upon the question of whether it is the truth to which the knower is related. If only the object to which he is related is the truth, the subject is accounted to be in the truth. When the question of the truth is raised subjectively, reflection is directed subjectively to the nature of the individual's relationship; if only the mode of this relationship is in the truth, the individual is in the truth even if he should happen to be thus related to what is not true.** Let us take as an example the knowledge of God. Objectively, reflection is directed to the problem of whether this object is the true God; subjectively, reflection is directed to the question whether the individual is related to a something *in such a manner* that his relationship is in truth a God-relationship. On which side is the truth now to be found? Ah, may we not here resort to a mediation, and say: It is on neither side, but in the mediation of both? Excellently well said, provided we might have it explained how an existing individual manages to be in a state of mediation. For to be in a state of mediation is to be finished, while to exist is to become. Nor can an existing individual be in two places at the same time—he cannot be an identity of subject and object. When he is nearest to being in two places at the same time he is in passion; but passion is momentary, and passion is also the highest expression of subjectivity.

* The reader will observe that the question here is about essential truth, or about the truth which is essentially related to existence, and that it is precisely for the sake of clarifying it as inwardness or as subjectivity that this contrast is drawn.

The existing individual who chooses to pursue the objective way enters upon the entire approximation-process by which it is proposed to bring God to light objectively. But this is in all eternity impossible, because God is a subject, and therefore exists only for subjectivity in inwardness. The existing individual who chooses the subjective way apprehends instantly the entire dialectical difficulty involved in having to use some time, perhaps a long time, in finding God objectively; and he feels this dialectical difficulty in all its painfulness, because every moment is wasted in which he does not have God.* That very instant he has God, not by virtue of any objective deliberation, but by virtue of the infinite passion of inwardness. The objective inquirer, on the other hand, is not embarrassed by such dialectical difficulties as are involved in devoting an entire period of investigation to finding God—since it is possible that the inquirer may die tomorrow; and if he lives he can scarcely regard God as something to be taken along if convenient, since God is precisely that which one takes *a tout prix,* which in the understanding of passion constitutes the true inward relationship to God.

It is at this point, so difficult dialectically, that the way swings off for everyone who knows what it means to think, and to think existentially; which is something very different from sitting at a desk and writing about what one has never done, something very different from writing *de omnibus dubitandum* and at the same time being as credulous existentially as the most sensuous of men. Here is where the way swings off, and the change is marked by the fact

---

* In this manner God certainly becomes a postulate, but not in the otiose manner in which this word is commonly understood. It becomes clear rather that the only way in which an existing individual comes into relation with God, is when the dialectical contradiction brings his passion to the point of despair, and helps him to embrace God with the "category of despair" (faith). Then the postulate is so far from being arbitrary that it is precisely a life-necessity. It is then not so much that God is a postulate, as that the existing individual's postulation of God is a necessity.

that while objective knowledge rambles comfortably on by way of the long road of approximation without being impelled by the urge of passion, subjective knowledge counts every delay a deadly peril, and the decision so infinitely important and so instantly pressing that it is as if the opportunity had already passed.

Now when the problem is to reckon up on which side there is most truth, whether on the side of one who seeks the true God objectively, and pursues the approximate truth of the God-idea; or on the side of one who, driven by the infinite passion of his need of God, feels an infinite concern for his own relationship to God in truth (and to be at one and the same time on both sides equally, is as we have noted not possible for an existing individual, but is merely the happy delusion of an imaginary I-am-I): the answer cannot be in doubt for anyone who has not been demoralized with the aid of science. If one who lives in the midst of Christendom goes up to the house of God, the house of the true God, with the true conception of God in his knowledge, and prays, but prays in a false spirit; and one who lives in an idolatrous community prays with the entire passion of the infinite, although his eyes rest upon the image of an idol: where is there most truth? The one prays in truth to God though he worships an idol; the other prays falsely to the true God, and hence worships in fact an idol.

*   *   *   *   *   *   *   *   *

The objective accent falls on WHAT is said, the subjective accent on HOW it is said. This distinction holds even in the aesthetic realm, and receives definite expression in the principle that what is in itself true may in the mouth of such and such a person become untrue. In these times this distinction is particularly worthy of notice, for if we wish to express in a single sentence the difference between ancient times and our own, we should doubtless have to say: "In ancient times only an individual here and there knew the truth; now all know it, except that the inwardness of its appropriation stands in an inverse relationship to the extent of its dissemination."* Aesthetically the contradiction that truth becomes untruth in this or that person's mouth, is best construed comically: In the ethico-religious sphere, accent is again on the "how." But this is not to be understood as referring to demeanor, expression, or the like; rather it refers to the relationship sustained by the existing individual, in his own existence, to the content of his utterance. Objectively the interest is focussed merely on the thought-content, subjectively on the inwardness. At its maximum this inward "how" is the passion of the infinite, and the passion of the infinite is the truth. But the passion of the infinite is precisely subjectivity, and thus subjectivity becomes the truth. Objectively there is no infinite decisiveness, and hence it is objectively in order to annul the difference between good and evil, together with the principle of contradiction, and therewith also the infinite difference between the true and the false. Only in subjectivity is there decisiveness, to seek objectivity is to be in error. It is the passion of the infinite that is the decisive factor and not its content, for its content is precisely itself. In this manner subjectivity and the subjective "how" constitute the truth.

But the "how" which is thus subjectively accentuated

* *Stages on Life's Way,* Note on p. 426. Though ordinarily not wishing an expression of opinion on the part of reviewers, I might at this point almost desire it, provided such opinions, so far from flattering me, amounted to an assertion of the daring truth that what I say is something that everybody knows, even every child, and that the cultured know infinitely much better. If it only stands fast that everyone knows it, my standpoint is in order, and I shall doubtless make shift to manage with the unity of the comic and the tragic. If there were anyone who did not know it I might perhaps be in danger of being dislodged from my position of equilibrium by the thought that I might be in a position to communicate to someone the needful preliminary knowledge. It is just this which engages my interest so much, this that the cultured are accustomed to say: that everyone knows what the highest is. This was not the case in paganism, nor in Judaism, nor in the seventeen centuries of Christianity. Hail to the nineteenth century! Everyone knows it. What progress has been made since the time when only a few knew it. To make up for this, perhaps, we must assume that no one nowadays does it.

precisely because the subject is an existing individual, is also subject to a dialectic with respect to time. In the passionate moment of decision, where the road swings away from objective knowledge, it seems as if the infinite decision were thereby realized. But in the same moment the existing individual finds himself in the temporal order, and the subjective "how" is transformed into a striving, a striving which receives indeed its impulse and a repeated renewal from the decisive passion of the infinite, but is nevertheless a striving.

When subjectivity is the truth, the conceptual determination of the truth must include an expression for the antithesis to objectivity, a memento of the fork in the road where the way swings off; this expression will at the same time serve as an indication of the tension of the subjective inwardness. Here is such a definition of truth: *An objective uncertainty held fast in an appropriation-process of the most passionate inwardness is the truth,* the highest truth attainable for an *existing* individual. At the point where the way swings off (and where this is cannot be specified objectively, since it is a matter of subjectivity), there objective knowledge is placed in abeyance. Thus the subject merely has, objectively, the uncertainty; but it is this which precisely increases the tension of that infinite passion which constitutes his inwardness. The truth is precisely the venture which chooses an objective uncertainty with the passion of the infinite. I contemplate the order of nature in the hope of finding God, and I see omnipotence and wisdom; but I also see much else that disturbs my mind and excites anxiety. The sum of all this is an objective uncertainty. But it is for this very reason that the inwardness becomes as intense as it is, for it embraces this objective uncertainty with the entire passion of the infinite. In the case of a mathematical proposition the objectivity is given, but for this reason the truth of such a proposition is also an indifferent truth.

But the above definition of truth is an equivalent expression for faith. Without risk there is no faith. Faith is precisely the contradiction between the infinite passion of the individual's inwardness and the objective uncertainty.

If I am capable of grasping God objectively, I do not believe, but precisely because I cannot do this I must believe. If I wish to preserve myself in faith I must constantly be intent upon holding fast the objective uncertainty, so as to remain out upon the deep, over seventy thousand fathoms of water, still preserving my faith.

*   *   *   *   *   *   *   *   *

§ 4. *The Subjective Thinker—His Task, His Form, His Style*

If an excursion into the realm of pure thought is to determine whether a man is a thinker or not, the subjective thinker is *ipso facto* excluded from consideration. But in and with his exclusion every existential problem also goes by the board; and the melancholy consequences are audible as an undertone of warning accompanying the jubilant cries with which modern speculative thought has hailed the System.

There is an old saying that *oratio, tentatio, meditatio faciunt theologum.* Similarly there is required for a subjective thinker imagination and feeling, dialectics in existential inwardness, together with passion. But passion first and last; for it is impossible to think about existence in existence without passion. Existence involves a tremendous contradiction, from which the subjective thinker does not have to abstract, though he can if he will, but in which it is his business to remain. For a dialectic of world-history the individuals vanish in humanity; you and I, any particular existing individual, cannot become visible to such a dialectic, even by the invention of new and more powerful magnifying instruments for the concrete.

The subjective thinker is a dialectician dealing with the existential, and he has the passion of thought requisite for holding fast to the qualitative disjunction. But on the other hand, if the qualitative disjunction is applied in empty isolation, if it is applied to the individual in an altogether abstract fashion, one may risk saying something infinitely decisive and be quite correct in what one says, and yet, ludicrously enough, say nothing at all. Hence it is a psychologically noteworthy phenomenon that the absolute disjunction may be used quite disingenuously, precisely for the purpose of evasion. When the death-penalty is affixed to every crime, it ends in no crime being punished at all. So also in the case of the absolute disjunction. Applied abstractly it becomes an unpronounceable mute letter, or if pronounced, it says nothing. The subjective thinker has the absolute disjunction ready to hand; therefore, as an essential existential moment he holds it fast with a thinker's passion, but he holds it as a last decisive resort, to prevent everything from being reduced to merely quantitative differences. He holds it in reserve, but does not apply it so as by recurring to it abstractly to inhibit existence. Hence the subjective thinker adds to his equipment aesthetic and ethical passion, which gives him the necessary concreteness.

All existential problems are passionate problems, for when existence is interpenetrated with reflection it generates passion. To think about existential problems in such a way as to leave out the passion, is tantamount to not thinking about them at all, since it is to forget the point, which is that the thinker is himself an existing individual. But the subjective thinker is not a poet, though he may also be a poet; he is not an ethicist, though he may also be an ethicist; he is not a dialectician, though he may also be a dialectician. He is essentially an existing individual, while the existence of the poet is non-essential in relation to the poem, the existence of the ethicist, in relation to his doctrine, the existence of the dialectician, in relation to his thought. The subjective thinker is not a man of science, but an artist. Existing is an art. The subjective thinker is aesthetic enough to give his life aesthetic content, ethical enough to regulate it, and dialectical enough to interpenetrate it with thought.

The subjective thinker has the task of understanding himself in his existence. Abstract thought is wont to speak of contradiction, and of its immanent propulsive power, although by abstracting from existence and from existing it removes the difficulty and the contradiction. The subjective thinker is an existing individual and a thinker at one and the same time; he does not abstract from the contradiction and from existence, but lives in it while at the same time thinking. In all his thinking he therefore has to think the fact that he is an existing individual. For this reason he always has enough to think about. Humanity in the abstract is a subject soon disposed of, and likewise world-history; even such tremendous portions as China, Persia, and so forth, are as nothing to the hungry monster of the historical process. The abstract concept of faith is soon disposed of; but the subjective thinker who in all his thinking remains at home in his existence, will find an inexhaustible subject for thought in his faith, when he seeks to follow its declension in all the manifold *casibus* of life. Such subjective reflection is by no means a light matter; for existence is the most difficult of all subjects to penetrate when the thinker has to remain in it, because the moment is commensurable for the highest decision, and yet again a vanishing instant in the possible seventy years of a human life.

*   *   *   *   *   *   *   *   *

While abstract thought seeks to understand the concrete abstractly, the subjective thinker has conversely to understand the abstract concretely. Abstract thought turns from concrete men to consider man in general; the subjective thinker seeks to understand the abstract determination of being human in terms of this particular existing human being.

*   *   *   *   *   *   *   *   *

There is a sense in which the subjective thinker speaks quite as abstractly as the abstract thinker; for the latter speaks of man in general and of subjectivity in general, while the former speaks of the one man (*unum noris, omnes*). But this one human being is an existing human being, and the difficulty is not evaded.

To understand oneself in existence is also the Christian principle, except that this "self" has received far richer and deeper determination, still more difficult to understand, in conjunction with existence. The believer is a subjective thinker, and the difference that obtains, as was shown above, is only that between the simple man and the simple wise man. Here again the "self" is not humanity in general, or subjectivity in general, in which case everything becomes easy because the difficulty is removed, and the whole task transferred to the realm of abstract thought with its shadow-boxing. The difficulty is greater than it was for the Greek, because still greater contradictions are conjoined, existence being accentuated paradoxically as sin, and eternity accentuated paradoxically as God in time. The difficulty consists in existing in such categories, not in abstractly thinking oneself out of them; abstractly thinking, for example, about an eternal God-becoming and the like, all of which ideas emerge as soon as the difficulty is taken away. As a consequence, the believer's existence is still more passionate than the existence of the Greek philosopher, who needed a high degree of passion even in relation to his *ataraxy;* for existence generates passion but existence paradoxically accentuated generates the maximum of passion.

To abstract from existence is to remove the difficulty. To remain in existence so as to understand one thing in one moment and another thing in another moment, is not to understand oneself. But to understand the greatest oppositions together, and to understand oneself existing in them, is very difficult. Let anyone merely observe himself, and take note of how men speak, and he will perceive how rarely this task is successfully realized.

*   *   *   *   *   *   *   *   *

In spite of all his exertion the subjective thinker enjoys only a meager reward. The more the collective idea comes to dominate even the ordinary consciousness, the more forbidding seems the transition to becoming a particular existing human being instead of losing oneself in the race, and saying "we," "our age," "the nineteenth century." That it is a little thing merely to be a particular existing human being is not to be denied; but for this very reason it requires considerable resignation not to make light of it. For what does a mere individual count for? Our age knows only too well how little it is, but here also lies the specific immorality of the age. Each age has its own characteristic depravity. Ours is perhaps not pleasure or indulgence or sensuality, but rather a dissolute pantheistic contempt for the individual man. In the midst of all our exultation over the achievements of the age and the nineteenth century, there sounds a note of poorly conceived contempt for the individual man; in the midst of the self-importance of the contemporary generation there is revealed a sense of despair over being human. Everything must attach itself so as to be a part of some movement; men are determined to lose themselves in the totality of things, in world-history, fascinated and deceived by a magic witchery; no one wants to be an individual human being. Hence perhaps the many attempts to continue clinging to Hegel, even by men who have reached an insight into the questionable character of his philosophy. It is a fear that if they were to become particular existing human beings, they would vanish trace-lessly, so that not even the daily press would be able to discover them, still less critical journals, to say nothing at all of speculative philosophers immersed in world-history. As particular human beings they fear that they will be doomed to a more isolated and forgotten existence than that of a man in the country; for if a man lets go of Hegel he will not even be in a position to have a letter addressed to him.]

CHAPTER XII

The Return to Enlightenment:
Ernst Mach (1838-1916)

WITH THE EXCEPTION OF KANT, NO PHILOSOPHER hitherto considered in this book made any contribution to physical science; few of them, indeed, had any first-hand knowledge of it at all. In marked contrast to the Age of Reason, philosophical interest in physical science remained largely dormant during much of the nineteenth century. Progress continued to be rapid, but most scientists were content to do their work rather than talk about it. One reason for this is that fundamental philosophical adjustments to the new scientific conception of the natural world had already been made in the preceding period. Moreover, the very success of the natural sciences in providing systematic and verifiable descriptions dispelled any remaining doubts concerning the validity of its methods, at least within the domain of inorganic phenomena. With the gradual assimilation of the Newtonian physics into the blood stream of European intellectual life, there remained, then, no basic point of conflict between physical science and the other major institutionalized interests of society. Even the ever-reluctant Church had finally begun to reconcile the articles of its Faith with the scientific picture of the physical world. The remaining argument concerned the extension of the methods of physical science to the domains of life, mind, and history.

Toward the end of the nineteenth century, however, philosophical interest in the physical sciences and in their methods again revived. This interest, in the first instance, came from the scientists themselves rather than from the professional philosophers. This was due primarily to the fact that within both physics and mathematics new basic ideas were beginning to emerge which required fundamental rethinking on the part of physicists and mathematicians concerning the nature of their disciplines and the relation of the concepts of those disciplines to experience and to "reality." Kant had regarded Euclidean geometry, almost as a matter of course, as the one universal and necessary science of space. But after the appearance of the revolutionary non-Euclidean geometries of Riemann Lobachevski, it was no longer possible to conceive pure geometry as a science of a priori synthetic truths concerning spatial phenomena given in experience. What, then, *is* the subject matter of geometry, and of what, if anything, can the new non-dimensional geometries be said to be true? Analogous refinements and complications within physical theory presented similar problems of interpretation to scientists and philosophers who continued to adhere to the thesis that the cardinal virtue of the scientific method consists, above all, in its stubborn refusal to countenance expressions which have no empirical referents.

These problems were complex and difficult. But some solution to them had to be found if the status of physics as an empirical science was still to be maintained, and if the science of physics was still to be upheld as the paradigm of human knowledge. The need for such solutions was all the more pressing at this time precisely because the empiricist theories of knowledge that had for so long been supposed to justify the claims of the scientific method as the only vehicle of rational belief were themselves under heavy fire from other quarters. Not only the philosophical idealists and their allies in the fields of history and social theory, but also theologians and political revolutionaries had much to gain and nothing to lose from the increasing confusion within the ranks of the scientists themselves. If that darling of positivism, physics itself, could no longer be regarded as a purely empirical discipline, then what was to stand in the way of the pretensions of other, avowedly unempirical, "disciplines," to give us knowledge, one way or another, of "the real world?"

Empiricists since the time of Hume felt that the characteristic feature of science which radically distinguishes it from transcendental theology and metaphysics is its rejection of any concept which cannot be defined in terms referring to discernible items of sense experience. Now, however, it was becoming evident that the paradigmatic science of physics was itself increasingly committed to the employment of concepts for which no such reduction seemed possible. In that case, however, what sort of argument could be made against those philosophers who maintained that the mere empirical indefinability of such notions as God, Freedom, and Immortality, constitutes no serious objection against them? If the great science of physics inevitably has recourse to transempirical conceptions when merely trying to explain correlations between observable phenomena, is not a tacit warrant provided within science itself for the theological concepts and the metaphysical explanations which Comte and his followers had repudiated in the name of positive science? And what are we to make of Mill's claims concerning the philosophy of experience, if not only mathematics but also physics itself becomes indifferent to the question whether its conceptual models have any experiential basis?

In this confused and embarrassing situation it was the Austrian physicist and philosopher Ernst Mach, who once again took up the defense of the program of positivism against its detractors. Mach was convinced that if science is to be consistently defended as the only form of rational belief, then, at whatever cost, the scientists must continually discipline themselves against the use of terms and theories that have no deducible connection with the facts of experience. He proposed, therefore, a radical therapeutic regimen which would strip the physical sciences to their fighting weight as empirical disciplines, and would thereby remove from the body of accredited scientific theory all its accumulated fat of unverifiable theoretical constructions. He proposed this, however, not so much in the name of the positive philosophy, but in the name of science itself. He spoke, that is to say, as a physicist to physicists, and not as a mere philosophical propagandist.

According to Mach, the sole aim of science is to describe and predict observable relations among phenomena. But what are we to accept as phenomena? Our everyday uncritical perceptions notoriously contain elements of subjective interpretation that go beyond what we may be said, strictly, to see or hear. What we ordinarily call "observation" cannot be relied on to provide veridical representations of the sensory data which are the beginning and end of all scientific generalization and prediction. It is essential, therefore, that any scientific theory of knowledge should develop an adequate theory of phenomena from which every trace of subjectivity has been eliminated. By allowing only sensations themselves as the "elements" of human knowledge, and only terms designating such elements as referential, Mach thought that a decisive test could be provided for veridical perception and for distinguishing cognitively meaningful from meaningless expressions. He was aware however, that science cannot get along without certain other terms which do not designate sensory elements or combinations of them. For example, science cannot do without "thing words" or such concepts as cause or number. According to Mach, all such concepts are merely "auxiliary concepts." They are admissible into scientific discourse only in so far as they enable us to economize our thinking about phenomena. These concepts, so to say, are calculating devices, not terms of reference. In so far, then, as they make possible the organization of hypotheses into a compendious, perspicuous, and systematic body of scientific theory, Mach was prepared to admit auxiliary notions into scientific discourse, but only with the explicit understanding that they are not to be taken as designating anything unless definitions can be provided which show how they can be reduced without remainder to conjunctions of other terms that refer directly to sensory elements.

Thus there are two methodological principles at work in Mach's theory of knowledge. According to the first principle, which may be called the thesis of empiricism, sensations alone provide the real data or "stuff" of knowledge.

For Mach this thesis had the important corollary that the only terms of reference are those which, directly or through definition, refer to sensations. We may call this the corollary of phenomenalism. According to the second principle, which may be called the pragmatic principle of economy, auxiliary concepts may be admitted into scientific discourse, but only for the purpose of organizing hypotheses into a coherent system. These principles, it must be confessed, produce a certain tension in Mach's thought. Nor did he succeed in providing an account of auxiliary terms which would sufficiently explain their use without requiring us to suppose that they designate mysterious entities in the real world. In order to relieve this tension, and to explain the symbolic function of non-designating terms within science, Mach required a philosophy of language and of logic of greater power and subtlety than he himself possessed. And it was not until the next century that the positivists and their pragmatic allies began to make good this deficiency.

Mach, like Comte before him, was essentially a program maker. His ideas were germinal, and have had a great influence in the period since his death. But he did not provide analyses of particular auxiliary concepts which would show in detail how they operate in the process of "saving experiences." His theory, moreover, was too psychological; what was wanted was not so much a statement of the psychological value of such notions, as an explanation of their logical functions within discourse. What was needed, above all, was a clearer conception of mathematics and logic themselves. But this could be provided only after these disciplines had been more completely systematized and the purely logical foundations of mathematics had been revealed. Then, and then alone, could the non-referential meaning of the auxiliary concepts of science be properly explained.

The aims of Mach's theory of knowledge were radically antisubjectivistic, and were wholly opposed to metaphysical idealism. In view of this, it is interesting to observe that in his book *Materialism and Empirio-Criticism,* Marx's greatest disciple, Lenin, attacked Mach's philosophy as merely the most recent and subtle form of the subjectivism and idealism which dialectical materialism had been combating for over half a century. It may be questioned, however, whether Lenin fully grasped the point of the doctrines which he attacked. He was shrewd enough to see that they presented a fundamental threat to any metaphysics or philosophy of history which pretended to be at once scientific, dialectical, and materialistic. But he was mistaken in construing Mach's theory of sensation as merely a sophisticated form of subjective idealism. Mach did not in the least regard what he called "sensations" as mental entities which exist only in perception or as the objects of a transcendental mind or ego. All such "metaphysical" issues Mach himself considered to be quite meaningless. Properly understood, indeed, the concepts of mind, body, and matter are themselves what later philosophers have called "logical constructions." They are, that is to say, wholly analyzable in other terms which refer only to sets of correlations among the elements of experience. From this standpoint, the so-called "mind-body problem" resolves itself into the problem of determining the particular higher-order correlations that hold between those lower-order correlations of phenomena which we compendiously refer to as "mental" or as "physical." For both physics and psychology alike there is only one basic subject matter: sensory experience. The difference between them is wholly a difference in their respective ways of classifying phenomena and in the particular types of correlation with which they are respectively concerned.

The issue here at stake is fundamental to the program of the unity of science in which Mach, like Comte before him, had a vital stake. For according to this program there are no basic methodological differences between the natural sciences and the sciences of life and mind. Nor are there any features of the phenomena dealt with by biology and psychology that render them intrinsically unamenable to the intersubjective methods of verification that are employed in the physical sciences. At least by intention, Mach's theory of sensations as the only elements of knowledge is quite compatible with that form of behaviorism or physicalism, as it is sometimes called, which countenances no "private" mental entities whatever. For him "mind" has no meaning apart from the correlations of sensation to which it may refer, and sensations themselves are neutral entities which can be correlated and recorrelated in innumerable ways. There is no reason whatever, on Mach's view, why any given sensation should not be both "physical" and "mental," nor why any sensation should not be in principle perceivable by more than one person.

Not all empirical theories of knowledge have so sharply denied inescapable differences in method between those sciences that deal with physical objects and those having to do with mental phenomena. It is logically possible to acknowledge that all knowledge refers finally to items of experience and still leave it an open question whether all forms of experience are, in principle, public. And indeed there have been a good many philosophers who have considered themselves to be empiricists who have still held that there is a certain class of data (Hume called them "impressions of reflection") which can be apprehended only by a special mode of observation, which is variously referred to as "introspection," "self-observation," or "self-awareness." Such admissions would be fatal to such a program as Mach's. For once it is admitted, on principle, that access to the facts of emotion, feeling, and memory can be gained only through certain private modes of observation, then the whole ideal of the unity of science is doomed from the outset. And in that case at least one basic contention of the idealists would have to be sustained, namely, that there is an ineradicable difference in kind between the sciences of nature and of behavior and those disciplines which have to do primarily with the inner life.

For Mach's purposes, then, it is not enough to announce that nothing shall be accepted as a scientific hypothesis which cannot meet the test of observation. For what is to count as "observation?" Is there one fundamental sort of observation only, or are there many? Are some classes of phenomena public and others private, or are all phenomena, at least in principle, intersubjectively observable? These questions were pressing in Mach's time; they remain so to this day. Nor is it sufficient, from Mach's point of view, to hold that all questions concerning causal connections among phenomena are questions of observable correlation. For what if such connections cannot be intersubjectively verified in all cases? If some of the correlated phenomena are accessible only to one individual, then there would seem to be no adequate ground for holding that the methods employed in the physical sciences are essentially the same as those required for knowledge of "physical" phenomena.

The intention of Mach's doctrine is, then, radically anti-subjectivistic. To put the point in Mill's language, he contends that there are no possibilities of sensation which cannot in principle be shared. Loneliness, on such a view, is due to isolation from one's fellow men, not to the presence in one's experience of sensations or feelings from which others are cut off by necessity.

Whether, as some have held, this thesis of positivism is itself "metaphysical" or merely a rule of inquiry or method, is a matter upon which philosophers are not all agreed. The question of names is of no great importance, so long as it is realized that the principle of the intersubjectivity of sensations is a basic commitment which is not itself capable of verification by the methods of science. How could it be, since it is, at bottom, a claim concerning the procedures and ideals which are proper to science itself? That, however, is nothing against it, if, as many nineteenth-century philosophers maintained, every philosophy, and above all every metaphysics, is involved in certain basic commitments or posits which are incapable of, because antecendent to, all demonstration.

The underlying motives of Mach's philosophy are clear. In his view, science, as the institution concerned with cumulative knowledge, has achieved its remarkable successes only by adhering rigidly in practice to the principle that every admissible hypothesis must be capable of meeting intersubjectively observable tests. Once the authority of this principle is impugned, even if only in the name of a supposedly more tolerant empiricism which permits the acknowledgment of private sensations known only through introspection, the way is already cleared for obscurantists who claim "truth" for propositions whose only warrant is prejudice, revelation, or the authority of particular individuals. The ideological consequences which follow from the admission of such forms of "knowledge" are immense.

Mach knew very well the essentially ideological import of his own philosophical commitments. And it is perhaps fitting that a book such as this, which is concerned with ideological conflicts of the greatest importance to our own lives should close with a selection from the writings of a philosopher who is able, in good conscience, to reaffirm the underlying spiritual ideals of the Enlightenment itself. Toward the end of Mach's great work *The Science of Mechanics,* there occurs the following passage: "Rationalism does not seem to have gained a broad theatre of action till the literature of the eighteenth century. Humanistic, philosophical, historical, and physical science here met and gave each other mutual encouragement. All who have experienced, in part, in its literature, this wonderful emancipation of the human intellect, will feel during their whole lives a deep, elegaical regret for the eighteenth century." Mach felt that the beneficent ideals of the Enlightenment had not only been rejected by antipositivistic philosophers, but were now in danger of being undermined unconsciously by the scientists themselves. Some contemporary positivists, aware of deviations within their own ranks, have lately been crying, "Back to Mach." From Mach's standpoint, what they should mean by this is "Back to Enlightenment."

Since Mach's time the validity of Mach's program for the decontamination of science has been hotly argued. The distinguished physicist Max Planck, for example, maintained that Mach's principle of economy, if generally accepted, would fatally impair the progress of science itself by crippling the scientific imagination and the scientist's faith in his own work as a true representation of reality. Others have held that the dignity of science as the supreme vehicle of human knowledge would disappear if the theories of natural science should generally be thought of as nothing more than a system of convenient summary formulas for predicting the occurrence of sensations. Even Einstein, despite his great admiration for Mach, sometimes seems to have opposed positivism, in his later years, for some such reasons as these.

Such objections, however, are primarily psychological; they do not affect the philosophical cogency of Mach's program. A more serious difficulty has to do with the phenomenalistic side of Mach's theory of knowledge. This may be seen in the following statement made by Professor Philip Frank in his defense against misconceptions of Mach's doctrine. "It is not," says Frank, "a question of actually expressing all physical statements as statements about relations among sense perceptions. It is important, however, to establish the *principle* that only those statements have a real meaning which *could* in principle be expressed as statements about relations among our perceptions." This defense is inadequate. Why, it may be asked, is it not a question of actually doing what the principle says could be done? How, indeed, are we to know whether the principle is significant if, as is generally agreed, no one has ever provided one clear example in which statements about physical objects have been translated without loss of meaning into other statements about relations among sensations? At the present time, a great many philosophers who are otherwise sympathetic to the philosophy of scientific empiricism believe that Mach's phenomenalistic theory of meaning cannot be carried out at all. The reason for this, so they contend, has essentially to do with irreducible logical differences between statements about physical objects and processes and the reports of immediate experience which are used to confirm them. Even if this aspect of Mach's doctrine must be abandoned, it still does not follow that the fundamental thesis of positivistic empiricism must be abandoned, the thesis, that is, that intersubjective observation is the fundamental and only test of all statements of fact. For this thesis concerns not the translatability of factual statements into statements about the relations among sense perceptions, but the more important question concerning the nature of the evidence which may be adduced in support of any factual belief. It is no small matter whether this thesis is abandoned, for upon it, in no small degree, depends the possibility not only of cumulative knowledge and the advancement of learning, but, to a great degree, of a society of free men who share a common world. On this point there is little difference between Mach and Kant himself. And so, in this way, our story comes to full turn.

The following selections are taken from Chapter IV, "The Formal Development of Mechanics," of Mach's *The Science of Mechanics.**

¶ 6. The idea that theology and physics are two distinct branches of knowledge, thus took, from its first germination in Copernicus till its final promulgation by Lagrange, almost two centuries to attain clearness in the minds of investigators. At the same time it cannot be denied that this truth was always clear to the greatest minds, like Newton. Newton never, despite his profound religiosity, mingled theology with the questions of science. True, even he concludes his *Optics,* whilst on its last pages his clear and luminous intellect still shines, with an exclamation of humble contrition at the vanity of all earthly things. But his optical researches proper, in contrast to those of Leibnitz, contain not a trace of theology. The same may be said of Galileo and Huygens. Their writings conform almost absolutely to the point of view of Lagrange, and may be accepted in this respect as classical. But the general views and tendencies of an age must not be judged by its greatest, but by its average, minds.

To comprehend the process here portrayed, the general condition of affairs in these times must be considered. It stands to reason that in a stage of civilisation in which religion is almost the sole education, and the only theory of the world, people would naturally look at things in a theological point of view, and that they would believe that this view was possessed of competency in all fields of research. If we transport ourselves back to the time when

* *The Science of Mechanics,* translated by T. J. McCormack from the 2nd German edition. Chicago: The Open Court Publishing Co., 1893, pp. 456–65 and 481–85. This work originally appeared in 1883, under the title *Die Mechanik in ihrer Entwicklung.*

people played the organ with their fists, when they had to have the multiplication table visibly before them to calculate, when they did so much with their hands that people now-a-days do with their heads, we shall not demand of such a time that it should *critically* put to the test its own views and theories. With the widening of the intellectual horizon through the great geographical, technical, and scientific discoveries and inventions of the fifteenth and sixteenth centuries, with the opening up of provinces in which it was impossible to make any progress with the old conception of things, simply because it had been formed prior to the knowledge of these provinces, this bias of the mind gradually and slowly vanished. The great freedom of thought which appears in isolated cases in the early middle ages, first in poets and then in scientists, will always be hard to understand. The enlightenment of those days must have been the work of a few very extraordinary minds, and can have been bound to the views of the people at large by but very slender threads, more fitted to disturb those views than to reform them. Rationalism does not seem to have gained a broad theatre of action till the literature of the eighteenth century. Humanistic, philosophical, historical, and physical science here met and gave each other mutual encouragement. All who have experienced, in part, in its literature, this wonderful emancipation of the human intellect, will feel during their whole lives a deep, elegiacal regret for the eighteenth century.

7. The old point of view, then, is abandoned. Its history is now detectible only in the form of the mechanical principles. And this form will remain strange to us as long as we neglect its origin. The theological conception of things gradually gave way to a more rigid conception; and this was accompanied with a considerable gain in enlightenment, as we shall now briefly indicate.

When we say light travels by the paths of shortest time, we grasp by such an expression many things. But we do not know as yet *why* light prefers paths of shortest time. We forego all further knowledge of the phenomenon, if we find the reason in the Creator's wisdom. We of to-day know, that light travels by *all* paths, but that only on the paths of shortest time do the waves of light so intensify each other that a perceptible result is produced. Light, accordingly, only *appears* to travel by the paths of shortest time. After the prejudice which prevailed on these questions had been removed, cases were immediately discovered in which by the side of the supposed economy of nature the most striking extravagance was displayed. Cases of this kind have, for example, been pointed out by Jacobi in connection with Euler's principle of least action. A great many natural phenomena accordingly produce the impression of economy, simply because they visibly appear only when by accident an economical accumulation of effects take place. This is the same idea in the province of inorganic nature that Darwin worked out in the domain of organic nature. We facilitate instinctively our comprehension of nature by applying to it the economical ideas with which we are familiar.

*　　*　　*　　*　　*　　*　　*　　*　　*

The question may now justly be asked, If the point of view of theology which led to the enunciation of the principles of mechanics was utterly wrong, how comes it that the principles themselves are in all substantial points correct? The answer is easy. In the first place, the theological view did not supply the *contents* of the principles, but simply determined their *guise;* their matter was derived from experience. A similar influence would have been exercised by any other dominant type of thought, by a commercial attitude, for instance, such as presumably had its effect on Stevinus's thinking. In the second place, the theological conception of nature itself owes its origin to an endeavor to obtain a more comprehensive view of the world;—the very same endeavor that is at the bottom of physical science. Hence, even admitting that the physical philosophy of theology is a fruitless achievement, a reversion to a lower state of scientific culture, we still need not repudiate the *sound root* from which it has sprung and which is not different from that of true physical inquiry.

*　　*　　*　　*　　*　　*　　*　　*　　*

The conception of a will and intelligence active in nature is by no means the exclusive property of Christian

monotheism. On the contrary, this idea is a quite familiar **one to paganism** and fetishism. Paganism, however, finds this will and intelligence entirely in individual phenomena, while monotheism seeks it in the All. Moreover, a pure monotheism does not exist. The Jewish monotheism of the Bible is by no means free from belief in demons, sorcerers, and witches; and the Christian monotheism of medieval times is even richer in these pagan conceptions. . . .

8. Physical science rid itself only very slowly of these conceptions.

It is natural that these ideas so obstinately assert themselves. Of the many impulses that rule man with demoniacal power, that nourish, preserve, and propagate him, without his knowledge or supervision, of these impulses of which the middle ages present such great pathological excesses, only the smallest part is accessible to scientific analysis and conceptual knowledge. The fundamental character of all these instincts is the feeling of our oneness and sameness with nature; a feeling that at times can be silenced but never eradicated by absorbing intellectual occupations, and which certainly has a *sound basis,* no matter to what religious absurdities it may have given rise.

9. The French encyclopaedists of the eighteenth century imagined they were not far from a final explanation of the world by physical and mechanical principles; Laplace even conceived a mind competent to foretell the progress of nature for all eternity, if but the masses, their positions, and initial velocities were given. In the eighteenth century, this joyful overestimation of the scope of the new physico-mechanical ideas is pardonable. Indeed, it is a refreshing, noble, and elevating spectacle; and we can deeply sympathise with this expression of intellectual joy, so unique in history. But now, after a century has elapsed, after our judgment has grown more sober, the world-conception of the encyclopaedists appears to us as a *mechanical mythology* in contrast to the *animistic* of the old religions. Both views contain undue and fantastical exaggerations of an incomplete perception. Careful physical research will lead, however, to an analysis of our sensations. We shall then discover that our hunger is not so essentially different from

the tendency of sulphuric acid for zinc, and our will not so greatly different from the pressure of a stone, as now appears. We shall again feel ourselves nearer nature, without its being necessary that we should resolve ourselves into a nebulous and mystical mass of molecules, or make nature a haunt of hobgoblins. The direction in which this enlightenment is to be looked for, as the result of long and painstaking research, can of course only be surmised. To *anticipate* the result, or even to attempt to introduce it into any scientific investigation of to-day would be mythology, not science.

Physical science does not pretend to be a *complete* view of the world; it simply claims that it is working toward such a complete view in the future. The highest philosophy of the scientific investigator is precisely this *toleration* of an incomplete conception of the world and the preference for it rather than an apparently perfect, but inadequate conception. Our religious opinions are always our own private affair, as long as we do not obtrude them upon others and do not apply them to things which come under the jurisdiction of a different tribunal. Physical inquirers themselves entertain the most diverse opinions on this subject, according to the range of their intellects and their estimation of the consequences.

Physical science makes no investigation at all into things that are absolutely inaccessible to exact investigation, or as yet inaccessible to it. But should provinces ever be thrown open to exact research which are now closed to it, no well-organised man, no one who cherishes honest intentions towards himself and others, will any longer then hesitate to countenance inquiry with a view to exchanging his *opinion* regarding such provinces for positive *knowledge* of them.

When, to-day, we see society waver, see it change its views on the same question according to its mood and the events of the week, like the register of an organ, when we behold the profound mental anguish which is thus produced, we should know that this is the natural and necessary outcome of the incompleteness and transitional character of our philosophy. A competent view of the world

can never be got as a gift; we must acquire it by hard
work. And only by granting free sway to reason and experience in the provinces in which they alone are determina-
tive, shall we, to the weal of mankind, approach, slowly,
gradually, but surely, to that ideal of a *monistic* view of
the world which is alone compatible with the economy of
a sound mind. . . .

IV. THE ECONOMY OF SCIENCE

1. It is the object of science to replace, or *save,* experiences, by the reproduction and anticipation of facts in
thought. Memory is handier than experience, and often
answers the same purpose. This economical office of
science, which fills its whole life, is apparent at first glance;
and with its full recognition all mysticism in science disappears.

Science is communicated by instruction, in order that
one man may profit by the experience of another and be
spared the trouble of accumulating it for himself; and thus,
to spare posterity, the experiences of whole generations are
stored up in libraries.

Language, the instrument of this communication, is itself
an economical contrivance. Experiences are analysed, or
broken up, into simpler and more familiar experiences,
and then symbolised at some sacrifice of precision. The
symbols of speech are as yet restricted in their use within
national boundaries, and doubtless will long remain so.
But written language is gradually being metamorphosed
into an ideal universal character. . . .

2. In the reproduction of facts in thought, we never
reproduce the facts in full, but only that side of them which
is important to us, moved to this directly or indirectly
by a practical interest. Our reproductions are invariably
abstractions. Here again is an economical tendency.

Nature is composed of sensations as its elements. Primitive man, however, first picked out certain compounds of
these elements—those namely that are relatively perma-
nent and of greater importance to him. The first and oldest

words are names of "things." Even here, there is an abstractive process, an abstraction from the surroundings of the things, and from the continual small changes which these compound sensations undergo, which being practically unimportant are not noticed. No inalterable thing exists. The thing is an abstraction, the name a symbol, for a compound of elements from whose changes we abstract. The reason we assign a single word to a whole compound is that we need to suggest all the constituent sensations at once. When, later, we come to remark the changeableness, we cannot at the same time hold fast to the idea of the thing's permanence, unless we have recourse to the conception of a thing-in-itself, or other like absurdity. Sensations are not signs of things; but, on the contrary, a thing is a thought-symbol for a compound sensation of relative fixedness. Properly speaking the world is not composed of "things" as its elements, but of colors, tones, pressures, spaces, times, in short what we ordinarily call individual sensations.

The whole operation is a mere affair of economy. In the reproduction of facts, we begin with the more durable and familiar compounds, and supplement these later with the unusual by way of corrections. Thus, we speak of a perforated cylinder, of a cube with beveled edges, expressions involving contradictions, unless we accept the view here taken. All judgments are such amplifications and corrections of ideas already admitted.

3. In speaking of cause and effect we arbitrarily give relief to those elements to whose connection we have to attend in the reproduction of a fact in the respect in which it is important to us. There is no cause nor effect in nature; nature has but an individual existence; nature simply *is*. Recurrences of like cases in which A is always connected with B, that is, like results under like circumstances, that is again, the essence of the connection of cause and effect, exist but in the abstraction which we perform for the purpose of mentally reproducing the facts. Let a fact become familiar, and we no longer require this putting into relief of its connecting marks, our attention is no longer at-

tracted to the new and surprising, and we cease to speak of cause and effect. . . .

The natural and common-sense explanation is apparently this. The ideas of cause and effect originally sprang from an endeavor to reproduce facts in thought. At first, the connection of *A* and *B*, of *C* and *D*, of *E* and *F*, and so forth, is regarded as familiar. But after a greater range of experience is acquired and a connection between *M* and *N* is observed, it often turns out that we recognise *M* as *made up of A, C, E,* and *N* of *B, D, F,* the connection of which was before a *familiar* fact and accordingly possesses with us a higher authority. This explains why a person of experience regards a new event with different eyes than the novice. The new experience is illuminated by the mass of old experience. As a fact, then, there really does exist in the mind an "idea" under which fresh experiences are subsumed; but that idea has itself been developed from experience. The notion of the *necessity* of the causal connection is probably created by our voluntary movements in the world and by the changes which these indirectly produce, as Hume supposed but Schopenhauer contested.

Much of the authority of the ideas of cause and effect is due to the fact that they are developed *instinctively* and involuntarily, and that we are distinctly sensible of having personally contributed nothing to their formation. We may, indeed, say that our sense of causality is not acquired by the individual, but has been perfected in the development of the race. Cause and effect, therefore, are things of thought, having an economical office. It cannot be said *why* they arise. For it is precisely by the abstraction of uniformities that we know the question "why."]

CHAPTER XIII

Concluding Unscientific Postscript

AS WE HAVE OBSERVED IN THE CASE OF MACH, A REACTION had already begun to set in toward the end of the nineteenth century against the modes of philosophizing which prevailed during much of it. This reaction has continued, particularly in English-speaking countries, through most of the twentieth century. It was a necessary and, in many ways, a desirable revolt. Philosophers were weary of the language of paradox, the obscurity and the jargon of the Hegelians. They were repelled by a dialectical method which enables its practitioners never to say what they mean or mean what they say. The characteristic nineteenth-century propensity to promulgate grandiose philosophies of history and irrefutable laws of historical development fell increasingly into disrepute, as did also the ambiguous historical relativism which seemed to imply that anything is right or true so long as it expresses the spirit of its age. And after the heyday of the evolutionary theory, philosophers and scientists alike began increasingly to question the historical method as the key which would unlock all the doors to the house of knowledge. The fair hopes for that method, as things turned out, did not materialize, and the sciences of man were obliged to revert to less spectacular techniques, more similar to those employed in the physical sciences. Indeed, the very historical consciousness itself became suspect, as influential philosophers, such as Bertrand Russell, once again proclaimed the timelessness of truth and the universality of the methods to which they themselves were addicted.

As the old century drew toward its close, America finally came of age, philosphically, in the persons of Charles Peirce, William James, and John Dewey. These advocates of the brash new philosophy of pragmatism asserted, with increasing conviction and force, that the whole function of thought is to produce habits of action. According to Peirce, the meaning of any idea can be determined only by observing the habits of action which it produces; "what a thing means," said Peirce summarily, "is simply what habits it involves." The implication was clear: If no habits of action can be shown to be associated with any term, it is, for all practical purposes, without meaning. Thus, at a single stroke, the pragmatic criterion of meaning seemed to impugn all idealistic talk about the Absolute, not simply as false, but as senseless. But the justice of the criterion was even-handed, and the pragmatists were no friendlier to the materialistic metaphysics of a Spencer than to the idealism of a Hegel. To put the question in William James' breezy way, What is the "cash value" of all the hoary controversies between the idealists and the materialists? Save for James himself, most pragmatists, it must be confessed, did not stay for an answer. They were more concerned to point out that proponents of the "block universe" were blockheads than to look for the habitual role of metaphysical assertions in human life. Nor did they stop to consider how much they themselves owed to the plain anticipations of pragmatism that are to be found in the writings of Kant, Fichte, and Nietzsche. Had they considered the matter more carefully, as Josiah Royce enjoined them to do, they might have found that the underlying spirit of idealism was, in many ways, akin to the spirit of their own philosophy.

Along with questions concerning the meaningfulness of many nineteenth-century philosophical theses, went other no less central objections to the then prevailing conceptions of the philosophical enterprise itself. James, and his younger English contemporaries G. E. Moore and Bertrand Russell, objected to the turgid system-building of the more famous nineteenth-century philosophers. They insisted that philosophical progress comes only from detailed analysis of particular concepts and piecemeal examination of particular problems. This new pluralistic temper resulted in a distaste for the grand old philosophical "isms" and the large-scale syntheses of Hegel and Spencer, which produce a vague feeling of assurance without contributing anything to our understanding of nature. Moore attacked the paradoxes of idealism in the name of common sense; Russell attacked them in the name of science. Both of them rejected a mode of philosophizing which had no use for the Cartesian demand for clear and distinct ideas. They flatly rejected the idealistic coherence theory of truth and the doctrine of internal relations, insisting as Hume had done earlier, that there are no "internal" or "necessary" relations among matters of fact. And they argued that the test of truth cannot be mere internal coherence or consistency of propositions, but that the final test of any proposition is its correspondence with observed fact. They claimed to be "realists," not always realizing, perhaps, how far their basic position had been compromised by the critique of reason which had been the supreme achievement of Kant and his idealistic followers.

Beyond all this, however, the new pragmatic and realistic philosophies that were emerging at the turn of the new century were determined to bring philosophy itself into closer relation with mathematics and empirical science. Like his seventeenth-century predecessors, Russell aspired to a new scientific philosophy which acknowledged no essential difference between philosophy and science. He went so far, in fact, as to claim that ethics and political philosophy are not, properly, a part of philosophy at all, since they are concerned, not with truth, but merely with the expression and organization of attitudes.

The achievements of these distinguished thinkers, in my opinion, have contributed greatly to human enlightenment. Yet there are signs, after more than fifty years in which James, Peirce, and Dewey in this country, and Moore and Russell in England, have been the predominant influences, that a more just and sympathetic evaluation of nineteenth-century philosophy is in the offing. We are beginning to remind ourselves, first of all, that the spirit of the Enlightenment never really disappeared in the nineteenth century, and that the dominant philosophies of our own age are essentially continuous with philosophical positions which were strongly and ably defended throughout this period. Positivism itself, as we have seen, is a child of the nineteenth century, and in Mill and Spencer, and even Nietzsche and Marx, the attitudes of empiricism and naturalism continued to prevail. It could be argued, in fact, that after the time of Hegel, idealism ceased to be a dominant force in continental philosophy, and that after 1850 its major influence was limited to the more backward English-speaking countries of England and America. We must not forget, in short, that, for all its romantic reaction against the Age of Reason, the nineteenth century was itself a great age of science. Indeed, the hysterical opposition of orthodoxy to the new ideas of evolutionary biology and the new "positive" sciences of psychology and sociology itself indicates the growing strength of the scientific conception of man throughout this period. Not only scientists and philosophers, but also novelists like George Eliot and Samuel Butler, testify to the general power of the scientific outlook among intellectuals during the nineteenth century. Even Matthew Arnold, who fought a desperate rearguard action in defense of the Hellenic and Hebraic traditions, was profoundly impregnated with the naturalistic and scientific temper of the age. His *Literature and Dogma* is, in some ways, a prophetic anticipation of those latter-day liberal or positivistic theologies which try to preserve the authority and moral appeal of the Bible by removing it altogether from the sphere of factual discourse and placing it within the domain of "literature," whose business, according to Arnold, is not so much knowledge but the "criticism of life."

But there are other signs that contemporary philosophers are beginning to acknowledge their affinities with the great thinkers of the nineteenth century. This is due, in part, to the fact that we are becoming aware that the great cultural issues with which nineteenth-century philosophers were concerned are still with us. With the emergence of such irrationalist ideologies as Fascism and Nazism, the spread of Communism, and the more recent revival, in the West, of supernatural religion, twentieth-century philosophers have been forced to rescrutinize their own faith in reason and their unquestioning commitment to the gospels of science, or what they call "common sense." After a period of detailed analysis of the logical foundations of science, philosophers are beginning to see that the more fundamental critique of reason, initiated by Kant and continued by the idealists, is still an indispensable philosophical task, and that without it the obscurantists and the mystagogues may win by default.

There was a depth and spiritual freedom inherent in nineteenth-century philosophy at its best which we might do well to try to recover. Scientific philosophers may disdain ideology; but they do so at their peril, and their own hard-won intellectual gains may well be lost in a tide of philosophical and theological irrationalism and anti-intellectualism if they continue to refuse to emulate their own great predecessors, Comte, Mill, and Mach. The cause of Enlightenment is never wholly won, and in order to keep its spirit alive in an age of profound ideological opposition to it, the friends of science must themselves once again enter the ideological lists. And whether one likes it or not, this means doing metaphysics in at least one sense of that ambiguous term.

Here, however, a leaf may be taken from the book of the idealists. For them, metaphysics did not mean superscience, but the formulation and defense of basic human commitments. Their insistence upon coherence as the test of metaphysical adequacy itself suggests that fullness of life rather than correspondence to facts is the ultimate aim of metaphysical discourse. Their talk about "reality" has confused many commentators; but the fact that it is always an "ideal reality," not "existence," with which their metaphysical theses are concerned, makes it quite clear that the fundamental business of metaphysics, for them, is not a description of the nature of things, but the formulation of a coherent world-view, adequate to the conduct of life.

The fact is, as Hegel knew, that man has use for many different kinds of symbolic forms, so that the adequacy of any proposition must be judged by criteria that are relevant to the ends which it serves. To argue that moral judgments, for example, are meaningless merely because "good" and "right" do not designate any observable characteristics of things, is to assume, in advance, that the assignment of such characteristics to phenomena is the only aim of discourse. Why should we make such an assumption? The point is simply that any form of discourse which has a rationale and is directed to the satisfaction of some serious human purpose, has a meaning, in one well-established sense of that term.

This much the pragmatists themselves acknowledge. What nineteenth-century philosophers call metaphysics may be significant, or even necessary to the conduct of life, even if it has no "scientific" meaning. Here we may make use of the pragmatic principle that the meaning of any utterance is found, not in "clear and distinct ideas" but rather in the habits of action connected with it. Different forms of discourse are geared into different patterns of action, of which the institution of science is one, but only one, major type. This being so, the reflective analyst will not declare metaphysics meaningless without first inquiring into its characteristic social role. Nor will he judge its propriety in advance by criteria that are relevant only to some other form of human activity. This, if I mistake not, is precisely what Kant's theory of the "two reasons" implies. It is also part of what was implicit in Fichte's doctrine of knowledge.

It is my conviction that, along with other more dubious benefits, the transcendental turn taken by Kant and his followers at the beginning of the nineteenth century accomplished results of lasting importance for philosophy. We are only now, however, beginning to see them in perspective. By insisting upon the necessity of basic critique in the domains of knowledge, morality, metaphysics, and religion, Kant introduced into the mainstream of philosophical reflection a degree of critical self-consciousness about its own prerogatives, methods, and goals which has been

wholly salutary. Contemporary philosophers have frequently been dissatisfied with the upshot of Kant's own
results. Some of them look back nostalgically to the day
when metaphysics was still regarded as the great queen of
the science, majestically laying down the necessary laws of
all being. Such a day is irrevocably past. This does not
mean the whole enterprise of metaphysics is unimportant
or should be abandoned. It means, rather, that it must be
conceived and practiced in another spirit. After Kant, metaphysics was freed to do its own integral work of clarifying,
organizing, and defending the basic human attitudes and
commitments implicit in any way of life or culture. In the
light of that aim its own standard of reasonableness must
remain, as the idealists argued, that of coherence. An adequate metaphysics must be, certainly, compatible with and
indeed hospitable to the findings of science; but there are
other basic human commitments with which it must reckon, and other patterns of action which it must take into
account in attempting to formulate an adequate picture of
"reality."

The term "picture," here, is crucial. The aim of a picture is not to describe things in themselves, but to present
a composition which, as a whole, will be enduringly satisfying to the beholder. A picture is not, so to say, "asser-
tive," and its adequacy is not to be measured by its point-
for-point correspondence to some ulterior state of affairs.
A metaphysical system is not unlike a picture in this respect, although its ends are perhaps closer to those of
morality than to those of art. But its aims are more comprehensive than those of morality, for the adjustments
which it envisages are not merely those of justice between
persons but rather those of the whole person to his total
environment, natural, social, and internal. If we take seriously, as I do, both Kant's and Comte's conceptions of
human knowledge, neither absolute idealism, nor evolutionary naturalism, can properly be thought to provide
extensions of man's scientific knowledge of the world. On
the contrary they are both "metaphysical" efforts to formulate critical answers to the most comprehensive, limiting
questions which the individual can ask about the organiza-

tion of human life and action as a whole. Whether such answers are "cognitive" and "true" or "false" in the scientific sense is unimportant. What does matter is that the pictures of reality which they present to us may enable us to organize our energies more adequately for the satisfaction of our total needs as men. Then they will be "true" in the only sense of the term which is worth considering.

We are once again beginning to realize, as men invariably do in periods of great cultural crisis, that the metaphysical need, the need for an integrating vision of Man's fate and hope, can never be permanently overborne. When, for a brief period, it disappears from view, what this means is that the members of a given society are either so well-adjusted to the major demands which their institutions place upon them that they do not need to raise limiting questions about those institutions, or else that their basic commitments are so deeply rooted and so universally accepted that there is no occasion to bring them into consciousness and submit them to radical critique. Such periods of social complacency and cultural cohesion are very rare, especially in a dynamic, "open" society such as our own. In the normal course, vigorous metaphysical reflection is both an essential sign of cultural growth and an essential condition of institutional and personal self-correction. In an age, such as ours, which is so overwhelmingly involved in ideological struggles, it once again becomes an indispensable tool for the clarification, purification, and self-maintenance of our own integral way of life. To oppose Communism, for example, without continually rescrutinizing and reclarifying our own fundamental commitments, would be to run the risk of allowing the conflict to degenerate into a mere struggle for power, or, which is worse, of losing our own heritage of freedom in the process of trying to defend it.

But we may perhaps learn a lesson here from the fate of idealism in Germany. Beginning as a philosophy of freedom, which insisted on relating every social norm to the demands of each man and every principle of reason to the work which individual men must do in order to fulfill themselves, it ended, ingloriously, as a semi-official defense of the existing order and a half-slavish invocation of "tradition." In discovering that reason itself is inevitably conservative, and that rational standards in any society must be rooted in a commonly accepted cultural tradition, the idealists made the mistake of forgetting what Santayana called the "pre-rational" needs and "post-rational" satisfactions which reason itself must serve, in the light of which and for the sake of which any critique of reason is justifiably undertaken.

The primary spiritual evil inherent in any traditional and hence "rational" scheme of things consists in the fact that we invariably tend to make a fetish of it. It is, indeed, as though the very condition of rationality, in any sphere, is that it become a fetish for those who are governed by it. But here, again, the nineteenth century provides both the explanation and the cure. It was through his historical consciousness that Hegel became aware that reason itself has its historical roots, and that as cultural conditions change, so do conceptions of rationality also change. Hegel himself was "freed" from the importunate claims to universal validity in previous philosophical systems because he saw them as historically determined and hence mutable adjustments to a changing social environment. The irony is that he failed to recognize that his own philosophy is similarly time-bound, and that the dialectic of history was not frozen, once and for all, within his own logic.

Hegel lacked the saving humility which can be learned from Mill's philosophy of experience. What Mill shows us is the possibility of a self-correcting tradition which provides the antidote to its own tendency to become a fetish. Here, in short, is a conception of reason—I have called it "reasonablism"—which adjusts itself in advance to the limiting questions which men may ask about any proprieties, however sacred. This is the essential liberty which Mill defended. To defend it, however, is to defend the idea that the critique of reason, and hence of culture, is always in order, and that the possibility of revolution against particular forms which reason may take is itself always legitimate. The request for reasons, if sufficiently prolonged, is always a threat to any established order. The great thing about Mill's philosophy is that it defends and even solicits such threats, and in so doing domesticates them. What Mill offers us, in effect, is a tradition to end all traditions, which is committed, at bottom, only to the principle of reasonableness itself, the principle, that is, that a reason may be properly requested for any proposition whatever, and that no principle is ever exempted from critique, so long, at any rate, as the latter is conducted honestly and in good faith.

It seems to me, then, that the idea and the ideal of the critique of reason, to which all schools of philosophy in the nineteenth century made essential contributions, remains perhaps the greatest of all of the contributions of nineteenth-century philosophy. This does not in the least imply irrationalism or lack of faith in the principles of science. Many men of enlightenment, unfortunately, seem to think that the prerogatives of science are or should be kept beyond the peradventure of criticism, and that once the identification of "rationality" and "validity" with the principles of formal logic and experimental science is subject to challenge, the whole edifice of positive science is threatened. This indicates, however, nothing more than an underlying failure of nerve and a fear that the scientific outlook cannot preserve its integrity in the free market place of ideas. One does not have to be a traitor to the ideals of science in order to acknowledge that science should be subject to critique in the same way that any other institution must be. Immanuel Kant did not turn his back upon enlightenment and rationality when he sought to provide a critique of theoretical reason which would at the same time establish its proper limitations. Quite the contrary; by defining those limits, he hoped to strengthen its claims to sovereignty within its own sphere. If the methods of science, or of the "understanding," are the only proper procedures for the acquisition of factual knowledge, this thesis has not been self-evident in every age. In each generation, such procedures must be reclarified, reappraised, and defended against misrepresentation and opposition. But if they can be defended, they also can be criticized, and in either case there is no alternative, whether one likes it or not, to "first philosophy" or metaphysics.

No doubt the nineteenth-century philosophers failed, for the most part, to meet the demands of contemporary analytical philosophy for clarity and rigor. But the proof that these demands may be met without sacrificing wholeness and comprehensiveness of philosophical vision may be found in at least one of the philosophers with whom we have had to do, namely, Kant. Kant, in principle at least, satisfies in great part our "metaphysical" demand for positive total adjustment to our total environment. But he does this without sacrificing the counterdemand for detailed analysis and painstaking critique of particular concepts. Many of Kant's particular analyses are no longer acceptable to analytical philosophers; nor is his general scheme, with its profoundly dualistic conception of human nature, its unknowable thing-in-itself, and its poorly grounded and unsatisfying postulates of practical reason, satisfactory to contemporary philosophers. But Kant still represents the ideal of what the philosophical mind at its best can be: uncynically disillusioned, highly critical and self-conscious of its limitations, yet still loyal to the standards of reasonableness and humanity whose grounds it seeks; steadfastly devoted to the principles of human self-enlightenment, yet aware that self-enlightenment is compatible with respect for the principle that man is a social being responsible to and for others as well as himself; and, finally, hospitable not only to the demands of knowledge but also to the proper claims of art, morality, and religion.

One is tempted to cry once again, as so many others have done in the past, "Back to Kant!" But this would be as futile as the comparable cries "Back to Plato!", "Back to Aristotle!", or "Back to Aquinas!" which we hear so often in these days. As Hegel has taught us, we can never go back again; we can only try to do for ourselves and for our own culture what these great men attempted for their own ages. If, in our time, a new Kant were to emerge, his own critique of reason would have to take a very different form than that of Kant himself. Among other things, he would have to place the life of reason more firmly than Kant was able to do within the natural and social contexts in which it must be lived. For reason is a form of life, not a noumenal cookie-cutter. It is a form of life, moreover, which, as the irrationalists in their own misleading ways have helped us to see, is grounded in active urgencies that alone provide its only ultimate justification. To say this is not to capitulate to unreason; it is merely to save oneself from the futile and finally unreasonable claims of dogmatic "realism" and "rationalism"; it is only to acknowledge that if we cannot go back to Kant, neither can we go back to the Ages of Reason and Faith which lie behind him. To acknowledge that the regulation of human thought and action is a wholly human affair, and that their principles are rooted, in the end, only in our commitment to them, is a sober and chastening reflection. But it is also, at long last, to realize our own great burden of responsibility for the perpetuation of the ideals of a truly free society, for which alone the critique of reason can have any real meaning.

Recommended Further Reading

Note: This selected list includes important works and collections of writings that are available in English. Some entries are out of print, but all of them can be found in most college and in many city libraries. In most cases, no special mention has been made of works from which selections included in this volume have been made. At the end of the list, I have mentioned a few critical or interpretive works by major contemporary philosophers in order to provide the reader with appraisals and analyses that may differ, to some extent, from my own. It should be emphasized, however, that these latter works are primarily opinions of individual philosophers or schools of philosophers, and not contributions to scholarship. Santayana's *Egotism in German Philosophy*, for example, is a brilliant, penetrating, but occasionally malicious study of German philosophy from Kant to Nietzsche, and taken for what it is, I highly recommend it; but it is not to be taken as a product of impartial, historical research. When the reader is ready for works of this last sort, he will already have passed beyond the stage at which such a bibliography as this is necessary.

IMMANUEL KANT

The Critique of Pure Reason, translated by N. K. Smith. New York and London: The Macmillan Company, 1934. This, in my judgment, is the best and certainly the most readable translation of Kant's greatest work.

Critique of Practical Reason and Other Writings in Moral Philosophy, translated by Lewis W. Beck. Chicago: The University of Chicago Press; London: Cambridge University Press, 1949. Excellent translations of Kant's more important writings in ethics.

JOHANN GOTTLIEB FICHTE

The Vocation of Man, translated by W. Smith. Chicago: Open Court Publishing Company, 1922. A characteristic work, more readable than most.

Addresses to the German Nation, translated by R. F. Jones and G. H. Turnbull. Chicago: Open Court Publishing Company, 1923. Necessary, if not entirely agreeable, reading for anyone who wants to understand Fichte's more nationalistic phase.

The Science of Rights, translated by A. E. Kroeger. London: Trubner and Company, 1899. An important and difficult book in an adequate, if somewhat old-fashioned, translation.

G. W. F. HEGEL

The Phenomenology of Mind, translated by J. B. Baillie (rev. ed.). New York: The Macmillan Company; London: George Allen & Unwin, Ltd., 1931. The most important of Hegel's earlier works, essential for an understanding of his thought.

The Philosophy of Fine Art, translated by F. P. B. Osmaston. London: G. Bell & Sons, Ltd., 1920 (4 v.). In my opinion, this work, edited posthumously from lecture notes, is one of Hegel's masterpieces. Profound, stimulating, and fantastic by turns, its influence upon aesthetics is still very great.

Science of Logic, translated by W. H. Johnston and L. E. Struthers. New York: The Macmillan Company; London: George Allen & Unwin, Ltd., 1929 (2 v.). No doubt an indispensable book for anyone who seeks to penetrate the "secret" of Hegel. I would suggest that it be deferred until the above-mentioned works have been read.

The Philosophy of Hegel, edited by Carl Friedrich. New York: Random House, 1953. (Modern Library.) An excellent selection of Hegel's major writing.

ARTHUR SCHOPENHAUER

The World as Will and Idea, translated by R. B. Haldane and J. Kemp (6th ed.). London: Kegan Paul, Trench, Trubner and Co., Ltd., 1907 (2 v.). Schopenhauer's masterpiece, excellently translated.

Selected Essays, edited by Ernest Befort Bax. London: G. Bell & Sons, Ltd., 1914. Charming, witty, and characteristic pieces.

Two Essays. London: G. Bell & Sons, Ltd., 1889. (Bohn's Philosophical Library.) Includes *On the Fourfold Root of the Principle of Sufficient Reason,* one of Schopenhauer's important earlier works.

AUGUSTE COMTE

Positive Philosophy, freely translated and condensed by Harriet Martineau. London: Trubner & Co., 1853 (2 v.). The translation is free but quite readable. The work is Comte's best.

JOHN STUART MILL

Philosophy of the Scientific Method, edited by Ernest Nagel. New York: Hafner Publishing Company, 1950. A first rate edition of the most important parts of Mill's *Logic,* together with an illuminating introductory essay by the editor.

Utilitarianism, Liberty, and Representative Government, edited by A. D. Lindsay. New York: E. P. Dutton & Co., Inc., 1910. (Everyman's Library.) This volume contains the most important of Mill's contributions to moral and social thought. The essay *Liberty* is a masterpiece.

HERBERT SPENCER

The Principles of Ethics. New York and London: D. Appleton and Co., 1892 (2 v.). One of Spencer's most interesting and influential works; a key work of the "synthetic philosophy."

Illustrations of Universal Progress, A Series of Discussions. New York: D. Appleton & Co., 1864. A characteristic work which illustrates Spencer's evolutionary philosophy from a number of different angles.

KARL MARX and FRIEDRICH ENGELS

A Handbook of Marxism, edited by Emil Burns. New York: Random House; London: Victor Gollancz, Ltd., 1935. A first-rate selection of major works, including works of Marx, Engels, Lenin, and Stalin.

FRIEDRICH NIETZSCHE

The Philosophy of Nietzsche, edited by W. H. Wright. New York: Random House, 1937. (Modern Library.) This volume includes five important works: *Thus Spake Zarathustra, Beyond Good and Evil, The Genealogy of Morals, Ecce Homo,* and *The Birth of Tragedy.* The translations leave something to be desired, but the works included are all of major interest.

SÖREN KIERKEGAARD

Either/Or, A Fragment of Life, translated by David F. Swenson and Lillian Marvin Swenson. Princeton: Princeton University Press, 1944. One of Kierkegaard's most stimulating books.

The Concept of Dread, translated by Walter Lowrie. Princeton: Princeton University Press, 1946. A strange, puzzling book which contains some of the ideas which have most influenced the existentialists.

ERNST MACH

The Analysis of Sensation, translated by C. M. Williams. Chicago: Open Court Publishing Company, 1914. A classic work in the development of the philosophy of positivism.

GENERAL

Popper, Karl. *The Open Society and Its Enemies* (rev. ed.). Princeton: Princeton University Press, 1950; London: Routledge & Kegan Paul, Ltd. (2 v.), 1952. This work is highly controversial, and extremely stimulating. Not so good on Hegel, but the chapters on Marx are first rate.

Royce, Josiah. *The Spirit of Modern Philosophy.* Boston: Houghton Mifflin Company, 1892. To my mind the best sympathetic treatment of the German idealists in English, and one of Royce's best works. Royce is perhaps the greatest of American idealists. Well worth reading.

Santayana, George. *Egotism in German Philosophy* (new ed.). London: J. M. Dent & Sons, Ltd., 1939; New York: Charles Scribner's Sons, 1940. A somewhat unsympathetic but brilliant discussion by a master.

Index

280

281

The Mentor Philosophers

The distinguished series of paperbound books which presents philosophical thought from medieval times to the present.

THE AGE OF BELIEF

The Medieval Philosophers

By Anne Fremantle

Here, in one volume, is the wisdom of the most spiritually harmonious age that Western man has known. In this age of belief, the period from the fifth to the fifteenth centuries, when religion and social institutions were closely related, philosophers discussed the nature of God, of Being, and of Man, with an intensity not known before or since.

In this remarkable book, Anne Fremantle, religious scholar and author, presents selections from the basic writings of such dominant philosophers of the medieval period as St. Augustine, St. Thomas Aquinas, Boethius, Erigena, Anselm, Abelard, Bonaventura, and Averroës, with an interpretation of their work woven throughout the texts. (Mentor #MD126—50¢)

ANNE FREMANTLE, an associate editor of Commonweal, an editor of the Catholic Book Club, an associate professor at Fordham University, an editor-on-loan to the United Nations during the General Assembly, is also the author of numerous books, reviews, and articles, including "The Papal Encyclicals in Their Historical Context" (Mentor #MD177—50¢)

THE AGE OF ADVENTURE

The Renaissance Philosophers

By Giorgio de Santillana

THE RENAISSANCE was a time when men turned from abstractions, from thoughts of other-worldly perfection, to explore new seas, new continents, new notions, new images of man. They studied the giants of the past in the belief that they had already discovered man's true nature and then brought forth such bold creations—in art, psychology, politics and manners—as were never known in the ancient world.

Giorgio de Santillana presents in this volume the basic writings of the great innovators of the Renaissance—Da Vinci, More, Machiavelli, Michelangelo, Erasmus, Copernicus, Montaigne, Kepler, Galileo, and Giordano Bruno—and contributes an introduction and connecting commentary which illustrates the love of life that characterized this age of adventure. (Mentor #MD184—50¢)

GIORGIO de SANTILLANA was born in Rome in 1902. He studied and worked in Rome and Paris until 1935, when he came to the United States. Dr. de Santillana has taught at Harvard and is currently professor of History and Philosophy of Science at M.I.T. He edited Galileo's Dialogue on the Great World Systems and is the author of The Crime of Galileo.

Century of Genius

THE AGE OF REASON

The 17th Century Philosophers

By Stuart Hampshire

THE *Age of Reason*, edited by the outstanding teacher and author, Stuart Hampshire, presents selections from the basic writings of such great 17th century philosophers as Bacon, Pascal, Hobbes, Galileo, Descartes, Spinoza, and Leibniz, with a penetrating introduction and interpretive commentary illuminating their works.

The 17th century was the great formative era of modern philosophy, marked by the decline of medieval conceptions of knowledge, by the rise of the physical sciences and by the gradual transition from Latin to French and English as instruments of philosophical thought. In this age of reason, philosophers began to explain natural processes in mathematical terms. They also developed vital concepts of knowledge and certainty, appearance and reality, freedom and necessity, mind and matter, deduction and experiment. (Mentor #MT367—75¢)

STUART HAMPSHIRE is a Fellow of All Souls College, Oxford. Author of many articles on logical theory and on ethics, he has published a book on Spinoza. A lecturer in philosophy at Oxford since 1936, he has been a visiting professor at Columbia University.

The Emergence of Science

· THE AGE OF ENLIGHTENMENT

The 18th Century Philosophers

By Isaiah Berlin

THE PHILOSOPHY of the 18th century begins with a systematic effort to apply to the study of man those methods which Newton had so triumphantly applied to nature. The editor of this volume, Isaiah Berlin, traces the development of the influence of scientific thought through the writings of the great philosophers and popularizers whose work remains the foundation of liberal humanism and rationalism in the West.

Berlin's selections, and his penetrating introduction and interpretive commentary, shed light upon the philosophy of Locke, Berkeley, Voltaire, Hume, Reid, Condillac, and their German critics. (Mentor #MD172 —50¢)

ISAIAH BERLIN is a Fellow of All Souls College, Oxford, and a University Lecturer in Philosophy. Born in 1909, he is a graduate of Corpus Christi College, Oxford, where he took First Class Honors in Philosophy and Ancient History, Politics and Economics. He has been a visiting lecturer at Harvard University and Bryn Mawr College, and has written widely on philosophical, historical and political topics.

The Philosophers of Our Time

THE AGE OF ANALYSIS

20th Century Philosophers

By Morton White

THIS VOLUME emphasizes those ideas of the philosophers of the 20th century which are most important to philosophy and least familiar to the general reader —ideas in the field of logic, and of philosophical and linguistic analysis. Yet the better-known studies of time and instinct, existentialism, phenomenology, and organism are also represented.

Philosophy in the 20th century is by no means remote from the concerns of the ordinary man and the problems of culture. In his introduction and commentary, Morton White illustrates this, and illuminates the background of the selections themselves. The 20th century philosophers included are: Peirce, Whitehead, James, Dewey, Bertrand Russell, Wittgenstein, Croce, Bergson, Sartre and Santayana. (Mentor #MT353—75¢)

MORTON WHITE, now chairman of the Department of Philosophy at Harvard University, has taught at Columbia University and at the University of Pennsylvania. He has also held a Guggenheim Fellowship and was visiting professor at Tokyo University. The author of numerous articles and reviews, he has written three books, The Origin of Dewey's Instrumentalism, Social Thought in America, *and* Toward Reunion in Philosophy.